*"Banished
from
Their
Father's
Table"*

Jewish Literature and Culture
Series Editor, Alvin Rosenfeld

"Banished from Their Father's Table"

LOSS OF FAITH AND HEBREW AUTOBIOGRAPHY

Alan Mintz

Indiana University Press
BLOOMINGTON & INDIANAPOLIS

Manufactured in the United States of America

Library of Congress Cataloging-in-Publication Data

Mintz, Alan L.
    Banished from their father's table : loss of faith and Hebrew
autobiography / Alan Mintz.
        p.   cm.—(Jewish literature and culture)
    Includes index.
    ISBN 0-253-33857-3
    1. Autobiographical fiction, Hebrew—History and criticism.
2. Feuerberg, Mordecai Ze'ev, 1874–1899—Criticism and
interpretation.   3. Berdichevsky, Micah Joseph, 1865–1921—Criticism
and interpretation.   4. Brenner, Joseph Hayyim, 1881–1921—Criticism
and interpretation.   I. Title.   II. Series.
PJ5029.M45   1989
892.4'35'09—dc19   88-45755
                                                                                CIP

1 2 3 4 5 93 92 91 90 89

For Susanna

CONTENTS

Acknowledgments

My interest in the autobiographical strain in Hebrew literature began in 1976 in a tutorial with Dan Miron, and his suggestions have remained a source of fruitful influence throughout. Discussions with Gershon Shaked at various stages of the writing have likewise been of inestimable value in shaping the direction of this work. Robert Alter has been a reliable friend in helping the project move forward. Arnold Band offered much encouragement and advice in the initial stages of the work.

Versions of chapters 2 and 3 originally appeared in the *Association of Jewish Studies Review,* and I am grateful to the Association for permission to use portions of that material. I recall with great appreciation and sense of loss the founding editor of that journal, the late Frank Talmage, who gave me much encouragement and providing so much editorial care and probity. A Hebrew version of chapter 4 appeared in *Mehkerei yerushalayim besifrut ivrit,* and I thank my friend and mentor Ezra Fleischer for providing this opportunity.

Many individuals have been kind enough to give valuable suggestions as the work developed: Arnold Eisen, Paula Hyman, Natalie Zemon Davis, Mark Cohen, Shmuel Verses, Menahem Brinker, and David Ruderman. I owe a special debt of gratitude to David Stern for his unflagging intellectual companionship and to David Roskies for his cheerful encouragement.

I acknowledge with pleasure the hospitality extended by the Department of Hebrew Literature of the Hebrew University of Jerusalem in 1985 and the substantial support given me by the General Research Board of the University of Maryland. To Adele Berlin, Marsha Rozenblit, and Charles Manekin of the Meyerhoff Center for Jewish Studies at Maryland I give my thanks and appreciation for creating a warm atmosphere which encourages the serious pursuit of scholarship.

To my wife Susanna Morgenthau this book is dedicated in happy but meager acknowledgment of a vast and profound debt. Her wisdom and insight pervade these pages.

*"Banished
from
Their
Father's
Table"*

ORIGINS AND ANTECEDENTS

Part One

ONE

The Turn toward Autobiography in Hebrew Literature

Woe to the Father who has banished
his children from His table; and woe to
the children who have been banished
from their Father's table.
   —Bavli Berakhot 3a

A parable is told in the Talmud of a father who was obliged to exile his sons because of their rebellious behavior. The punishment was unavoidable, the act of a father who would chastise those whom he loves. The deed done, however, the father now sits alone, mournfully bereft of his children, while his children wander in exile bereft of their father. The father in the parable is God and the sons are the Children of Israel. The story is told by the Rabbis to describe the changed nature of Jewish existence in the aftermath of the destruction of the Second Temple and to place new emphasis on the pathos of God's suffering for the exile he has had to impose on his people.[1]

The generation of Hebrew writers that came of age in the 1880s and 1890s read their situation in the words of the midrash. They experienced the metaphysical anguish of life after the sudden collapse of religious faith in their time as analogous to the spiritual plight of the Jewish people in the years after the fall of Jerusalem. Yet in their reading of the parable the emphasis fell on the figure of the children rather than the father. They, too, were "sons who had been banished from their Father's table," and this phrase was used self-consciously in the literary criticism and journalism of the period as a tag for the generation as a whole and its condition.[2] Their "banishment" was in fact twofold. Most recently, they had lost faith in the plausibility of the Haskalah (Hebrew Enlightenment), and that failure had in turn triggered a tragic reevaluation of the earlier break with traditional belief and practice.

For a time earlier in the century, the Haskalah had offered a model of accommodation and transition. Judaism would be purified and strengthened by virtue of being purged of obscurantism and superstition. Belief in God would endure, but the God worshiped would now be a God of reason who presided over a religion of reason. Jewish society would be modernized in its education, organization, and occupational structure, and in

3

return Jews would be allowed greater participation in the larger culture. By the 1880s, however, the Haskalah vision had mostly collapsed, its failure due in large measure to the intractable and intensifying force of Russian antisemitism. For the young Hebrew writers who reached adulthood at the end of the century, then, the Haskalah was no longer a credible option; it had been overtaken by history.

The turning point in the biographies of these young writers is the moment of apostasy: the sudden realization that the received belief in the God of Israel—and therefore the authority of the Torah and the command-ments—is no longer possible. (The term apostasy is used here as a transla-tion of the Hebrew *kefirah*, which was used by the Rabbis to designate a denial of the fundamental principles of Jewish belief; "apostasy" is not used in this study, as it sometimes is in modern parlance, to designate con-version to another religion.) The pathos of this event is underscored by the origins of these young men.

Typically, they originated from the most devout and scholarly circles of Jewish society, and many distinguished themselves as child prodigies of talmudic learning in whom the pride and resources of family and com-munity were heavily invested. Often already in adolescence the "infection" of religious doubt was contracted through contact with Haskalah writings; the process was hastened after the writers left their towns and villages for the yeshiva and there formed bonds with other youths who harbored the same hesitations.

For this group, the moment of apostasy was experienced very dif-ferently from their precursors, the maskilim, earlier in the century. For these Hebrew *philosophes* there had been a comfortable deism to turn to, and they could therefore view their apostasy as a deliverance from error and a rebirth into a religion of reason. Their apostasy, then, was a kind of fortunate fall; rather than losing the experience of belief, they transferred their faith to a different, more enlightened set of doctrines. For their belated descendants, however, this middle ground no longer existed, and the experience of apostasy became much more cruelly desolating. It was not so much that the world of faith had been purposefully rejected but that at a certain point its plausibility had simply collapsed. The world that had once been thick with symbols and texts, sacred times and covenanted obliga-tions, providential signs and redemptive promises was, suddenly, not there. What had been lost, moreover, even if it was no longer tenable, was also no longer replaceable. The new ideologies of the times, which pre-sented themselves as functional replacements for religious fervor and ad-herence, were no more acceptable to these sensitive minds than such cruder forms of evasion as immigration, assimilation, and careerism. This intellectual and metaphysical negation was deepened by the loneliness that resulted from the break with family and community. Into the resulting void rushed erotic obsession and other demons against which there were few defenses.

The attempt in Hebrew literature to represent and explore the shape of experience in the immediate aftermath of the collapse of faith is the subject of the present study. I shall argue that the need to tell this story resulted in the creation of a new mode of writing in Hebrew prose narrative—the autobiography, both inside and outside of fiction. At this moment in literary history there occurs a substantial intersection between a particular theme, which I shall call the apostasy narrative, and a particular form, the autobiographical mode. (The theoretical definition of autobiography and the critical assumptions concerning it will be discussed later in this chapter.) To comprehend the force and the novelty of autobiography we must first understand something of the literary norms that were shattered by its emergence in the nineteenth century. The novel was the regnant form in Hebrew prose at the time, and it was as an alternative to the novel that autobiography arose.

In the thirty years following the publication of the first Hebrew novel in 1853 (Mapu's *Ahavat tsiyyon,* "The Love of Zion"), dozens of examples of the genre appeared, as well as an even larger number of translations into Hebrew from European languages. The sources of influence are not to be found in the contemporary novels of such writers as Balzac, Dickens, Flaubert, or Eliot, but, because of various cultural mediations, in the sentimental and melodramatic tradition of the eighteenth century. The Hebrew novel of the period, whose principal practitioners included Abraham Mapu, Sh. J. Abramowitsch (Mendele), Peretz Smolenskin, and Reuben Asher Braudes, is a large, sprawling affair, peopled by many characters, in which the action often switches back and forth among settings widely distant from one another. The plot is organized episodically and threads its way through a variety of deceptions, coincidences, and changes of identity. The characters are not "rounded" but represent different values or positions in the religious and social struggles of the day. The rather straightforward third-person telling of the story is frequently interrupted by didactic digressions and familiar appeals to the reader. The themes of the novels concern the ideological and social turmoil of contemporary East European Jewry as observed from the slant of Haskalah values. The plot often revolves around the adventures of a young man with an enlightened outlook who is being persecuted by hypocritical representatives of the old order. Behind all the satirical indictments of superstitious beliefs and corrupt communal practices, there lies a confident implicit model of an ideal society based on reason, science, and justice.

In the 1870s when Moses Leib Lilienblum, the author of the most important autobiography of the Haskalah period, (*Ḥat'ot ne'urim, Sins of Youth*), sought to describe his struggles to liberate himself from outmoded beliefs and to secure an enlightened education, the Hebrew novel must have struck him as an entirely unsuitable means for doing so. The story Lilienblum had to tell was one of self-delusion, loneliness, and disappointment, and there would hardly be a place for such emotions and experiences in the novel's melodramatic plot reversals and coincidences. In portraying adolescence, Lilienblum is in fact wickedly funny in parodying his *own* pretensions to being a hero who represents the forces of light and justice; the mature writer insists again and again that he is not a hero, and by this he means very clearly the kind of hero featured in the novel of the times. The novel, in short, was perceived to be overconventionalized. Romantic love, happy endings, and irrepressible protagonists were all part and parcel of the genre, and these conventions, which were wildly inappropriate to the realities of Jewish society in the minds of this new generation, led the novel into what was felt to be an unacceptable tension with the lived truth of individual existence as it had been transformed by the crisis of apostasy. What was sought, therefore, was an alternative tradition of narrative prose writing which could take on life closer to the bone. This was found in the Rousseauean autobiography as imported to Jewish literature by Solomon Maimon. It was from Maimon's example in German (the *Lebensgeschichte*) that autobiographical writing in Hebrew took its point of departure. The important autobiographies in the Haskalah period by Lilienblum and M. A. Guenzburg *(Aviezer)* are "straight" autobiographies in the sense that, despite their artistry, they are presented as factual stories whose narrators and whose authors are one. At the end of the century during the Revival (Tehiyah) period, the autobiographical impulse crosses over into fiction. The model, with all its by-now familiar generic expectations, is appropriated by such fiction writers as M. Z. Feierberg, M. Y. Berdichevsky, and Y. H. Brenner as the basis of a new kind of authentic narrative in which the ironic divergence between hero and author can be exploited to the full.

Now Rousseauean autobiography, like all differentiated literary models, is itself replete with conventions, and Hebrew writers felt the force of these norms no less than those of the novel. When Maimon, for example, shamefully admits to having lied about the theft of some trinket and this confession seems curiously out of place in the story, it is impossible not to see it as an obligatory gesture toward a similar incident in Rousseau's *Confessions.* Even if the autobiography had its own conventions—although it *was* at the time a less convention-laden genre—the conventions by their very nature were experienced as something of a liberation. Telling the truth, even if it was an unflattering truth, was one of the rules. The kind of truth, moreover, was linked to the reality of an individual life. While the Hebrew novel of the time may have told the truth about society in its extensive and historical dimensions, it is only in autobiography that the central unit of representation could be the self and its inner experience.

Before describing the outcome of the meeting between Hebrew literature and Rousseauean autobiography, it is worth reflecting on the utter novelty of this encounter. *The Confessions* constitutes a grand departure precisely because of the rich and continuous tradition of autobiography in classical and Christian Europe which Rousseau's enterprise both breaks with and renews. The many-volume life-work of the German scholar Georg Misch, for example, is devoted to sorting out autobiographical literature only up until the early Middle Ages.[3] After the magisterial figure of Augustine, whose *Confessions* inaugurate the major categories of the genre, there is a nearly unbroken succession of strong texts: Abelard, Teresa of Avila, Montaigne, Cellini, Dante, John Bunyan, Benjamin Franklin, Goethe, and many others.[4] Such a canon, moreover, excludes memoirs, diaries, *res gestae*, lives of the philosophers, and other forms of writing that are not true autobiographies in the sense that they are not acts of self-reflection displaying genuine inwardness.[5]

There could be no greater contrast than with the classical Hebrew literary tradition. If we search for instances of autobiographical writing, we find virtually nothing until the Renaissance. In the Bible the prayerful voices that beseech on their own behalf and the retrospective wisdom of Kohelet can barely be said to belong to self-reflective writing. In rabbinic literature there is a definite sense of the importance of individual lives in the case of the great masters, but the *exempla* that relate didactic stories about their lives were never cast in terms of *self*-understanding and were never gathered into collections and given the same stature as code and exegesis. In the Middle Ages the closest we come to such a work is Maimonides' *Epistle on Resurrection,* in which a scholar explains and defends his earlier teachings against critics who misrepresent them. If, in short, the urge to self-portraiture is universal, then Judaism must impose upon this generalization considerable constraints. In the classical tradition the individual is so firmly embedded within communal, legal, and historical structures that his or her separate inner drama is simply not viewed as a significant source of meaning for the tradition as a whole.

So how is it, then, that such an alien growth as autobiography eventually comes to be domesticated within Jewish literature? The answer begins in the Renaissance and early modern periods, in which the field of autobiography widens out considerably while at the same time remaining something of a hidden garden. We know of a number of Jewish literary self-portraits, if not full-scale autobiographies: in the sixteenth century, the diaries of the court Jew Jossel of Rosheim, the legendary accounts of the messianic pretender David Reuveni, Yomtov Lipman Heller's account of his imprisonment in Prague, the family history of an Alsatian Jew named Asher Halevi, the confessional autobiography of Leon Modena and an account by his grandson Isaac Minhaleviim, the visionary apologetic statement by the physician Abraham Yagel; in the seventeenth century, Jacob Emden's story of his pursuit of secret followers of Shabbetai Zevi, the Yiddish memoirs of Glückel of Hameln, and an autobiographical fragment by a nameless Bohemian Jew published by Alexander Marx. This may not be all; as additional texts are published by historians, we may find that this kind of writing was more widespread than previously supposed.[6]

At first glance this flowering of self-portraiture would seem to provide the modern Hebrew autobiography with a worthy and substantial lineage. Yet in only the most qualified sense can we see the makings of a tradition in these texts, because of the simple fact that these writers were not aware of each other's works, nor were they read in later times. Virtually all of these texts existed only in manuscript, and they were circulated, if at all, within the family circle or among descendants; this situation did not change until the late nineteenth and twentieth centuries when the manuscripts were published by Jewish scholars as historical documents. The reasons why these works were not widely circulated among contemporary audiences bear in the main on the family-centered motives for the writing. Authors usually attempted to confirm the worthiness and antiquity of their genealogies and to establish their own place within the cycle of family fortunes and misfortunes. Allied to this impulse was the encouragement provided by the literary model of the Hebrew ethical will, the *tsava'ah*, in which a man set out to communicate his moral and spiritual legacy to his children. In the case of Glückel of Hameln, the motives were even closer to home; she wrote her memoirs to console herself after her husband's death. Only Leon Modena's autobiography—and perhaps Jacob Emden's as well—contains a true confessional theme, the admission of his compulsive gambling and its baleful consequences. In a European Christian world in which the "character" of the Jews was richly debated, the self-disclosed failings of such an important writer as Leon were best kept well within the orbit of the community.

Of the many memoirs and family chronicles written in this period, Leon Modena's *Life of Judah (Hayyei Yehudah)* may be said to be one of the few true autobiographies, and this for two reasons.[7] Here the chronicle of a public career and family fortunes is combined with the subjective confession of personal deficiencies and the subjective expression of lament. Here also is an attempt to represent the entirety of an individual life, from "cradle to grave," rather than a single phase or episode. Modena was a rabbi active in the Venetian ghetto during the first half of the seventeenth century and the highly reputed author of Jewish-Christian apologetics. He was employed by the community as a preacher and a teacher, and he worked at many other occupations in order to underwrite a compulsion for games of chance. Modena began writing his *Life* at the age of forty-seven in the grief following the death of one of his sons, and he contributed to the work during the thirty remaining years of his life. *The Life of Judah,* as Natalie Zemon Davis has suggested, comprises three themes: confession, lament, and self-praise. Modena confesses his addiction to games of chance; its ruinous effect makes him search for income by any means possible.[8] (In contrast to contemporary Christian autobiography, incidentally, the pattern of sinning leads to no climactic act of repentance.) Modena's lament is occasioned by a cluster of calamities involving his three sons: one died from lead poisoning as a result of alchemical experiments; one was murdered by Jewish rivals in the ghetto; and one went into exile abroad. These are not, however, the sins and sorrows of an Italian Jewish Everyman. After the manner of other Renaissance writers, Modena has large claims to make on his own behalf. From a child prodigy he developed into a renowned preacher whose sermons attracted churchmen and visiting dignitaries as well as regular synagogue worshipers. To document his fame as a writer he presents the many treatises and pamphlets under his authorship. Modena's life is told in a year-by-year fashion, with the length of the entries varying with the importance of the incidents. Since the work was begun in midlife, the narrative of the early years represents a different kind of self-disclosure from the material entered on a yearly basis. Yet despite this linear method of composition, *The Life of Judah* is far from a naive chronicle of life events. The reselection and ordering of these events reflect a desire to bring the three themes of the work into a conspicuous liturgical pattern of sin and punishment.[9]

Leon Modena died in Venice in 1648. It was not until 1911 in Kiev that Abraham Kahana published the Hebrew text of *The Life of Judah* from a copied version of the only manuscript. Natalie Zemon Davis has suggested that Modena, like other early modern Jewish autobiographers, was sensitive to a living a life observed both by Jews and by gentiles. Certain of his writings represented Judaism to the Christian world, others were written for a large and learned rabbinical world, and still others, such as the autobiography, for family, friends, and descendants. This latter belongs to the kind of literature written by insiders for insiders. There are secrets both about the self and about the Jews as a religious group that must be told, but must also be kept within a trusted circle.

The other major pre-modern Hebrew autobiography is Jacob Emden's *Megillat sefer.*[10] Emden (1698–1776) was a rabbi, scholar, and polemicist who lived in Germany and traveled to Amsterdam and Poland; he is best known for his prosecutorial campaign against rabbinical authorities he believed to be secret followers of Shabbetai Zevi. Compared to Modena's *Life of Judah,* Emden's autobiography is a large and sprawling composition which gives the impression of being overstuffed with information. The literary models Emden emulated are not clear to us, but they were not the results of the same training in humanistic rhetoric Modena received. This inclusiveness, however, gives *Megillat sefer* great interest as an historical source, for it comprehends many facets of Emden's life and activities. The work is concerned less with his ideas and scholarly accomplishments than with the conflicts and controversies surrounding them. Emden gives a particularly detailed account of the marital arrangements with each of his three wives. His various health problems are described, including his fondness for tea drinking and his bout with a tapeworm. Emden goes into his business transactions and financial ventures and misadventures, since he strove to remain independent of the paying rabbinate. A chapter is devoted to the houses he bought in Altona. *Megillat sefer* is not without its intimate details:

the author's impotence on the night of his marriage at the age of eighteen, the gentile servant girl who tried to seduce him, the wellborn Jewish lady to whom he was attracted. Nearly a full third of the book is taken up by a tribute to his father, who died when the son was twenty years old. This grand gesture of filial piety accords well with the purpose Emden avows for undertaking the work as a whole. As a man embroiled in controversy all his life, he was driven by a great desire to be understood by his sons and their descendants just as he extended the same understanding to his father. He seeks to vindicate himself and counter the aspersions cast on him by his enemies. He wishes, in other words, to set the record straight for his progeny and posterity.

Like Modena's autobiography, Emden's was in fact never read beyond the family circle. It, too, existed as a single manuscript until it was published in Warsaw one hundred and twenty years after his death, also by the historian Abraham Kahana. The insider-to-insider norm needs to be stressed because it was a boundary dramatically crossed in 1792 by the Berlin philosopher Solomon Maimon with the publication of his *The Autobiography of Solomon Maimon (Lebensgeschichte)*.[11] As a child in rural Poland, Maimon had distinguished himself as a Talmud prodigy and had therefore been married off at the age of eleven. His thirst for knowledge led him beyond the traditional Jewish curriculum in search of Western learning. He abandoned his family and set out for Germany, where he lived as an itinerant tutor, often resorting to begging between employments. After many hardships and after toiling to acquire a mastery of German philosophy, Maimon was finally granted the right to reside in Berlin. There he became a friend of Mendelssohn, frequented the mixed salons of the city, won philosophy competitions, and came to be regarded by Kant as one of the few minds that truly understood him. The autobiography, which is written in German, follows Maimon's life from early childhood until his admission to Berlin. In addition to relating the events in his life, the work also provides a great deal of information about Jewish life in Poland in the mid-eighteenth century and devotes several lengthy digressions to such discrete subjects as the Talmud, Hasidism, and Kabbalah.

Maimon's *Lebensgeschichte* is one of those rare books that legitimately deserves to be called seminal. Reading it from the vantage point of two hundred years later, one is astonished to discover the first and freshest telling of a story that was to be reworked, elaborated, and adapted in many succeeding times and places, a story which became the very cornerstone of modern Jewish literature: the narrative of acculturation.[12] It was only at this moment in time that the telling of such a story became possible. Virtually for the first time since the tenth and eleventh centuries in Spain, certain Jews were allowed to participate in European professional, commercial, and cultural life without being required to renounce their Judaism. Maimon's journey from the heart of pious village Jewry in Poland to the philosophical and literary salons of Berlin, this journey outward, provided the model for a new conception of the shape of a Jewish life, a new trajectory. The will to move beyond and the trials and deprivations endured along the way carry the burden of the narrative, which is brought to a close the moment the hero makes his successful entry into the new world. The retrospective point of view in Maimon's autobiography is one of *achieved* position, and the tribulations of the journey can therefore be brought under a sign that is essentially comic.

Maimon's *Lebensgeschichte* is notable as well for being the first importation into Jewish literature of the new autobiographical norms determined by *Les Confessions* of Rousseau, published only some ten years earlier. This was hardly a gesture to a passing cultural fashion. Most literary historians view Rousseau's confessions as a paradigm-setting event in the modern age on the same order of importance as Augustine's *Confessions* in the post-classical age. Rousseau shifted the audience/addressee for his confession from God to the world; his quarrel was with society, that is, the civilized society that had misunderstood him. What was to be laid bare in the confession was not problems of sin and faith but the "truth of the heart," the flow of genuine sentiments and affects. Because in an over-civilized age such feelings are closer to nature than the practices of society, writing of the ways of the heart became tantamount to revealing the truth. Confession merges with self-justification. Rousseau admits having done some unworthy act, but then claims credit for having had the sincerity to admit it, and he goes on to explain why, given the pressures of society and the truth of the heart, he is in fact not responsible.[13] Rousseau's revision of the autobiographical enterprise had a strong and immediate impact on European writing. In Maimon's case, the influence was significant but imperfectly assimilated, and the mixed results tell us a great deal about the constraints on Jewish autobiography.

Rousseau's example had the positive effect for Maimon of opening up the field of representation to include the life of sentiments and domestic relations. Marriage became something more than a simple rite-of-passage to be noted for its marking a change of status and circumstances; it was moved to the foreground and made a major condition, a limiting condition, of life, together with the domestic politics surrounding it. While retaining its centrality, the history of scholarly accomplishment is broadened to include an affective dimension: how the acquisition of knowledge feels, and how the self responds to the rebuffs of society. Childhood comes into new focus as the spawning ground of adult sentiments rather than as simply a record of teachers and subjects. The audience for the autobiography was reconceived as well. It became the wide world rather than the family circle. The family, in fact, makes its appearance as an impediment to enlightenment rather than as a reality whose future enfolds the prospects for the author's immortality. Since the attainment of truth can abide allegiance to no received institutions, the very shape of experience is recast into the form of a quest. Maimon leaves home and wanders forth in search of true enlightenment, and his episodic journey makes him something of the *picaro*. Seen from the point of view of the worthiness of his quest and its eventual success, Maimon views others he comes across on his path not as persons with their own moral claims but as actors who perform the role of helping him on his way or detaining him.

Yet Maimon's will to follow Rousseau's example exceeds his willing-ness—and his capacity—to do so. Very little is actually shown to us con-cerning the emotional realities of the hero's domestic relations. Maimon was subjected at the age of eleven to an arranged marriage, which he was incapable of consummating until several years later. For his readers this was undoubtedly an exotic and troubling phenomenon, and Maimon promises in his chapter heading to reveal "the mysteries of the marriage state." But instead the reader is treated to a comic account of the positioning of the two families before the wedding and of the young husband's political situation in his mother-in-law's household after it. Maimon's desire to fulfill their expectations is expressed in rather mechanical borrowings from Rousseau's repertoire of sincere gestures. In chapter 9 Maimon admits an infatuation with a servant girl and in the previous chapter he confesses a petty theft for which others are blamed; he even labels the incident in the chapter heading as a "Theft à la Rousseau." Maimon's incapacity to deliver on these prom-ises stems from a basic difference between his experience and Rousseau's. If Rousseau's truth can be said to be of the heart, Maimon's is of the head. His eventful accession to the position of Berlin philosopher represents a true fulfillment of a life which has been presented throughout as a struggle to realize mental gifts and to strive for truth at its most universal level. The most emotionally affecting scenes in the book, the painstaking decipher-ment of the German alphabet and the banishment from the gates of Berlin, are in fact episodes in the struggle for enlightenment. The supremacy and sufficiency of this goal is never questioned, and consequently the life of sentiments can never become more than an adjunct to it.[14]

A curious compositional feature of the *Lebensgeschichte* is the several long chapters devoted to the Kabbalah and Hasidism. These are full-scale descriptive essays, and as eye-witness accounts as well they have been heavily drawn upon by modern scholars as important historical sources. Because these excursuses are self-contained and because they interrupt the story of Maimon's progress in life, they have been considered bothersome by editors and translators and have often been removed from the narrative and made into appendices. These free-standing chapters are the most conspicuous instances of an information-delivering function which is part of the main, rather than incidental, business of the book. At every turn Maimon provides his readers with explanations about the Jews, their reli-gious practices, their marriage customs, their occupational structure, their sectarian divisions, their communal organization, and hierarchy. As much as the *Lebensgeschichte* is an autobiographical account, then, it is also an anthropological act, an essay in ethnology on the subject of the Jews. This fact helps to clarify the question of audience. Although many young Jews in Eastern Europe throughout the nineteenth century found their way to Maimon's autobiography, the motive for writing the book was to reach a *gentile* readership, with the addition, perhaps, of those "non-Jewish" Jews whose acculturation into German life had gone so far as to make Maimon's explanations necessary. We thus arrive at a point at the opposite extreme from the insider-to-insider practice of Leon Modena and other pre-modern Jewish autobiographers. Having left the traditional, closed Jewish community, Maimon addresses himself to the citizens of the new rational order in whose midst he has arrived. To such an audience the story of Maimon's life prior to his arrival would be unintelligible without the ethnographic background. This is an audience, however, which one senses is not entirely satisfied by being provided with information or at least information about the Jews. Maimon must also flatter and entertain.

The question of language here is paramount. Maimon's choice of audience determines his use of German, and his choice of German determines his audience. The *Lebensgeschichte,* together with works by Mendelssohn and later by Heine, constitute the first moments in the emergence of a modern European Jewish literature. Within this larger stream, the lesser current of autobiography over the next century will come to include self-portraits written by Jews in German, French, Russian, English, and Italian. At the outset of the modern period, thus, we have before us at least *two* Jewish literatures: one written in non-Jewish languages by Jews about Jewish themes and another written in Hebrew. (Yiddish becomes still another option.) The distinction is important for the understanding of literary history in general and crucial for the purposes of this study, which will take up the path of Hebrew literature. The interplay among these literatures and their audiences becomes more complex as the nineteenth century progresses; it no longer resembles the relatively clear-cut communicative transaction enacted by Maimon's autobiography. To write in a European language does not necessarily mean to write for gentiles, as more and more Jews come to participate in European culture. And while writing in Hebrew did mean being read largely by Jews, these Hebrew readers knew or were aware of European literature; nor did writing in Hebrew mean to write for *all* Jews (a purpose for which Yiddish would have been the appropriate choice), but for members of an intelligentsia. The distinctions between insiders and outsiders therefore became elusive. Nevertheless, the choice to write in Hebrew remains highly significant. About this choice, as we shall see, there was nothing natural or inevitable, and in the course of this study we shall have several occasions to return to this phenomenon and wonder at the mystery it presents. Two aspects of the question are relevant at this juncture. In contrast to European languages, writing in Hebrew makes available to the writer—and creates a connection with—the great classical literary tradition and its repertoire of

sources and allusions. To write in Hebrew was also a contemporary ideological choice; it was an act of identification with and participation in a
movement for cultural and social reform called the Haskalah and, later in
the century, in a more actively nationalist movement for Jewish revival. As
we return to the career of autobiography, it is this track we shall follow.

Haskalah autobiography, as S. Werses has surveyed it, is a wide field
which includes such well known figures as I. S. Reggio, S. D. Luzzatto,
M. H. Letteris, A. Gottlober, S. Y. Fuenn, J. L. Gordon, M. A. Guenzburg,
and M. L. Lilienblum.[15] The fact that these names are well known—and
known to us from works other than their autobiographies—is significant.
Most of these works are accounts of the author's literary and cultural
activity, and they interest us now, if they do at all, as portals to a more
complete comprehension of that activity. Reggio, for example, describes his
call to Jewish learning and the progress of his career as a scholar; in
provoking detail in the pages of *Ha-maggid*, Luzzatto gives an authorized
version of the canon of his works; Letteris and Fuenn offer not so much
portraits of themselves as reminiscences of such famous figures from the
milieu in which they worked as Rappaport and Krochmal; and Gottlober
deflects attention from himself in another way by confining himself to an
ethnographic account of the Volhynia and Podolia of his youth. In contrast
to this conception of autobiography as reflections on a public career, there
are two outstanding exceptions: Mordecai Aaron Guenzburg's *Aviezer*[16]
and Moses Leib Lilienblum's *Sins of Youth (Ḥat'ot ne'urim)*.[17] These two
works are concerned with what might be crudely called the personal life
independent of, or intermixed with, the public career; as texts, these
autobiographies ask to be taken seriously for the intrinsic truth of the
experience they portray rather than for their association with the famous,
or not so famous, authors who wrote them. And so it is: we now honor
Guenzburg more for *Aviezer* and less for his *Devir* and his historical works,
and we honor Lilienblum's publicistic activity because of the existential
authority given it by *Sins of Youth*.

To sharpen the distinction between *Aviezer* and *Sins of Youth* and the
other autobiographies, we can profitably use Guenzburg's own terms in the
methodological preface to his book. For Guenzburg there are two ideal
types, biography and autobiography, which are distinguished not so much
by the point of view (whether one is writing about oneself or about
another) but by the nature of the subject. Biographies are written about
men who have become famous because of their great spiritual powers or
because of the outstanding events of their lives; it is the task of the biog-
rapher, according to Guenzburg, "to choose with wisdom and discrimination all that is lofty and precious in their life histories, as well as the spirit
that urged them on to accomplish their wonderful deeds"—in other words,
to select from among a multiplicity of personal attributes those special ones
that conduce greatness.[18] The autobiographer, in contrast, is positively

forbidden selectivity. He need not be a great man; what he needs instead of achievements is comprehensive self-knowledge and a commitment to truth so unflinching that there will be no hesitation in confessing any sin or shortcoming. Of the biography type, Guenzburg says there are many examples in Hebrew—Nahmanides and Naphtali Herz Wessely, for instance (and, we would add, the self-told biographies of Reggio, Luzzatto, and others); of true autobiography, there have been very few, or more precisely, none in modern times until *Aviezer.*

These categories, it need hardly be said, are not original with Guenzburg; the mention of confessing should give away his indebtedness to the climate of assumptions concerning the genre created by Rousseau, whose ideas, we have seen, entered Jewish literature through the conduit of Solomon Maimon's autobiography. (Although Maimon's autobiography was not translated into Hebrew until 1899, it was widely read in the original.) It is to Rousseau's simple but previously unacknowledged assumption that childhood and youth are essential to understanding the mature person that we owe the first substantial accounts of those stages of development in Hebrew in the works of Guenzburg and Lilienblum. Rousseau's primary influence was, of course, in identifying the autobiographical act with confession and sincerity—what our writers would call "the love of truth"—and in creating a literary norm that requires revealing what is indiscreet, foolish, and shameful in a life as well as what is noble, and that further requires that no dimension of the personal life remain above scrutiny. There are, however, two other conditions of Rousseauean autobiography which Hebrew writers had much more difficulty in assimilating. One is Rousseau's assertion, trumpeted in the famous opening lines of *The Confessions*, of the absolute originality and unrepeatability of his experience and the literary account of it. "I have resolved on an enterprise which has no precedent, and which, once complete, will have no imitator."[19] One need only mention the Haskalah writer's belief in reason, reform, and the correctibility of human behavior to know that he had a greater interest in stressing the typicality of his experience than its originality. It is the actual content of the Rousseauean confession which presented the most difficulties for the Haskalah autobiographer. What is being confessed are the passions of the heart, the search for love, the continual attempts to satisfy a need for total intimate companionship which includes physical union but goes far beyond it. In the face of confessions such as these, our autobiographers, Lithuanian scholars married at the threshold of puberty, must stand with empty hands: there was simply nothing in their experience that answered to Rousseau's preoccupation with passionate intimacy.

There is a conspicuous discontinuity in the Hebrew autobiographical tradition between these works of Guenzburg and Lilienblum and the spate of activity at the turn of the century in the works of Feierberg, Berdichevsky, and Brenner. The gap reflects in part the differences between the worldview of the Haskalah and that of the Revival (Tehiyah) Period that succeeded it. The pogroms of 1881 that figured so prominently in the resolution of Lilienblum's own identity became a symbolic marker between the end of one era and the beginning of another.

In the Revival Period, the autobiographical impulse took a different turn: it crossed over into fiction. By the 1890s, the imposing edifice of the Haskalah novel had been dismantled, and fiction therefore no longer had to be avoided in order to serve as a medium for telling the story of one's life. Novelists could now hark back to the Haskalah autobiography and exploit *its* conventions as a technique for leavening their work with authenticity. The crossover into fiction also opened up a new avenue of aesthetic possibility. In the Haskalah autobiography, the author of the work and the retrospective narrator of the story are presumably the same person. The Lilienblum who tells the story of his life in *Sins of Youth* presents himself as the same Lilienblum who lived the life and now exists as a real public person. From the point of view of poetics, we may designate the teller as a narrative persona, but from the experience of the reader and the "compact" he enters into with the author, there is no difference.[20] In the fictional text, however, the expectations, and hence the possibilities, are otherwise. Elimelekh, the young hero who tells his story in Berdichevsky's *A Raven Flies* (*'Urva parah*), is not presumed to be Berdichevsky. There remains a potentially fast distinction between the implied author (Berdichevsky) and the retrospective narrator (Elimelekh), however much the one may have shared the experiences of the other. This gives the author the opportunity to ironize the distance between himself and the narrator, who can then be tinged with various degrees of unreliability. This is a freedom, we shall see, of which both Berdichevsky and Brenner take full advantage.

Mordecai Ze'ev Feierberg (1874–1899), Mica Yosef Berdichevsky (1865–1921), and Yosef Hayyim Brenner (1881–1921) are the three Hebrew writers from the Revival Period who make the fullest fictional use of the autobiographical tradition to tell the story of a generation's spiritual uprooting. The three works that partake of this tradition were all published around the turn of the century: Feierberg's *Le'an?* (*Whither?*) in 1899, Berdichevsky's *A Raven Flies* in 1900, and Brenner's *Bahoref (In Winter)* in 1903. Although the appearance of these novels and novellas is highly clustered, there is a clear progression among them in which each work comments upon and proceeds from the other. The shared theme undergoes a rapid elaboration within a very short period of time.

Most conspicuous is a sense of a division of labor among these works, as if a common story were being told by diverse hands. This was already evident in an earlier period in Lilienblum's explicit acknowledgment that he was beginning with adolescence because the account of childhood had been adequately dealt with in Guenzburg's *Aviezer*. Similarly, Berdichevsky concentrates on the years of young adulthood as if the story of the earlier stages of life had already been told by Feierberg. But it is not so much in the chronological apportioning of the narrative that this interdependence is evident as in the division of themes. Feierberg accomplishes what no one else does in all of Hebrew literature; he reconstructs from within the post-Haskalah ordeal of apostasy, experienced as nothing less than a personal and cosmic catastrophe. Berdichevsky, on the other hand, explores the deferred consequences of this event for the psychic organization of the young intellectual. Cut off from family and community and trusting in the sufficiency of reason, Berdichevsky's hero easily falls prey to the forces of erotic obsession. *A Raven Flies* is a brilliant examination of the unsuccessful defenses mobilized to neutralize this threat; the novella is the first representation in Hebrew literature of neurotic repetition.

The true sign that these works comprise an identifiable and self-consciously organized tradition is indicated by the intertextual nature of Brenner's autobiographical first novel *In Winter*. That Brenner, the great modernist prose writer of the Revival Period, should altogether have chosen the Hebrew autobiography (as opposed to the several Russian and European versions available) as the literary model for his debut as a novelist is a fact of signal importance. His deep and self-aware engagement of these earlier Hebrew texts operates on several planes. As to the partition of the apostasy narrative into several developmental stages, Brenner presumes, unlike any of his predecessors, to comprehend the whole, that is, to undertake an account of childhood, adolescence, and young adulthood. Similarly, he attempts to overcome the thematic division between the spiritual-intellectual dimension of experience after faith and the sexual-psychological dimension by incorporating both and making the one dependent on the other. In each of the sections of *In Winter* there are scenes which are not only recognizably dependent upon Brenner's precursors but which deal with thematic territory that has been pioneered and, in a sense, owned by others. From Feierberg Brenner takes the depiction of childhood piety, the delight in the *mitsvot,* and the dread of the consequences of sin. From Lilienblum Brenner reevokes the account of the young man's move to the city and his humiliating ordeal of belated education. And from Berdichevsky, of course, there is the intellectual's descent into the mire of erotic obsession.

Now it might seem from this that Brenner's *In Winter* is merely a pastiche that summarizes a genre rather than an original work that redefines one. But this would be a mistaken impression. Brenner's originality is radical and far-reaching. Each instance of apparent borrowing is in fact a case of determined appropriation in which Brenner undertakes a thoroughgoing revision of his received material. Feierberg, for example, is invoked but undercut; the dour piety that repressed the growth of his hero is revalued and presented in Brenner as a medium which was vital and nurturing but one which is now so completely lost as to be irrelevant. Not only is each thematic component revised but the organization of the whole has been redesigned. In order to grasp Brenner's revisionary stance toward the tradition of Hebrew autobiography, I propose in chapters 5, 6, and 7 to understand *In Winter* as a text created by the interplay of thematic codes. I shall argue that Brenner takes the autobiographical tradition and breaks it down into three codes: the cognitive-cultural code, which treats religious and ideological belief and intellectual development; the existential-psychological code, which examines the impact of family and education upon the formation of the self; and finally the erotic code, which represents the unconscious motives for behavior as they are triggered by the male hero's response to women. Brenner's novel is rigorously divided into three parts, in each of which there is a different disposition of the three codes and different narrative techniques for presenting them.

In Winter is a complex and important enough work to warrant such involved analysis on its own. But its true significance derives from its location at the end of a tradition and its status as its culmination. It is on the basis of that claim—plus the desire to convey to the non-Hebrew reader something of the texture and aura of Brenner's fictional world—that more than a third of the present volume is devoted to this one work. *In Winter* does nothing less than rewrite the whole of the Hebrew autobiographical tradition and in so doing brings it to an accelerated end—at least for the time being. (The subsequent career of the autobiographical impulse in Hebrew literature will be the subject of the conclusion to this study.)

For all the large issues raised in this study about the fate of the self in the aftermath of belief, the compass remains purposefully circumscribed. The confessional tradition inspired in Hebrew by Rousseau and Maimon is a stream that runs deep but never turns into a torrent. Guenzburg's and Lilienblum's are the classical models that are appropriated in fiction by Feierberg and Berdichevsky and given an authoritative reworking by Brenner. This tradition can be understood as an intersection between a formal and a thematic axis. The formal axis is the autobiographical premise of self-portraiture and retrospective narrative; the thematic axis is what we have called in a kind of shorthand the apostasy narrative (*sippur hahitpakrut*), which describes a young man's break with religion, family, and community, and his attempts to live in a world empty of those beliefs and institutions.

If these two axes were disentangled, each could certainly be followed with profit on its own path. The autobiographical direction would lead us to the childhood recollections of such great writers as Sh. Y. Abramowitsch (Mendele) in his *Of Bygone Days* (1894–1911, *Bayamim hahem*) or to the first-person memoirs of the famous and the obscure who participated in the wars and revolutions and social movements that shaped the age and who wrote of their experiences in Hebrew. In these works the events witnessed are more important than the mind and soul of the autobiographer; at most his individual experience is presented as paradigmatic of the ordeal of some larger collective.

The subtle exploration of inwardness absent from this group is present in abundance if, in turn, we isolate the thematic axis. U. N. Gnessin pushed Brenner's dissections of inner emptiness even farther; his work represents the most radical extrapolation of this direction. In a lesser vein, the novels of I. Bershadsky break new ground in the development of a psychological realism and an appreciation of subconscious motives. Within a more social and less introspective framework, the fiction of Y. D. Berkovitch and H. D. Normberg depicts the predicament of the uprooted intellectual, the *talush,* at home in neither the old order or the new. Yet here it is the confessional, self-reflexive dimension that is missing.

There remains a context in which the two axes do come together brilliantly: the poetry of Bialik.[21] Alongside the stately prophetic image of Bialik as the national poet—and perversely at odds with it at many turns— is an autobiographical myth that is in a continual process of being elaborated and revised throughout Bialik's career. We find here many of the themes familiar to us from prose fiction: early emotional deprivation, Torah and the commandments as alternative sources of nurturing, the catastrophic loss of faith, the seductions of nostalgia and the torments of guilt, and the search for new modes of identity. Bialik's quest brings him to the mystery of nature, to the negative capability of the imagination, and to the vocation of poetry.[22] Bialik's attachment to these new sources of strength and authority is precarious and in the end tragically beyond reach. Yet those powers to which the poet seeks to bind himself reveal just how different is his situation from that of the writers in the prose autobiographical tradition. Bialik's lyric poetry is generated by a romantic mythos which assumes a sympathetic rapport between the soul of the poet and the soul of world. This rapport is often no more than a memory of loss or the ghost of a presence, yet it makes possible a metaphysical middle ground which is not available to a writer such as Brenner. When the autobiographical speaker in Bialik's "Before the Bookcase" ("Lifnei aron hasefarim") is banished from the world of the study house, he is received into the arms of the night, which, as Dan Miron has eloquently shown, represents an alternative plenum of mystery and meaning.[23] Bialik and those who followed him in the poetic revolution he began were, in short, influenced by romantic and symbolist models of literary discourse that are different from those of the writers who followed the Rousseauean breakthrough in prose and prose fiction. Even the one gem of Bialik's *prose* that is genuinely autobiographical, "Aftergrowth" ("Safiah"), falls outside the bounds of the present study because it is attached to a wholly different tradition which is concerned with the birth of the imagination in the child rather than with the loss of faith and its consequences later in life.

After years of neglect, autobiography has recently become an attractive object of theoretical study in literary criticism.[24] The first phase of this new interest centered on the design the autobiographer imposed on the flux of his or her experience and the metaphors fashioned to express that pattern.[25] The second phase was initiated by the deconstructionist skepticism about fixing the self in language. More than any other genre, autobiography promises to tell the truth about a life, and this claim has provoked the scrutiny of critics like Paul De Man who see in this presumption an illusion of escape from the constraints of language and reference.[26] Whereas James Olney would point with pride at the opportunity autobiography affords for the expression of man's self-making capacities through language, De Man would point to a sense of absence produced by man's having been dissolved into language.[27]

The terms of this debate are not directly relevant to the autobiographers, real and fictional, discussed here. None of them believes in language enough to fear that his ontological status will be supplanted by it or to assume that a misspent life can be reinvented through a linguistic act of self-creation. The earlier discussion about the design and patterning of a life is, as will become evident, more to the point. The thorny definitional issues about what constitutes an autobiographical text in the absence of first-person telling do not present a problem in our case. The works of the five authors discussed here belong to a discrete literary-historical phenomenon, and they are identified with each other by virtue of their overt thematics as well as by a network of intertextual references.

Rather than imposing a theoretical schema on this material, we can learn more by asking what are the critical issues urgently suggested by the texts themselves. Some of these issues are common to the autobiographical enterprise in other climates and venues, while others take on a particular inflection within the context of Hebrew literature.

First is the issue of inwardness. This may seem axiomatic in a discussion of autobiography; yet it is surprising in how many examples of the genre the focus falls on many things other than the inner life of the narrator: the times, the folkways of a culture, scholarly controversies, other family members, professional accomplishments, and so on. As Karl Joachim Weintraub has pointed out, this sense of inwardness is historically conditioned and becomes possible only when a society conceives of the value of individual experience in its individuality.[28] Although the heroes of the Hebrew autobiographies discussed here partake in a collective historical trauma, they never cease to experience their dislocation in distinctly personal terms. Their pain and inadequacy are not lessened by being part of the common woe.

The second issue concerns confession, the expressive and transactive realization of inwardness. Every utterance, we know, is said by someone to someone; who speaks in autobiography is usually self-evident, but who is addressed is not always clear. For Guenzburg and Lilienblum the conventions of the Hebrew ethical will still prevail. Having survived an ordeal of miseducation and error, they seek to bequeath their hard-won wisdom to their imagined spiritual descendants. Yet for their real followers, the fiction writers who took up the autobiographical mode at the end of the century, the conviction of having garnered from life a communicable knowledge had broken down. Is the narrator's speech only an ejaculation, an ungovernable outcry which is addressed to no one? Or does the narrator address himself in a solipsistic effort to exorcise his own demons? Whatever the case, the motive animating Rousseau—to explain himself to society and justify his "deviant" behavior—is no longer at the center of the Hebrew autobiographical endeavor. The question is a larger one than the relations between the dramatized narrator and the dramatized addressee within the text. In the sociology of Hebrew literature at the time (the relations between real authors and real audiences), a readership for the new, modernist Hebrew fiction seems not to have yet developed, and this void is palpably reflected within the narratives themselves.[29]

The third issue is the shape given to the narrated life.[30] At the most basic level there is the choice of which segments of a life to represent. Which years are considered to be the crucible of identity, and how is this choice governed by the stages of life that have already been exhaustively described in earlier autobiographical works by other writers? Like any narrator, the autobiographer makes continual choices about what is put in the foreground and what in the background, and which events can be summarized and which demand scenic depiction. What is special in the case of autobiography is the focus on a single life and the self-assumed responsibility of the narrator to make sense of his own history. Making sense means identifying a pattern of coherence within the welter of actions and circumstances. This pattern or design, as James Olney has shown, is often not explicitly stated but expressed through central metaphors. Lilienblum, for example, presents the shape of his life as a series of futile ploddings that, like grace from above, is suddenly transformed by yielding to the *force majeure* of history. A candle that blazes most brightly in the moment just before it exhausts its fuel and expires is the image used by Feierberg to convey the intensity of experience in the suicidal descent into apostasy. For Berdichevsky, the pattern is circular; his narrator's blindness to the meaning of his experience condemns him to the treadmill of neurotic repetition. In contrast, Brenner's hero grasps the nature of his ordeal and learns from it—up to a point; his understanding does not extend to his buried sexual needs, which end by destroying what he had achieved. The image here is of new life (the infant's emergence from the womb, the moth's metamorphosis into a butterfly) being beaten back in the enclosure whence it came.

The fourth issue concerns the rhetoric of authenticity. The autobiography in Hebrew arose, we have seen, as an alternative to the melodramatic and sentimental conventions of the Haskalah novel. Yet persuading the reader that the "true" truth was indeed being told required its own rhetoric. Lilienblum made the breakthrough by making his text a melange of letters, telegrams, journal entries, and quotations from books, as well as continuous narrative. Later writers in the tradition develop other strategies to produce the effect of authenticity: revealing shameful behavior, recording dreams and reveries, cultivating a deliberately anti-literary style, constructing plots that are episodic and fragmentary. Most of all, the autobiographer relies upon the generic expectations surrounding his text generated by what Philippe Lejeune calls "the autobiographical compact."[31] According to the terms of this compact, the reader accepts as truthful or sincere the claim that the narrative is a retrospective account told by a real person about real events that have taken place in his own existence. It is precisely this credulity, this inclination to accept as authentic a text that bears the markings of autobiography, that was so successfully exploited by fiction writers such as Brenner who violated the autobiographical compact for the sake of a higher autobiographical truth.

The final and most fundamental critical issue is the retrospective premise of autobiography. The narrator tells a story about himself in which he is both the teller of the tale and its subject. This entails the splitting of the self into a narrating "I" and a narrated "I" or, put differently, the narrator as retrospective analyst and the narrator as experiencing character.[32] So, for example, in Brenner's *In Winter* Yirmiah Feuerman, the narrator, sits in an isolated village and chronicles the development of Yirmiah Feuerman, the character. His interjections into the story and his meditations on the difficulty of telling it take place within the present time of the writing, while the account of his development is located at various removes in the past. What complicates this situation from the point of view of narrative poetics is the fact that neither of these poles is stable. As for the narrator as character, it goes without saying that he is not one but many as he develops from child to youth and approaches the present time of the writing. But there is no guarantee that the narrator as retrospective writer will not change during the actual course of the writing and as a response to his encounter with his previous selves. This is precisely what happens in *Sins of Youth;* the Lilienblum who begins telling his story is very different from the Lilienblum who concludes it.

This is a complexity that a reader takes in his stride because of necessity it creates an engaging dramatic tension: Will the narrator succeed in the end in overcoming the split between his past and present selves? This can be achieved in many ways; the most obvious is based on the psychoanalytic model in which the goal is to accept the past and thereby become free of its constraints. This ideal of integration, or at least the honest struggling toward it, becomes, then, the implicit test for the success of the autobiographical undertaking. Does the narrator succeed in recovering his self or does he fail? This is a test, however, which does not easily apply to Hebrew autobiography; or to put it another way, this is a norm which our authors, at least those following Lilienblum, feel constrained to violate. Berdichevsky's Elimelekh is more deeply mired in bad faith at the end of his story than at its outset, and Brenner's Feuerman is similarly overmastered by unbidden obsessions when he brings his account to an indeterminate conclusion. This "failure" to achieve integration is, to my mind, part of the great honesty of Hebrew autobiography. Just as it was impossible to conform to the romantic expectations of the novel *(roman)* form, so it was impossible to manufacture a harmony of self at a historical moment in which the world had fallen badly out of kilter. Given the futility of the goal, then, the willingness to expose the secrets of the self nonetheless becomes an act of courage.

Although our Hebrew writers may provide interesting cases for theorists of autobiography, it is not here that the drama of the material is primarily to be found. The signal service performed by these texts lies elsewhere; it lies in their giving us a window into the interior experience of the generation of Jews who lived through the great transformation of Jewish life in the modern era. We can examine the history of political and social institutions and the development of religious and ideological movements and thereby discover a great deal about this upheaval without penetrating this interior dimension. How was the loss of faith experienced by the individual and how did it affect the perception of reality? How were relations within the family changed: between parents and children, and between spouses? What was the nature of relations between the sexes in a world from which religious tradition had suddenly been withdrawn? What are the consequences of the feelings of shame, vulnerability, and loneliness on the capacity to reconstruct both Jewish collective life and individual existence? For answers to these questions the Hebrew autobiographical tradition is an important source.

The goal of the present study, however, is not directly historiographical; it aims instead at dramatizing the pathos of this moment in recent Jewish history and at understanding, through works of literature, the mentality of those who experienced it intensely. The pathos of the moment, we said at the outset, results from being born into Jewish history both too late and too early. Unlike their Haskalah predecessors, for our authors the experience of apostasy was not the happy prelude to an enlightened life but a vertiginous fall into an unexplored void. Feierberg projected this sense of dislocation backward and reimagined the inner religious world of the child as always having existed under the sign of loss. Later writers located the time of loss in the past and lived long enough to examine the vicissitudes of life in the void.

To be sure, these were lives lived under conditions of extremity, but it would be a mistake to take the writing as an unrelieved record of torment and complaint. While one cannot speak of uplift, there are several senses in which we are witness to the human spirit's transcending its constraints in a moment of violent cultural change. We are witness, to begin with, to the nearly instantaneous transmutation of the painfully raw stuff of experience into serious and enduring art. In this these Hebrew works do not resemble the monuments of the Western autobiographical tradition, many of which are recollected in the tranquility of age and from the security of an achieved career and identity. Our Hebrew writers are barely through with adolescence when they set about making their life into a literature in which they, or their personae, are the heroes. Their stories are infused with a sense of experiential immediacy, creations still molten from the crucible of the imagination. The very existence of this art, moreover, is evidence of an ineffaceable sense of self. Despite failures of achievement and deficiencies of character, one must nevertheless be convinced of the *significance* of the experiences one is living through in order to believe that the story is worth telling.

Most impressive of all is the honesty. Hebrew autobiographical literature is about the capacity to abide the great crisis in the modern Jewish mind without telling lies. The possibilities for evasion are many: minimizing the consequences of the loss of faith, romanticizing what was lost, making ideologies into functional substitutes for religion, or simply walking away from the burden of Jewishness. The great existential strength of our autobiographical heroes lies, then, in their willingness to withstand the full measure of pain caused by the disappearance of God while at the same time seeing through the premature schemes to create new orders of meaning. In the precarious business of abiding the void, their consciousness is both a consolation and an instrument of insight. Intelligence, careful observation, and analytic acumen make it possible to demystify the awesomeness of the catastrophe and understand its components and proportions, and thereby locate the often despairing ordeal of the individual within the drama of the nation and the cosmos.

Finally, the very act of writing in Hebrew at the turn of the century demonstrated no small amount of faith. At the time the revival of the Hebrew tongue was much more a slogan than a reality; the very existence of a readership for Hebrew literature was in doubt. Mass audiences did exist if one followed the example of the great progenitor of Jewish autobiography, Solomon Maimon, to become a Jewish author in a non-Jewish language. There was no bar to becoming a Russian, German, French, or English writer, and the histories of those literatures bear witness to how greatly they were enriched by the efforts of Jews who did precisely that. To write in Hebrew at the turn of the century represented a calling of a different sort. It represented a faithfulness in a troubled present and an unseen future.

TWO

The Haskalah Background:
In the Toils of Authenticity

Lilienblum's *Sins of Youth* was the monumental autobiography of the Haskalah period, but it is not the true link between Rousseau and Maimon and the novelists at the turn of the century. This distinction belongs to a lesser known autobiography written fifty years earlier: Guenzburg's *Aviezer*. In writing the account of his life, Lilienblum assumes that his reader is familiar with *Aviezer* and, secure in this knowledge, takes leave to describe issues and stages of life not already dealt with by his precursor. It is to Guenzburg we must first look to discern the contours of the Haskalah autobiography.

Mordecai Aaron Guenzburg (1795–1846) was born in Salant, Lithuania and earned a living as an itinerant tutor until he settled permanently in Vilna, where with the poet Solomon Salkind he founded a modern Jewish school and became one of the leading spokesmen for the Vilna Haskalah. In addition to *Aviezer* and *Devir*, a miscellany of translated letters and travel accounts, Guenzburg was best known for a popular and stylistically influential series of histories of contemporary Europe, which included *Toledot benei 'adam*, *'Ittotei rusya*, and *Hatsarfatim berusya*.

Aviezer, which was begun in 1828 and published posthumously in 1864, is a statement about the ineluctable connection between impotence and apostasy. Impotence is viewed in part figuratively, as the enforced passivity inherent in the heder system of rote learning and in the enforced dependence on superstition and *pilpul* in matters of dogma and belief. But impotence is also taken very literally: as the sexual dysfunction resulting from the premature confrontation with sexuality enforced by the system of arranged early marriage. The cumulative effect of these varieties of impotence, Guenzburg argues, was to deny him the inner strength necessary to stand up before the onslaught of metaphysical questions which assailed him upon reaching maturity and which brought him to the verge of apostasy, of which he was finally cured, together with his sexual impotence, by an outside agency in the person of an aging apostate doctor. This thesis is realized in the book's four-part structure: three sections devoted to different aspects of impotence and a fourth presenting the cure and the philosophical affirmations it made possible. In its proportions the book is laid out as follows: section one, chapters 1–16: the heder and the formal

25

education; section two, chapters 17–37: marriage and domestic politics; section three, chapters 38–41: faith and apostasy; section four, chapters 42–52: the cure.

If *Aviezer* was concerned only with the figurative aspects of impotence it would hardly be distinguished from other didactic literature of the Haskalah; but the depiction of real impotence, bearing a burden of humiliation that is intensely and inescapably personal, indicates the presence here of a subjective dimension that is strikingly new. As a literary work *Aviezer* contains two intentions or functions: one didactic and one confessional, the two representing the older and the newer autobiographical norms. The *didactic* intention is evinced in the use of the experience of the individual as an illustration of the larger abuses of the community; the function of discourse here is to move the reader, who is palpably apostrophized, to corrective action, and the rhetorical mode is neoclassical in its use of parable, generalization, and example. The *confessional* intention, on the other hand, is not to expose but to express; the function of discourse in this mode is to effect release from a burden of private distress and to gain sympathy for the history of a particular individual; the rhetorical mode is protoromantic: since the purpose is to tell the story of a life, emphasis is placed on the production of a continuous narrative, to which such static elements as digressions and examples are subordinated. What is impressive about Guenzburg in *Aviezer* is his ability to manage both intentions, making them function together to produce a transition work of high importance.[1]

The didactic intention is understandably most in force in the examination of the heder years in the first section of *Aviezer.* The fact that this section consists largely of critical descriptions of the pedagogical methods of his several melamdim is very much in keeping with Guenzburg's eighteenth-century assumptions about education. After Locke Guenzburg believed, simply, that a child's mind is a clean slate that registers whatever associations are impressed upon it. The immense formative powers accorded teachers and parents by this theory put the child in a much greater danger of victimization than any romantic theory that would have the natural self of the child struggling to emerge on its own. The kind of educational victimization Guenzburg describes—in addition to the unrelenting exposure to the caprices of adult will and to such idiosyncrasies as one melamed's obvious manic depression—involves the systematic denial of cognitive freedom and autonomy. As to method, the teacher can show the child how to make something his own by understanding and reasoning it from within or he can give him a cheap sense of mastery through memorizing and copying, the path Guenzburg calls "living by theft" (p. 26). As to exegesis, the teacher can demonstrate the use of reason in extracting religious truth from figurative and aggadic material or he can handicap the child's mind by leaving it forever chained to fancy and superstition. And as to curriculum, the teacher can nourish the soul with a mixed course of

Bible, language, and Talmud, or he can leave the soul impoverished with an exclusive regime of Talmud study. When teachers refuse, as Guenzburg claims most of his did, to show the path to the true acquisition of knowledge and to its rational interpretation and thus relegate the student to imitation and superstition, the child is unmanned and reduced to unremitting dependence.

To give legitimacy to his pronouncements—and to the audacity of the autobiographical act itself—Guenzburg frequently uses in this section some of the conventions of the Hebrew ethical will (the *tsava'ah*). The presence of a hypostasized son or student to whom the work is addressed makes it a dramatic act of communication in the present as well as a narrative of events in the past. It justifies Guenzburg's interrupting the narrative to address to his reader-beneficiary advice for the future in the form of lessons reaped from the past and reflections on the enduring effects of early education.[2] The narrative itself is of a certain kind which does not take on a continuous movement from the past toward the present. Rather, each chapter contains a generalized statement about one stage in life and then offers a dramatized illustration of it. In addition, each chapter contains a parable—usually an animal parable very much after the fashion of such writers as Erter—which expresses the truth of the chapter in compressed figurative form, as if to say that it is insufficient to rely upon statement and example alone to do the work of explanation. In concert these features constitute the very model of a neoclassical argument; first, a short parable whose relevance is at first not clear; second, the decoding of the parable in the form of a general statement of the subject's situation at a certain stage of childhood; third, a situational example; and fourth, a return to the present of the writing in which the author makes the reader-listener the recipient of the cautionary wisdom of his experience.

Behind the story of marriage and impotence in the second section of *Aviezer* is the grand indictment of Eastern European society for collapsing the distance between childhood and adulthood and refusing to acknowledge the claims of adolescence. Guenzburg feels that by being asked to become a man overnight he was cheated of his youth, which survived only in occasional acts of petty rebellion and theft by which he symbolically repossessed what was taken from him. With a fine eye Guenzburg describes the workings of the marriage system as a set of transactions in which each family tries to maximize its three basic sources of "capital": learning, ancestry, and money. In Guenzburg's case, his father prided himself overmuch on the value of the family's ancestry and on his son's fame as a scholar, and while he bided his time in search of a stunning match, the position of the family was greatly shaken by the shame brought on it by the conversion to "Islam" (probably a euphemism for Christianity) of a relative of the father. As a consequence, the boy was sold into bondage to a family of wealthy but vulgar tailors. Being traded like chattel is disabling enough, but in this section Guenzburg's powerlessness takes on the additional quality of forced feminization. His transfer from the wise and benevolent supervision of his father and his deliverance into the collusive society of his new wife and mother-in-law are sealed by his inability to perform his duties as a man. The ordeal of humiliation comes to a climax when, in a perverse version of the *sotah* ritual, he becomes dangerously ill after being forced by the women to drink a potion to restore his virtility. He is finally rescued by his father, who sends for him to return to Salant.

It is clear that what interests Guenzburg in these events is not the play of love and feeling, but the play of power and powerlessness to which human relations are reduced in the absence of other sentiments. Even the eventual reconciliation between the boy and his young wife is really a restoration of a balance of power which has nothing to do with romance. These scenes, highly dramatic and wonderfully executed, are, to the best of my knowledge, the first sustained treatment in Hebrew literature of the politics of domestic relations. Whether because of the dramatic interaction of these scenes, or because of the deep personal humiliation they explore, or simply because of the fact that there is a story pressing to be told, the effect is that the paraphernalia of neoclassical statement are swept away by the strong current of historical narrative. The conventions of the *tsava'ah* form with the frequent addresses to a son or student are conspicuously absent, as is the need to make generalizations and provide examples. A few parables do remain but they are used in a special way to control the flow of the story by heightening suspense at critical points.

Later on in *Aviezer* Guenzburg recounts how the experience of reading the *Josippon* engendered a passion for history and a desire to make the writing of history his vocation. "And that is the only aspiration from all my youthful hopes," he writes with pathos, "that ever truly came to fruition" (p. 129). Guenzburg did indeed go on to become the writer who, more than any other in the Haskalah, gave the Hebrew reader access to the drama of European history. Guenzburg's real contribution, however, was not as a historian but as a writer of history. The substance of his historiography is decidedly derivative, but his winnowing of the elevated diction of the middle Haskalah to make Hebrew a vigorous narrative instrument for dealing with war and political conflict was an immense achievement. What is exciting in reading the central sections of *Aviezer* is the sense that we are watching Guenzburg, under the pressure of describing the turbulent conflicts of his own history, forging that language which he will later use so effectively to describe the affairs of nations.

The portrayal of apostasy in the fourth section is the most conventional: *pilpul* as a set of empty dialectics, Judaism's evasion of philosophical formulations, the stream of doubts that enter the mind once the first question is asked. What remains important here is the insistent analogy between this and the preceding section: just as the denial of feeling had led to dysfunction in the sexual sphere, so too the denial of spiritual nourishment has led to a breakdown in the sphere of faith.

It is entirely uncoincidental that the man who cures one dysfunction should cure the other too. The author is put into the hands of a mysterious aged doctor, a convert from Judaism and a possible crypto-Sabbatean, who is well versed in modern medicine as well as in the alchemical sciences. The young Guenzburg is finally cured of his impotence, ending a long cycle in the book and causing great rejoicing in his household. But the spiritual cure takes much longer. It is a kind of talking cure, presented in a series of reconstructed Socratic dialogues in which Guenzburg is set on the right path concerning God and immortality in terms derived from Mendelssohn's *Phaedon*. The purpose of the dialogues is to relieve the metaphysical impotence of skepticism into which Guenzburg has fallen in his questioning of revelation and tradition. The aged doctor accomplishes his task by demonstrating that a belief in God and immortality can be secured through reason alone, and by understanding this the lad can become one of the enlightened, who know inner strength rather than emasculating dependence on received traditions.

But to his credit Guenzburg realized that for his condition there is no full recovery. Just as he admits that his relationship with his wife will always be complicated and that he will always have to conserve his sexual energy, so he admits that the doctor's teaching has raised more questions than it has resolved and that his teaching will have to remain only a partial answer to be used alongside the tradition, which itself has not ceased to be compromised.

As a text *Sins of Youth (Ḥat'ot ne'urim)*[3] begins by presenting itself as the completion of another text. Of the genre of autobiography, in which the story of a life gets told because of its intrinsic significance rather than its association (as in biography) with the name of a great man, Lilienblum holds that there is only one genuine example in Hebrew literature: Guenzburg's *Aviezer. Aviezer* was exemplary and exhaustive in its analysis of the years of the heder and the years of betrothal in the life of a Lithuanian boy, but its account had stopped short of the trial of experience which follows in the years of manhood and accomplishment. Now, fifty years later, as if there was to be told the story of a single collective life, another Lithuanian boy who has grown to a kind of maturity is prepared to complete the task.

In a dozen pages, enough space to supply the relevant *differentia* of family background, Lilienblum dispatches the first fifteen years of his life— the span of years to which *Aviezer* was devoted entirely. The ground has been ceded to Guenzburg; what is relevant was said by him. Even in the first period of life to receive serious treatment in *Sins of Youth*, the ages between fifteen and twenty-three (1858–1866), one finds the same thematics of insufficiency that preoccupied Guenzburg. Here too is the story of a young *'illui* (talmudic prodigy) who is sold like chattel to a domineering and ambitious mother-in-law. Here too is the story of a mind which, parched by the aridity of Talmud study and strained by the extravagance of legend and lore, is forced to make its way from Maimonides to the more radical rationalists to the Haskalah writers and finally to apostasy. Here too the domestic theme and the educational theme are brought together in the figure of nocturnal emission. As the inevitability of apostasy becomes apparent, doubts are pushed back with redoubled piety; the young man attempts to rid himself of polluting thoughts so as not to endanger himself on the night of Yom Kippur, when a nocturnal emission is said to be a harbinger of early death. But on the morning of the holiest of days Lilienblum awakes to find that the dread event has taken place, a symbol for the eruption of irrepressible forces of both doubt and need.

The *Aviezer* elements, however, are quickly left behind. A look at the disposition of the materials of *Sins of Youth*, expressed in terms of the ratio of years to pages, gives a sense of Lilienblum's priorities in presenting the story of his life.

Section	Number of Years	Number of Pages
Days of Confusion	15	15
Days of Darkness and the Beginning of the Transition	8 (to age 23)	40
Days of Apostasy	3 (to age 26)	80
Days of Crisis and Renunciation	4 (to age 30)	130
The Way Back	9	55

For Lilienblum, religious crisis is clearly no longer the central issue of autobiography. The loss of faith, which takes place in the "Days of Darkness" section, came to fruition over eight years, which are dispatched in forty pages, while the new life *after* heresy, spreading over roughly the same number of years, requires a treatment of over two hundred pages. That a young man of active imagination and intelligence will, given certain circumstances, lose his faith is a fact altogether taken for granted; it is for some an event not nearly so catastrophic as it once was. The present question is the nature of experience in the aftermath of crisis and in the newly opened space of apostasy. Lilienblum calls this new space the *'olam ha-ma'aseh*, the world of praxis and practicality; at issue is the passage from learning to doing and from religious mystification to acting in the world.

The distinction between these two domains is rendered by Lilienblum's statement at the end of the work (2: 128ff.) that his life could be summarized by reference to four sins or failures. (The subtitle of *Sins of Youth* is *Haviddui hagadol* [*The Great Confession*].) Two were committed by his father: forced early marriage and a useless, impractical education. Two were committed by Lilienblum himself: uncritical devotion to the romantic Haskalah and a pointless involvement with a young woman. The domain of *Aviezer* is constituted entirely by the first two sins, and in as much as these are sins of the fathers against the sons the autobiographical discourse of *Aviezer* had to remain within the limitations of the Rousseauean ethic of sincerity. Rousseau was willing to confess his frailties and humiliations, but only the better to excoriate the society that had inflicted them and to defend his version of the essential self that had been thereby trodden down. In this version of autobiography confession and complaint are not exclusive. Similarly, we are persuaded by the sincerity of Guenzburg's story without ceasing to feel that this is sincerity for a purpose. The disclosure of impotence, in all its manifestations, is surely an act of sensitivity and courage, but it is also an act which, beyond any self-therapeutic function, serves to point the finger of guilt away from the speaking subject toward those who he feels bear final responsibility: through parents to Jewish society as a whole.

Guenzburg's decision to end his narrative with adolescence allowed him to remain within the protective innocence of childhood. In contrast, Lilienblum's determination to extend the autobiographical project into the years of moral autonomy, in which the consequences of the sins of the fathers persist but do not determine, offers no such cover. Because he acknowledges freedom over his own life, he must also accept accountability for it. In exchange for this burden it was given to Lilienbum to eclipse the older confessional ethic and produce a work that is an act of genuine self-confrontation.[4]

For Lilienblum the achievement of such authenticity means the acceptance of his failure to realize his freedom. He yielded to the blandishments of the Haskalah: he misspent his emotions in a confused attachment which was never consummated; he became obsessed with a fruitless fantasy of university study. In *Sins of Youth* Lilienblum intends us to see the unfolding of a path along which these delusions are recognized as such and discarded, until a point of existential purity is reached at which expectation is finally renounced.

Like all autobiographies, the form of *Sins of Youth* is generated by the convergence of two axes of self: (a) the present self, which from a position of achieved knowledge writes the text before us and creates (b) a series of past selves which change until they merge with the present of the writing. (That the time of the writing of the text is itself a duration during which the act of narration may alter the identity of the writing self is an actual possibility in *Sins of Youth*, one which will be returned to later.) Because in autobiography the present self has the authority to arrange the past and valorize it according to its priorities—to assume, in effect, a sovereign retrospective point of view—it is crucial to be sure of the identity of the finished self. In the case of *Sins of Youth*, knowing who Lilienblum is at the end of the work is complicated by the fact that there is more than one ending. In 1876 Lilienblum published a book called *Sins of Youth*, which brought his life through his thirtieth year (1873). The retrospective voice is that of a man whose life has ended and who surveys a vast cycle of self-deception and renunciation from a point of view from which no further development can be expected. However, in the early nineties Lilienblum wrote another autobiographical document (published in 1899) which re-opened the account of his life he had so dramatically closed many years before. This narrative, called *The Way Back (Derekh teshuvah)*—the title carries the more formal meaning of the path of repentance—picks up at age thirty and tells the story of how during the next eight years Lilienblum did indeed manage to pursue his secular studies in preparation for the university, only to have this enterprise undercut by the pogroms of 1881 and the new national consciousness they forced upon him. *The Way Back* ends with a resurrection to life; Lilienblum has been quickened from the slumber of alienation and renunciation and given a vocation of leadership in the life of the people, which has itself been reinspirited with an idea of renewed possibility.

The complications arise from the fact that Lilienblum did not allow *The Way Back* to stand on its own but called it in a subtitle "Part Three of the Book *Sins of Youth*," the work he had published twenty-three years earlier. Thus for generations of readers the whole work in its expanded form could be read as a story with a "happy ending," a story tracing a passage from negation to affirmation, which was an adumbration in miniature of the future direction of Hebrew literature and the national experience. At this point, however, complication can become confusion. It is not overly rigorous to point out that the ending of *The Way Back* constitutes a retrospective point of view for that composition alone. In light of this later knowledge Lilienblum could have revised *Sins of Youth* proper, but he did not, and therefore that composition of 1876 remains an integral work to which *The Way Back* has the force of a sequel but not a reorganization. We are therefore required to deal with *Sins of Youth* in its own terms and then go on to its sequel.

For some young men the onset of religious crisis resulting in apostasy must have been like the discovery of a dread disease which leaves nothing to look forward to but the fatal spread of infection; for Lilienblum it was like being born again. In the substantial section, "Days of Apostasy," which deals with his life between the ages of twenty-three and twenty-six (1866–1869), Lilienblum demonstrates how successfully the Haskalah could function, for a time, as a substitute religion. The Haskalah gave Lilienblum a new set of dogmas in the tenets of rationalism, a new body of scripture in the writings of Mendelssohn, Krochmal, and the late maskilim, as new eschatology in a vision of a society of enlightened manners and productive activity, in addition to a framework of social explanation which provided a comprehensive critique of Jewish society. Like socialism, positivism, aestheticism, and many other nineteenth-century ideologies that were in fact secularized religions, the Haskalah made it possible for Lilienblum's apostasy to be experienced after a certain point as an arrival instead of a fall—a kind of successful deconversion.

The Haskalah additionally gave Lilienblum something that a prospective career as a fixture in the local beit midrash could not match: an arena for the dramatization of self. In the society of Vilkomir—the Lithuanian town of his inlaws in which his adolescence was spent—Lilienblum assumes the romantic role of both rebel and martyr: the rebel, purchasing suspect books, forming subversive societies, rallying the enlightened youth, and the martyr, insulted and persecuted, bravely enduring all the afflictions of ostracism, even to the point of being informed against to the Russian authorities and risking arrest. Even more significantly, the Haskalah encouraged Lilienblum to become a writer. For him the new pantheon was made up of writers, and the new means of transcendence was writing. It was as a way of using his privileged individual talents in defending himself against his detractors that Lilienblum first took up writing, and it was the writing life which provided him with an alternative dimension of being which, though not remaining unaffected by the vicissitudes of the social life, would continue to provide Lilienblum with a measure of transcendence. In the Hebrew periodical press, in which his name began to be well known, Lillienblum had achieved a kind of power and presence he never attained in his life.

The subject of Lilienblum's writing in those years was religious reform, the question, as he put it, of the "joining of religion and life." Like other conservative unbelievers elsewhere in the late nineteenth century, Matthew Arnold among them, Lilienblum knew that the capacity for belief had been permanently impaired by modernity; at the same time he was deeply shocked at the prospective consequences for the preservation of culture if disbelief was allowed to run unchecked. His solution was to argue that if the demands of religious observance could be lightened by removing the layers of rabbinic interdictions heaped upon the original biblical commandments, then observance could be rationalized and the wholesale abandonment of religion forestalled.

For the purpose of his autobiography, the important burden of Lilienblum's writing at this time was the implication that the correctability of institutions extended to the correctability of individual lives, and specifically to *his* life. Lilienblum was intoxicated with the possibility of his own perfectibility. He trusted in the hope of undoing the effects of the education his father had imposed on him by following the career of the maskil, that is, by acquiring the rudiments of a gymnasium education, studying as an extern, and becoming a merchant or entering one of the useful professions.

Such a career would require leaving his family and his shtetl and going off alone to the big city; far from being pained at this prospect, Lilienblum was eager to be translated to a great center of enlightenment like Odessa and to consummate the role of rebel and martyr by becoming an exile. Just before he was about to leave Vilkomir, at a time when the entire town had righteously cut off relations with him, Lilienblum found a source of sympathy in the person of a young woman named Feyge Novakhovitch (referred to throughout as "N"). He was attracted to her company because she had maskilic leanings and was the only person in the town who was prepared to regard him as the persecuted hero he regarded himself, and also because in his eyes her existence was touched with an aura of romantic love and romantic independence. To a man of twenty-five who had been married from the age of fifteen and had the burden of three children, the idea that someone like Feyge could fall in love was moving and inspiring, all the more so because she had survived being disappointed in love, remained single, and retained her sense of self-worth within shtetl society. It was to her room that he repaired during the days of his persecution to sit with her and read together Mapu's *'Ahavat tsiyyon* and *'Ashmat shomeron,* and it was to her that he addressed an ode of gratitude and praise on the eve of his departure for Odessa (1: 207–10).

It is important to stress that the portrait of the writer as a young heretic-martyr is a reconstruction of Lilienblum's experience of himself during his last years in Vilkomir. At the time of the writing of *Sins of Youth* four to six years later, however, after the existential baptism of the Odessa experience, Lilienblum came to repudiate completely the person he had been during the days of apostasy and to view this earlier self as saturated with self-intoxication and false consciousness. The problem of writing the autobiography then became the problem of how to evoke the full poignancy of that self and its dramatizing ambitions and at the same time pass judgment on them and show the distance traveled to the present standpoint of achieved understanding; how, in other words, both to evoke and to evaluate the past without losing the force of the disparity. If Lilienblum had chosen the conventional means of retrospective narration—the kind of story that inevitably reduces the past to variations of the sentence, "I mistakenly believed at the time that . . ."—he would have granted the present the power and moral authority to vitiate the past even before it had been recalled to being. If, on the other hand, Lilienblum had bowed to the imaginative integrity of the past by allowing it to speak in its own voice dramatically through documents reprinted from that time, the opportunity for judgment would have been lost.

As a way out of this dilemma, Lilienblum chose to mix narrative and documentation, and the special disposition of these materials he arrived at served him well on several counts.[5] Lilienblum, to begin with, was able to achieve a striking embodiment in language of his various selves by making maximum use of the stylistic gulf between the swelling voice of the young maskil and the illusionless voice of the mature autobiographer. A long letter dated 12 Av 1866 describes Lilienblum's attempt to establish a society for the collection of maskilic literature and his various persecutions for his efforts. He addresses his correspondent as follows:

Now you will ask me, dear brother, in what way this society seemed worthy in my eyes? Incline thy ear, dear friend, to the utterances of thy beloved companion, who has been subjected to the insults of the upholders-of-vain-superstitions, to the apostate, for whom the Torah of Moses has been a girdle for his hips and the Talmud a girdle for his loins. Let thy ears attend that they may hear his reply. (1: 138)

It is hard not to be overwhelmed by the maskilic inflation of biblical diction here, especially in the use of locution instead of direct description ("Incline they ear"), epithet instead of direct naming ("the upholders-of-vain-superstitions"), and redundant parallelism ("girdle for his hips"/"girdle for his loins"). The passage is particularly resonant of the invocations to the great biblical songs of Moses, Balaam, and Deborah, and establishes an epic height that signals the recitation of heroic exploits or the delivery of a prophecy. Hardly noticed in such grandiloquence is the fact that it is being mobilized for a purpose which in its essence is entirely apologetic.

When the narrative comment, written in the mid-1870s, picks up after the letter has been quoted, Lilienblum observes:

This letter, which I have presented with all the vanity and hideous expressions as I in my innocence used to write them, will clearly indicate everything that happened to me during that summer. Besides the uproar concerning me all over town, I was much pained to see my wife crying constantly over my having become an apostate and I was greatly concerned for the welfare of my youngest son, who at the time was still nursing at the breast, lest he should fall ill from his mother's milk, which may have been poisoned by the intensity of her anguish. (1: 151)

The syntax of the passage is the linear syntax of historical explanation, not the posturing of epic reiteration. The sentences perform the function of elucidating circumstances, making judgments, communicating emotion; in general, the coefficient of feeling to statement is much closer to the bone. The language is conspicuously free of mediations and ornamental tropes and determines a kind of plain diction which provides for the expression of such unheroic emotions as anxiety and pain and for the mentioning of such homely details as nursing babies. In addition to making an explicit judgment upon the discourse of the text it is commenting on, Lilienblum's retrospective narrative is radically revisionary in that it offers a substitute or supplemental account of the events described in the letter, an account that reveals the affective, existential dimensions previously denied or unreported. At other times the need for explicit judgment and revision is obviated by the simple proximate coexistence of the two styles, a juxtaposition that casts a light of irony and often bathos on what was once intended in earnest.

A second method for mediating the relationship between past and present selves is control of the rhythm and the variety of the epistolary materials themselves. Having established the angle of judgment, about a third of the way through the apostasy section Lilienblum lets go of retrospective narration altogether and gives himself over to the reconstruction through letters of the miniature epic of the young Lilienblum's near crucifixion. The correspondence is with several older, established maskilim in the capital city of Kovno who are outraged by the young writer's plight. Lilienblum describes how gossip and petty annoyances quickly grew into conspiratorial meetings, which issued broadsides against him, calling for him to desist from writing for *Hamelits*, stripping him of his pupils, and threatening banishment and excommunication. For a crucial few pages when Lilienblum's fate hangs in the balance, Lilienblum himself disappears as a correspondent (1: 172–77). The drama of intercession on his behalf unfolds first through a frenzied exchange of telegrams, then two grave and rotund appeals to the chief rabbis of Vilkomir by a committee of supporters in Kovno, another telegram, and then a summarizing letter by Lilienblum supplying from his point of view a continuous account of the events that had been ominously hinted at by the more official communications. After the immediate danger subsides, there follows a series of letters to his supporters in which Lilienblum describes his apprehension over a new round of confabulations and threats (1: 182–88), and interwoven here for the first time are references to the young woman "N" that are all the more significant because they signal the first instance of diary entries rather than letters in *Sins of Youth*. The drama is brought to a ringing climax when Lilienblum is informed against and hauled before the local police to explain the incitement caused by his articles; demonstrating to the Russian magistrate that the true message of the Hebrew articles is an appeal for the discarding of religious superstition among the Jews, he gains the admiration of the authorities and wins the day.

Just how disingenuous is Lilienblum's telling of his story becomes evident in the canny manipulations of pacing and point of view. (For the time remaining before his departure from Vilkomir the story is carried forward mostly in diary entries, with retrospective comment being formally parenthesized in two specially titled concluding sections.) The cumultive effect is to recast Lilienblum's experience in dramatic, even melodramatic terms, complete with a courageous, persecuted hero who comes close to being thrashed by the enemies of reason but who triumphs in the end and becomes a romantic exile. In short, a kind of Enlightenment Purim spiel, with its classic reversal "from mourning to festivity."

Now, it should be remembered that in the general prologue to *Sins of Youth* (1: 98–99), Lilienblum, like Guenzburg, argues that Hebrew *auto*biography should differ from biography in its commitment to tell the story of a subject who may have no great achievements to his credit but whose life experience is truly representative of the "Hebrew drama" of contemporary life. The drama of other cultures may unfold in grand passions and strong feelings but the drama of Jewish life, Lilienblum contends, has no strong effects to show other than trouble and wretchedness. Its ruling humor is stupidity and it is built out of mistakes and folly. To believe that the circuit of experience, crisis, and self-realization that the young Jew must go through can yield anything other than the knowledge of the essential *absence* at the bottom of the "Hebrew drama" is simply to live in a world of illusion and bad faith. And what is this if not a monitory description of precisely the fool's paradise Lilienblum inhabited during his career as an apostate in Vilkomir: he staged a theatrical invention of heroic persecution and resistance; he believed there was high drama when in reality there was only the spectacle of stupidity. It is Lilienblum's method of composition not to *tell* us about his folly from the vantage point of later disillusionment but to recreate this specious sense of drama through the orchestration of contemporary documents.

In the fall of 1869 at the age of twenty-six Lilienblum arrived in Odessa with all the fantasies of success that young men in literature have traditionally carried with them in their journeys from the provinces to the big city. Lilienblum saw himself sitting and learning European languages without worries or impediments; he saw himself completing a course of studies at an institution of higher learning; he saw himself returning home after several years crowned with good fortune, learning, happiness, and fame; he saw himself achieving a life of gentility and reason, tranquility and peace of mind (2: 14). As in the case of other young heroes, the city did not yield graciously to his expectations. Although grateful to be released from the "fanatical" society of Vilkomir, Lilienblum was dismayed to find Odessa a city of merchants who paid lip service to culture but who had little real interest in it and who could be counted on to make Lilienblum feel suitably abashed when he appeared in their office to peddle copies of his writings. The small initial stipend provided him by his Kovno supporters soon ran out, and letters of recommendation to potential employers proved ineffectual; to meet his obligation to send some support to his family in Vilkomir Lilienblum had to take on pupils as the only kind of work available to him. The result was that Lilienblum could make no progress in the elementary secular studies that were requisite for any higher learning. Lilienblum conspired with circumstance by persisting in giving over whatever intellectual attention remained to writing further articles on religious reformist themes for the Hebrew periodical press. Lilienblum's energies were additionally sapped by despondency over the monotony and dreariness of urban life; this was an anomic, faceless existence far removed from the flamboyant drama of which he had so recently placed himself at the center.

The conditions of Lilienblum's life did not change substantially during the remaining four years that filled out the time covered by the original version of *Sins of Youth*. There was a brief economic reprieve when Lilienblum obtained a job as a subeditor of a Yiddish newspaper and there were worse times when his wife visited him in Odessa, but all in all the sum of Lilienblum's troubles remained constant throughout. The end result was that Lilienblum came no closer to acquiring the limited rudimentary education—not to mention the more ambitious achievement—he had dreamed of. Simply put, he failed.

Sins of Youth, however, is not entirely a record of failure. Running across the grain of the account of arrested formal education is the story of a second kind of education, one that is concerned with the sustained "working through" of Lilienblum's response to his failure. Confronted with his own inadequacies and with the intransigence of the world, Lilienblum strove to understand the mechanism of illusion that had encouraged his own complicity in his fate and to determine an existential stance to his suffering to which he might adhere with increasing force of will. The representation of Lilienblum's ordeal belongs in a sense to the category of existential literature in its nineteenth-century Russian variety because it is not concerned merely with a series of cognitive denials and affirmations—though *Sins of Youth* has been rifled for its "ideas" often enough—but rather with the reluctance of the self to do what it is told. Lilienblum proliferates theories of experience to explain and control the vicissitudes of his life, while at the same time he relapses into states of expectation and nostalgia that vitiate his intentions. These two aspects of the self create the troubled polyphony of this last, major section of the original *Sins of Youth;* the conclusion of the book finally succeeds in striking a note of unitary consciousness, though the costs and incompleteness of this achievement are everywhere apparent.

The first illusion to be renounced was the belief that in his courageous leap from the beit midrash to the Haskalah Lilienblum had crossed the great threshold of life and arrived at a new state of being. Under the indirect influence of new positivist-materialist currents in Russian intellectual life, Lilienblum soon realized that the threshold he imagined was there was illusory, and that he had never in truth stepped outside the same spiritual edifice; sitting in his seat in the old study house or wielding his pen for the Hebrew periodical press—what difference did it really make?

It had been from the accomplished possession of this truth in later years—and with the full complement or irony it permitted—that Lilienblum told the story of his apostasy in the previous section; here in the account of his first year in Odessa Lilienblum describes with moving immediacy the suddenness with which the enormity of his false consciousness had dawned on him. A letter to a supporter, Ezra Cohen, from December, 1869, demonstrates how total and unrelenting was Lilienblum's judgment of the essential continuities in his life:

Formerly, I was enamored of the Tosafists, the *Tur,* the *Beit Yosef,* the *Shakh,* the *Noda' Biyehudah,* R. Akiba Eger, and others, and now I am enamored of Mendelssohn, Levinsohn, Krochmal, and the like; formerly I strove to comprehend the Talmud and its commentaries and now I toil to comprehend the works of the new literature; formerly I spoke against the Karaites, who did not observe the Talmud, and today I speak against charlatans and practicers of superstition; formerly I used to weep over the exile of the Shekhinah and today I weep over the persecutions of our people; formerly I strove to disseminate the religion [*dat*] of the Talmud and today I strive to disseminate the opinions [*de'ot*] that are according to my lights. (2: 20)

Lilienblum is particularly modern in his self-diagnosis. Contemporaries might have looked on the experience of breaking with the tradition in cataclysmic terms, either as revolutionary liberation or as a cosmic rent in the order of being—in either case the great dividing line in a man's life. Lilienblum saw what sociologists of religion and students of romantic literature now see in nineteenth-century conversions: not discontinuity but the displacement and reembodiment of varieties of the religious impulse.

The reembodiment Lilienblum discloses had two aspects. The passage above is based on the claim that the new identity is homologous with the old; that is to say, there exists a continuity of function in the way in which persisting needs are fulfilled and the way in which they organized his present life. More significant is the claim that the nature and content of Lilienblum's activity as a Talmud student and as a maskil partook of the same essential realm of human experience. Lilienblum calls this the realm of *'iyyun,* which he opposes to *ma'aseh. Ma'aseh* connotes materiality, practical accomplishment, the exact sciences, and productive occupations. This last is the world of doctors, engineers, merchants, industrialists, the world of the good men in Kovno who saved him from his persecutors in Vilkomir and who alone believed in him and took an interest in his fate in Odessa. Gaining entry into the world of *ma'aseh* became Lilienblum's professed goal, though the barriers which separated him from it—Russian, Latin, German, mathematics, geography, as well as his own secret unwillingness—must have made the distance seem vast. Measured against this goal, Lilienblum's prolonged dalliance with the Haskalah not only counted for nothing but immeasurably debilitated his capacity to separate himself from the world of books and ideas.

One of the most dispiriting consequences of the crisis was Lilienblum's changed valuation of his identity as a writer. According to the Haskalah faith, the Hebrew writer was the successor to the great biblical singers, and as a practitioner of the reasonable and the beautiful, he was thought to occupy a kind of priestly role superior in moral authority to political or religious leaders. Though young Lilienblum's gifts may not have been of the sublime sort, he was a figure to reckon with in the small world of Hebrew literature, and it was his pride in his membership in that world which allowed him to survive his ostracism in Vilkomir and which won him the support and respect necessary to establish himself in Odessa. With his loss of faith in the Haskalah, he denied himself this last means of transcendence; the only thing he was good at and was rewarded for became a conspicuous form of *'iyyun*. He continued for a time to write, but he knew his perseverance was, according to the new goals, mere perseveration. Abetted by his despair over the condition of Russian Jewry and by the temporary absence of hospitable periodicals, Lilienblum's literary enterprise eventually ground to a halt.

Lilienblum's rejection of ideologies and substitute religions was clearly produced not only from within his own experience. Advanced thought in Russian intellectual life in the 1860s, especially that associated with N. G. Chernychevski, demanded a "realism" that would expose and call into question the cult of art and abstract thought and any other form of transcendentalism or "illusionism."[6] The new realism was based on an abandoned belief in the truthfulness of empiricism and the scientific point of view and in the conviction that every certainty of fact, however much it is opposed by fantastic imaginings, must be accepted in their place.[7] The most radical critic of the sixties was Dmitri I. Pisarev, whose brief career laid down the principles of nihilism: admiration for materialism and the natural sciences, historiosophic optimism, radical individualism, the reduction of human motives to egotism, and the assault on aesthetics and "pure art."[8] Pisarev saw his ideal of the critically thinking individual nowhere more evident than in the depiction of Bazarov, the hero of Turgenev's *Fathers and Sons* (1862).[9] Bazarov, for Pisarev, is the example of the pure empiricist for whom the sole source of knowledge is sensation and experience. To him the ideals that young people thrill to are so much romanticism and nonsense. He "feels a natural, undefinable aversion to phrase making, to waste of words, to sweet thoughts, to sentimental aspirations, and in general to all pretensions not based on real tangible forces."[10] Though he loves no one, he is not a misanthrope; if people choose to attach themselves to him he does not drive them away, though he never relaxes his skeptical attitude toward human motives. He is, finally, possessed of the courage to live without the false comfort of transcendental beliefs—and to die without them, too.

After jettisoning the surrogate religion of Haskalah romanticism, Lilienblum aspired toward a reduction and steeling of the self along the lines of Pisarev's picture of Bazarov. But whereas Bazarov enters the novel with his enviably practical and self-sufficient character fully formed, Lilienblum enters this phase of his life history woefully unprepared for the pursuit of such aggressive autonomy. Caught in the toils of his profuse hopes and ambitions, Lilienblum, in fact, is just the kind of person Bazarov views with disdain, one of those "people who dream of love and useful activity, of the happiness of the whole human race, and yet are not capable of lifting a finger to improve even a little, whether he be a doctor, artisan, pedagogue, or even a writer."[11] In his isolation from people Bazarov is protected from boredom, need, and despair by the fullness of thought and by his work as a biologist: "observations and experiments on living nature, observations and experiments on living people fill for him the emptiness of his life."[12] Suffering through a purgatory of need and despair, Lilienblum in Odessa is entirely unprotected. Yet the same kind of emotional self-reliance and practical activity become the goal of Lilienblum's efforts at reconstructing his life—a goal seen from across an infinite distance.

Lilienblum in the end could never fully become Bazarov. Cognitively, Lilienblum did manage to achieve a nihilistic comprehension of the world, and emotionally, he succeeded in overcoming his relation of need to other people. But when it came to central tasks of practical doing in the world there could be no success. It is the thesis of *Sins of Youth* that by their nature the conditions of Jewish life deny the individual the possibility of such fulfillment. Lilienblum arrived in Odessa in 1869 suffused with desire for the things of life he could not have; the autobiography is the story of the gradual narcotizing and eventual deadening of desire. The real ordeal of experience in *Sins of Youth* arises not out of the loss of faith in religion and its substitutes but out of the necessity to be reconciled in their aftermath to the reality of absence. Of the four years in Odessa (1869–73) the first is called by Lilienblum "the year of the great crisis" (he uses the German in Latin characters, "Krisis," as well as the new Hebrew coinage *'et ma'avar* [2: 46]); the treatment of this year spreads over sixty pages, more than any other in the work.

During this tormented season Lilienblum was tossed unrelentingly between the poles of desire and despair. His repeated ordeal took the shape of a fated circle of disillusionment. The circle begins with an uncontrollable profusion of fantasies and hopes about future success and happiness (associated with a cluster of terms: *dimyon, tikvah, ḥefets*); the impossibility of these fantasies brings on a wave of tearful self-pity (*dema'ot* and *regesh*), which finally issues in wretchedness, despair, and resentment (*ye'ush*) and then finally lapses back into fantasy. "I hope," writes Lilienblum, "I build imaginary, airy chambers and in my fancy fly to the heavens" (2: 40). "I desire, I seek, but I don't know what; I quest for the goal but I don't know what to call it" (2: 54). In the emptiness left by the excision of religion Lilienblum's soul is flooded with the kind of engulfing, blank desire which, released from its generating conditions, becomes its own substitute metaphysical presence.

Given the miserable actualities of Lilienblum's life in Odessa, the flight of desire would abruptly collapse of its own weight. Lilienblum would come crashing to the ground, there to be assailed by swarms of unanswerable questions and overcome by nausea: "I loathed my family life, I loathed my loneliness, I loathed the new city [Odessa]. . . ." Essential to the account of each breakdown is the mention of uncontrollable weeping. Tears are a sign of feeling (*regesh*), and Lilienblum uses them as a kind of metonymical marker of the critical stages in his effort to liberate himself from bondage to emotion. Weeping would give way to desperation and withdrawal into moods of black hopelessness in which Lilienblum would persevere until an onrush of desire would begin the cycle anew.

Lilienblum's second year in Odessa so reinforced the conviction of failure that the faculty of hope could never quite function in the same way. During this time Lilienblum hit on the idea of leaving Odessa and making a fresh start at a university in Germany. He won the support of his benefactors in Kovno, who put him in touch with a potential sponsor in Germany, who in turn informed Lilienblum that he would be expected to know German and to undergo an entrance examination in ancient languages and in science (2: 87). Exhausted from working to keep body and soul together and from trying to strengthen his shaky hold on the Russian language, Lilienblum found these demands so beyond his capacities that the idea that he might never proceed beyond his present condition began slowly to be accepted. The growing despair over his own conditions was paralleled by a pessimism concerning the fortunes of the Jewish people as a whole. For years he and others had been enunciating the new ideas on the basis of which the life of the people should be rebuilt (2: 74–79). No one had listened; there had been few responses to his articles, and the conditions of the nation had not changed. Lilienblum had little reason to believe that his people were any more educable than he himself was. Finally, Lilienblum was coming to realize during this time that his relationship to the young woman "N" was impossible and had drained him of enormous reserves of feeling which could never be replenished. He was spent and he had nothing—and would never have anything—to show for it.

Such a mass of disappointments had to have some effect on the tormented cycle of desire and despair. In the face of reality, it became increasingly difficult to conjure up fantasies of alternative futures. The frequent repetition of the words from the end of Job (41:1), "my hope has been shown in vain" (tohalti nikhzevah), indicates a degree of recognition of the purposelessness of striving for inaccessible goals. Lilienblum's liberation becomes possible finally only by the death of the heart. Throughout the great year of crisis Lilienblum longed for the time when his susceptibility to painful disillusionment would be dulled and when the seemingly unstinting flood of tears would abate. With each new trial or recollection of the past Lilienblum would measure the intensity of his weeping, reporting with relief at one point during that year that "the day is near when my heart will be a void within me" (2: 86). By the end of the fourth year in Odessa he was able to record in his journal (with exquisite autobiographical self-consciousness) for August 23, 1875: "Today marks a full year from the day on which I last shed tears. This has been the first year of the death (lit. "freezing") of my emotions" (kefi'at rigshotai) (2: 123). The goal of Lilienblum's development in these years became the achieving of a stone-like state of complete renunciation (ye'ush muhlat) (2: 96). The idea of ye'ush, which once referred to the wretchedness, despair, and embitterment that were the inevitable results of his encounters with reality in his first years in Odessa, was now redefined to designate the new existential ideal: victory over expectation and the dread of future *(pahad he'atid)*.

Along the path toward renunciation the question of the other could not be ignored. It would have been convenient if Lilienblum had been endowed with Bazarov's easy aloofness from human entanglements, but instead Lilienblum—though never in fact very entangled—inhabited an emotional world of extreme need. Having voluntarily rejected Vilkomir society, he had hoped to flourish within the admiring company of the enlightened in Odessa, only to find himself forced deeper into exile in a city that was in reality a commercial center whose inhabitants took nothing more than a polite interest in Lilienblum and the great issues he wrote on. He felt his deprivation keenly and shed his compromising tears over it. As Lilienblum's project of attempting to annihilate hope and need took shape, it became clear that he must strive to transform his wretched loneliness into sanguine aloneness, and that to do so would require a divesting of emotional ties and responsibilities, a virtual elimination of the transitive extensions of the self.

Responsibility begins with the family. Lilienblum had been married for ten years and had several children when he was at the height of his heretical rebellion in Vilkomir at the age of twenty-five. *Sins of Youth* records the fondness he felt for his children and his unceasing efforts while alone in Odessa to provide support for the family he had left behind—deserted?— in Vilkomir. These signs of solicitude aside, the principal function of the family in Lilienblum's life was as an encumbrance.[13] Its support, in addition to his own, usually made it impossible to pursue any of his plans, and at the rare times that Lilienblum was free, he lived in constant dread of his family visiting him in Odessa and destroying the few scraps of independence he had gathered (2: 115). The felt exclusion of his wife's voice (or even name) from the text is a reminder not only of the autobiographer's autocratic control over his narrative but also of the truth of Brenner's observation that Lilienblum's illusionless knowledge of himself did not mean that he was capable of knowing anyone else.[14]

In a letter of August, 1871 Lilienblum addressed to his wife his grave denunciation of Jewish marriage (2: 89–95). He prefaces his remarks with the pathetic observation that this letter marks the first time in their twelve-year marriage that their conversation will rise in substance above the level of such domestic exchanges as "Is dinner ready? Are the children asleep?" In Jewish life, according to Lilienblum, a man needs a wife to fulfill three functions: to relieve sexual desire, to give birth to sons, and to keep house. For a Jew a son is only a "kaddish" and for Lilienblum the recitation of the kaddish is as efficacious for the dead as the recitation of *tehinnot* for the living. If a man has children, he cares for them and grieves for them if they die. But to *want* children in the first place can only be narcissistic. The other two functions of Jewish marriage, sex and housekeeping, Lilienblum says very simply can be bought elsewhere. Because for Jewish men, women are commonly no more than this—servants and chamber pots *('avit shel shofokhin)*—they are interchangeable and mourned over no more than a bathhouse that burns down.

There is potentially one role for which the services of a woman cannot be hired: the role of a helpmeet, the *'ezer kenegdo*. What a man needs most in life is a partner, a companion with whom to share the joys and burdens of a life. The success of such a partnership, like any similar arrangement in the business world, is predicated on a pooling of equal resources by both parties. In his own case, Lilienblum argues, not only typically from the beginning was his marriage never understood as an emotional partnership but from the first days of his heresy there began to be created in him an inner world of experience which was literally unimaginable to his wife, naturally taboo and emotionally turbulent. It was not just the subversive content of Lilienblum's experience that was the problem; the fact of the very existence of a space of differentiated individuality created a margin of subjectivity which existing social arrangements could not adequately handle.[15]

It was within this space that Lilienblum's curious affair with Feyge Novakhovitch, the elusive "Maiden N," unfolded. The facts of the relationship are simple enough: during his embattled last six months in Vilkomir, Lilienblum drew on Feyge's sympathetic reassurance, and upon relocation in Odessa there ensued a four-year-long correspondence in which Lilienblum poured out the vicissitudes of his passage from desperation to renunciation. What the meaning of this relationship was for the development of Lilienblum's self as presented in *Sins of Youth* is unclear. On the one hand Feyge seems to have been Lilienblum's grand passion, the subject of grand poetry, the "conqueror of his heart," and he the lover who had fallen into the "snare of love" (2: 128); on the other hand is the startling fact that the relationship had no existence other than an epistolary one: during all the years in Odessa—according to Lilienblum's account—he never saw Feyge nor did he take steps to effect a meeting or even suggest one.[16] As far as Feyge was concerned this was not enough. She was passionately devoted to Lilienblum and wrote to him urging marriage. The series of reasons Lilienblum gave for backing away from the idea casts light on the role that this act played in the larger drama of renunciation. Marriage, to begin with, meant the assuming once again of family responsibility, and this was precisely what Lilienblum was trying to disentangle himself from in order properly to set about his studies. The goal of freedom could not be served by new encumbrances (2: 68–71). Although he admits that in his last days in Vilkomir he had grown to love Feyge desperately, he was incapable of disclosing his feelings because as a typical product of the world of the beit midrash, an innocent *kloyzner,* he could not deal with the shame of telling a girl he loved her and because, given the ideas about romance he had picked up from books, he considered it impossible that a woman like Feyge, whose heart had been broken by another man, could ever love again (2: 104–5). By the second year in Odessa, Lilienblum realized that his feelings for Feyge were an essential part of the prisonhouse of emotion and fantasy (*regesh* and *dimyon*) he was trying so painfully to escape from; he indeed needed to maintain contact with her, but in their letters he was prepared to reveal only the story of his intellectual-spiritual struggles but not the more intimate secrets of his heart, where every expression would stir old yearnings and deflect him from his necessary course (2: 70). And when that course was realized in the death of feeling and expectation toward the end of the Odessa years, dead also was the capacity for the "poesy of love" and any thought of a future connection between them.

The meaning of Lilienblum's relationship with Feyge Novakhovitch finally seems fixed by the nature of its origins. Drawn by their mutual misery, the possibility of their love was first rendered imaginable and then catalyzed by reading together Mapu's novels. Within this literary network of pastoral-platonic sentiments, their own unacknowledged affections took their identity. It was natural that what had begun in mutual communion over a text should be continued—and have its only reality—in the exchange of written documents, and that no effort should be made to turn the literary into the real—at least on Lilienblum's part. The sharing and companionship aspects of marriage were not simply the most important functions of marriage for Lilienblum: they were the only ones he was willing and capable of accepting. To make the word flesh, to join companionship with sexuality, would have created a matrix of emotional demand before which the *kloyzner* could only be impotent. The mixture of confidence and distance in a purely epistolary relationship enabled Lilienblum to isolate the helpmeet function of the new idea of marriage while escaping from its more intimate and engulfing exigencies.

The last year of the narrative (1872–1873) is treated in a scant eleven pages, which are concerned entirely with documenting the suppression and disappearance of the last vestiges of fancy and emotionalism. This meant writing in its various guises: Lilienblum's vicarious love affair through letters and his vicarious public career through articles. Each was seen as a flight from the world of practical, productive activity into a sickly imaginary realm. The correspondence with Feyge ended by Lilienblum's driving her away. As she came to realize that Lilienblum had no intention of ever being anything more than epistolary in his attentions, Feyge's letters became increasingly desperate and effusive. Lilienblum saw in the abandoned expressiveness of the language of her letters symptoms of the same illness from which he had so recently recovered. He accused her of "emotional agitation that derives from naïveté and purple phrases which, together with all sorts of other fantasies, are outside reality and the world of action" (2: 120). Faced with such treatment, Feyge chose not to respond, and the correspondence, which had been an abiding presence in Lilienblum's years of crisis, was terminated.[17]

Surveying his seven years as a Hebrew writer, Lilienblum concluded that there is something in the very nature of the writing life which is corrupting. The condemnation of the ignorant and the adulation of the enlightened, the passion for controversy and the dread of obscurity—all the sentiments determining the writer's emotional milieu—derive from and conduce to states of fantasy-ridden agitation. Lilienblum's nihilism also left little to write about. Topics of religious reform were now out of the question, and more secular issues concerning the state of Jewish society, which would naturally then have become Lilienblum's subject, were in turn disqualified on the grounds that the idea of the Jewish people, collectively considered, was a mystified, transcendental concept which violated a truly empirical understanding of reality (2: 125). Only the individual and his experience are real.

In exchange for these numerous renunciations, for having systematically stripped himself of the consolations of love, religion, and imagination, it would have been hoped that Lilienblum would have been granted some sense of existential achievement. It was not so.

> What am I now? A poor ignoramus ['*am ha'arets*], who denies every kind of fancy and consoling belief! I don't even know the rudiments of the exact sciences—so what do I know? My knowledge of Hebrew theology in my eyes counts for nothing because it is fanciful, transcendental knowledge that is not grounded in nature—so what do I know? Neither European languages, nor mathematics, nor geometry, nor astronomy, nor physics, nor chemistry, nor engineering, and the like—so what do I know? I know how to criticize foolish doctrines, yet by negation alone man's spirit cannot be fulfilled. (2: 124)

Lodged between the successful annihilation of an unworthy past and the unsuccessful appropriation of the desired future, Lilienblum judged the final balance of his life to be null.

Sins of Youth is, in the end, a self-told obituary. Looking back from 1873, his thirty-first year, Lilienblum concluded that his life was over—life in any sense that still holds out hope for change. He had renounced expectation and hope of "resurrection," and had passed from the company of the "living dead" of the beit midrash to the ranks of the "dead living" of modern life, and it was this consciousness of closure that gave him the authority at the age of thirty to write an account of his life: not the story of a life in progress but the definitive autobiography of a life that struggled, withered, and once and for all died. This is not even death with a flourish. In the preface to *Sins of Youth*, Lilienblum had said that the tale of his life would be a kind of representative Hebrew drama because it was characterized by absence rather than incident or affect (1: 95–96). Lilienblum returns to this notion at the close of the narrative when he apologizes to the reader for not supplying at least a suicide, the *de rigueur* ending in modern literature to a story of ordeal and disillusionment. But Hebrew writing cannot even provide that satisfaction because its subjects continue to live even though their life has expired (2: 126–27). As a testament of the dead, then, the autobiography is free to revisit and to parody the conventions of the *tsava'ah* form which were so important in such an early work as *Aviezer.* Whereas in a traditional *tsava'ah* a patriarch would summarize the fruits of his wisdom and bequeath his children guidelines along the path of tradition, Lilienblum testifies to the failure of his experience and counsels against walking in his ways.

The drama that does exist in *Sins of Youth*, it was said, is produced by watching the gap close between the successive stages of the auto-biographer's earlier self, as embodied in quoted documents from past years, and the achieved knowledge at the present time of the writing, as embodied in retrospective commentaries on those documents. There *is* knowledge in *Sins of Youth*. Although in terms of accomplishment in the world Lilienblum judged his life to be a failure, he nevertheless succeeded in understanding the reasons for his failure, those assigned to society and to himself. Such illusionless consciousness would seem to be the work's consummate moment, hinted at in the ironic distance between commentary and document earlier in the text and steadily approached as the past converges on the present.

The final irony of *Sins of Youth* is that even this consummation is never fully authorized; it is undermined by the deconstructive forces of nostalgia. A gross conception of autobiographical form would see the documentary axis of the work as moving in time through the past toward the stationary axis of retrospective knowledge. The fact is that this second axis also has a temporal duration, however microscopic in comparison to the expanse of years in the narrative itself. This is the time that elapses during the writing itself; though the writer may begin with a finished conviction of knowledge, that conviction must be exposed to the vicissitudes of reevoking the past. In Lilienblum's case this meant reexperiencing both the intoxication of his years of heretical rebellion in Vilkomir and the emotional anguish of his "deeducation" in Odessa; and although over time he managed to renounce the first and to wean himself from the second, reliving these experiences through writing about them seems to have weakened Lilienblum's resolve. The epilogue to *Sins of Youth*, "The Last Sigh," lingers with special poignancy on the ecstatic agony of his persecutions in Vilkomir (2: 134–35). Lilienblum knows that he was benighted and deluded then, his rebellion an empty palace revolution, but that knowledge does not prevent him from feeling the glow of those years: the radiant sense of self-worth, the exhilarating possession of positive doctrines, the fearless confidence of the writer who knows that the truth of his experience is worth generalizing from. These were all the wrong feelings, but their vibrancy forms such a contrast to the burnt-out disillusionment of the present that the final, monumental negations of *Sins of Youth* cannot help being shaken.

Some of the compositional differences between *Sins of Youth* proper and the new work *The Way Back* are instructive. Whereas *Sins of Youth* brought the narrative of Lilienblum's life to within three years of the date of publication (1876), in the case of *The Way Back* the interval is significantly greater. *The Way Back*, which covers the years 1873–1881, was published only in 1899. Also, whereas the second section of *Sins of Youth* ("The Days of Crisis and Renunciation") took 135 pages to cover four years, *The Way Back* manages to get through eight years in 55 pages. And where the texture of *Sins of Youth* is heavy with tortured existential strivings, through the texture of *The Way Back* breathes the light air of a clear and steady intention.

From the vantage point of the nineties many things became clear to Lilienblum. The "great idea" with which *The Way Back* closes, the idea of Hibbat Zion, the pro-Zionist aspiration of settling the Holy Land, had not only firmly established itself by this time but had already become tied to the great engines of political Zionism. By then, too, Lilienblum's identification with this idea and his commitment to its practical realization were complete in their passion and tested in their duration. *Sins of Youth*, to be sure, was narrated from a position of achieved selfhood, but that final state of triumphant renunciation had been qualified by the very negativity of its identity and by a failure of nerve in the form of nostalgia. The retrospective point of departure in *The Way Back* is utterly self-assured in its positive program, in its absorption in a transcendent non-subjective idea, and in its security from regret and reservation. This conviction allowed Lilienblum to attempt a kind of compression and linearity in the reconstructive presentation of self in these eight years. Despite the apparent reversal that took place in 1881, Lilienblum saw these years as forming essentially one continuous, if not fully conscious, movement, and this unidirectional pressure and relative lack of complexity eliminated the need for elaboration. More than any of the earlier autobiographical writings, *The Way Back* displays a desire to evade false starts and regressions and to make the past an image of an ineluctable, teleological movement toward the present.

Although the years 1873–1876 saw no change in Lilienblum's state of material privation and spiritual exhaustion, in the next year circumstances combined to create a dramatic change in Lilienblum's life. Until this time Lilienblum's family had been living with him in Odessa and their presence made it impossible for Lilienblum to do anything but eke out a day-to-day existence. The threat of a Turkish invasion in April 1876 caused the inhabitants of Odessa to seek temporary refuge in the towns and villages of the interior, and Lilienblum used this opportunity to relocate his family in Vilkomir, while he returned, alone and disencumbered, to Odessa. *Sins of Youth* had just been published and the proceeds from the sales—its revealing, autobiographical content made it sell briskly in the enlightened city of Odessa—and the small income it brought enabled Lilienblum to cut down on the number of tutorial hours he was forced to give. In possession for the first time of a modicum of independence, Lilienblum dared to resuscitate the old dream of a university education. Though he was thirty-three years old and a father of adolescent children, Lilienblum figured that he could cover the gymnasium curriculum in two years and then be within reach of the university.

"Congratulate me," wrote Lilienblum to a correspondent on June 18, 1877, "wish me *en bonne heure*. Congratulate me on having valiantly reached my goal and attained a happy end. For yesterday I began to study" (2: 154). The result of finally overcoming the great disappointment in his life was an exhilaration that carried him undaunted through what turned out to be many years of patient application. The important thing was to have made a beginning. For so long Lilienblum had self-punishingly dreamed of the future while in reality being pushed farther and farther back from taking a first step in its direction. Now since he was completely absorbed in studies he could safely turn his fantasies into a source of propulsive motivation to keep him on the track. The preparatory course took four years instead of two, each day of it minutely calibrated into hours for geometry, Latin, and geography, into time for individual study and for tutoring by former Hebrew students who had gone on to university. No matter how tedious and exacting his studies, Lilienblum's will was not deflected from his plan. Nor for that matter would Lilienblum yield to the blandishment of certain kinds of patronage. Judah Leib Gordon had secured a German benefactor who was willing to underwrite Lilienblum's education if he would commit himself in advance to training as an orientalist. But having journeyed so far into the realm of practical actuality, the thought of retreating into the world of dead languages, yet another version of talmudism, was unthinkable.

This display of will indicated a fundamental change of identity. At the end of section two of *Sins of Youth*, summing up the years of despair and resignation, Lilienblum signed his name with the pseudonymous acronym "The Wretched One" (*'umlal ba'arets = 'Ani Moshe Leib Lilienblum Ben 'Avi Rabbi Tsvi*). Writing to his wife to plead that she stay in Vilkomir and leave him to his work, Lilienblum announced that now he should be known by another name: "The Stubborn One" (*kesheh 'oref*) (2: 165). He reminds her, rather threateningly, of the time in his early twenties when he was the heretical rebel of Vilkomir. No threats from parents, rabbis, the authorities—or from her—could shake the fierce disputant's will to pursue his goals. And so now, after the long night of remission, the *via negativa* of self-denial and renunciation has been put behind him and his spirit returned to the vigilant assertiveness which several years before had been recalled only as a temptation to nostalgia. A new era has been ushered in: hardships and distractions remain but in place of tortuous self-questioning a sense of self-possession and security (*shalvat nefesh, korat ruaḥ*) pervade the text.

Whence this sudden and great renewal? Could it be traced back to the threat of the Turkish invasion which Lilienblum playfully suggests gave him freedom by removing his family from Odessa? Was it on account of the slight independence provided by the sales of *Sins of Youth*? The triviality of these reasons are patent. *The Way Back* is in the end not concerned with origins and explanations. Lilienblum was preoccupied instead with creating a revisionary myth of his self in which the deep running continuity is shown to be the will to action, conceived of as a pressure that is bound to surface when circumstances allow. Alternatively, Lilienblum's new life of accomplishment was pictured as a resurrection, a restoration to something that had once flourished but had in the meantime been suppressed. The reader of the second part of *Sins of Youth*, that reader who followed Lilienblum as he suffered and struggled gradually to achieve freedom from the terror of his disappointments and who assented to the authenticity of those struggles, must be forgiven if he is less than convinced by the effortlessness of Lilienblum's rebirth and if he is vexed by Lilienblum's evasion of the task of explicating the origins of this change. As I have suggested above, it is possible that, having met and seized the great cause of his life, Lilienblum had so become another person by the late nineties that the person who he had been in the early seventies was no longer recognizable or admissible, and hence the unanswerableness of the question of how a sense of self so secure and empowered emerged from an impasse of negation and exhaustion.

If it had not been for his conversion to Zionism, Lilienblum's career might have been assigned to a dim footnote in the subsequently ascendant historiography of nationalism. But because his journey from belief to enlightenment and nihilism was capped in the end by an embrace of Ḥibbat Tsiyyon, Lilienblum was transmuted in the annals of Hebrew literature into a mythic figure: the great truth teller whose quest for truth could finally not resist the logic of Jewish history. *The Way Back* has thus been read as the story of Lilienblum's conversion, a story that comes to its climax at the conclusion of the book when the pogroms of 1881 burst into his life, sweep aside the playthings of learning and enlightenment, and press Lilienblum into communion with the fate of the People.

The actual text of *The Way Back* in fact urges a reading of considerably more complexity. There are *two* great moments of breakthrough in *The Way Back,* one at the beginning of the work and one at the end, and between these moments there obtains a relationship of dialectical continuity. The first concerns Lilienblum's return to studies. In an important sense, as I have tried to argue, this event constituted a greater discontinuity with Lilienblum's past than the concluding embrace of nationalism. The return to studies represented a breaking out of the cul-de-sac of resignation and a successful reentry into the world of praxis. Both the fact of Lilienblum's individual rebirth and the fact that it was a rebirth into practical accomplishment had of necessity to precede an awareness of the logic of national rebirth, which likewise was to come in the form of a reawakening to the need for the taking of practical, material measures. The individual foreshadowed the collective; as Lilienblum had learned to save his own life, so might the People learn also. The *via negativa* had been put behind and then it became a question of new life finding its fitting object.

The final conversion was additionally prepared for by glimmerings of renewed interest in the affairs of Russian Jewry. These concerns form a minor theme in *The Way Back,* which receives a more insistent articulation as the work progresses. As early as 1876 the abortive scheme of English philanthropists to buy Palestine from the Sultan provoked in Lilienblum a "stirring of the imagination" (2: 148). In July 1878, Lilienblum mentioned with enthusiasm reports of the plans of the Alliance Israélite to purchase large tracts of Russian land to be colonized by impoverished Jews from the Pale (2: 180). After 1879 Lilienblum began to be extremely concerned by the growing assimilation of young Russian Jews and wrote on the evils of it in the Russian-Jewish press (2: 182). An article of his in *Hamilits* (1879, nos. 41, 44; 1880, nos. 1, 2) gratified him greatly by the controversy it aroused.

The claim of continuity should not be stressed overmuch. The great arrival was the more powerfully realized for having been adequately prepared for. The pogroms that swept through southern Russia in the spring of 1881 (the Jews of Odessa were attacked in the first week of May) were given poignant expression in *The Way Back* in a series of pained elliptical diary entries; the real turning point in Lilienblum's situation, however, followed by several months and is presented in four journal entries, for Elul 28 and Tishri 4, 6, 7—entries whose superscription, it should be noted, is given for the first time according to the Hebrew calendar. In these entries Lilienblum made the significant and brilliant choice not to present his crisis of identity in directly discursive psychological or ideological terms. He created an astonishing effect by instead presenting a kind of battle of the books: combat by textual proxy. In each entry Lilienblum juxtaposed a lesson from his gymnasium studies with another text, and simply by the progress of these unexplicated juxtapositions he managed to indicate the course of this conversion.

The first entry, for Elul 28, begins with a Latin exercise. The text is from Cicero: "The virtuous man will desire no reward for his labors and hardships other than praise and honor." Lilienblum first notices the grammatical peculiarities of the sentence, then transposes its syntax, and translates into Hebrew—all this as if the matter of the text were arbitrary, a moment in the exertions of an aspiring extern. Lilienblum pauses to wonder bemusedly at these old Roman sages who regarded praise and honor as sufficient motives for civic virtue, and then he leaves the exercise. Without comment there follows an excerpt from an official Russian state communiqué urging the documentation of Jewish crimes against Russian society: ". . . to gather and submit to the proper location precise information together with presumptions of guilt on the question: which aspects of the economic activity of the Jews cause injury to the lives of the principal inhabitants . . ." (2: 192). On this text Lilienblum does comment, drawing out instead the implication that in the economic world every group or individual prospers at the expense of others and that in Russia the Jews will always be regarded as the party giving injury. The irony of the juxtaposition of Cicero and a document of official Russian antisemitism cuts in two ways; though the venality of Russian society is judged by contrast to an entirely different norm of human behavior in a polity, the very loftiness of the Ciceronian civic ideal proves itself utterly and dangerously irrelevant to an understanding of the political actualities of the Jewish question.

The entry for Tishri 4 (no mention is made of the intervening holiday of Rosh Hashana) juxtaposes a series of mathematical problems with a passage from Jeremiah. The problems and their solutions, which graphically seize the reader by pouring an extravagant display of numbers and symbols over the Hebrew page, are concerned with logarithms and algebraic equations and together describe an ideal language of rationality. Logarithms are a device for abridging calculation by transposing complex operations into simple steps of addition and subtraction. Algebraic equations are sets of artificially manipulated equivalences that are transformed and balanced by agreed-upon rules. The biblical text is Jeremiah 45:4-5: "Behold, that which I have built will I break down, and that which I have planted I will pluck up, even this whole land. And thou seekest great things for thyself? Seek them not!" The context is a short prophecy given to Baruch ben Neriah at the conclusion of his narrative of Jeremiah's life and prophecies. Exhausted and depressed by the visions he has recorded, Baruch complains that he has been given no rest or consolation. Traditional exegesis, especially Kimhi, interprets Baruch's complaint as a request for the mantle of prophecy, which was often given to a prophet's disciple, after the example of Elijah and Elisha; modern criticism understands the complaint as a request simply for the kind of power to which important scribes often acceded. In any case, Baruch is told by God not to seek such grandiose attainments. His reward will be more modest but not insignificant; in the general catastrophe that will soon engulf Judah, Baruch will be allowed to escape with his life.

The application to Lilienblum's situation is clear. Lilienblum is a latter-day Baruch, a scribe rather than an original visionary, who has been overreaching in his search for personal achievement and greatness, while his people are condemned to destruction, of which the recent pogroms were but a small adumbration. A text from the real world of historical catastrophe stands next to a text from the artificially elegant world of mathematics. In an equation nothing is ever lost: what is taken from one term of the equivalence or done to it must be given to the other term so that the symmetry not be violated; the verse from Jeremiah, however, describes a judgment of irrecoverable devastation in which what was built and planted will be forever torn down and uprooted. The diary entry for Tishri 4 concludes: "I put down my book and papers and went out into the awesome destruction . . ." (2: 194).

The Jeremiah verse is used again as the countertext in the third and fourth journal entries (Tishri 6, 7); with each repetition the authority of the verse increases in proportion to the insipid irrelevancy of the gymnasium lesson text. The first text is an excerpt from a geography book describing mineral deposits in a certain region of Russia and their discovery by merchants and explorers. The text runs consecutively for several lines before phrases begin to repeat in a jumble of sentence fragments, as if a distracted student kept forcing his mind back to the page and as if self-possession of the text was foundering on the bedrock of the Jeremiah verse, which immediately follows it. The matter of the passage is again not arbitrary. For a Jew to force himself to learn by rote the features and resources of a land which is not his and which does not want him is absurd and humiliating. Additionally painful is the obvious contrast between the firm substantiality of rich mineral deposits and the vulnerable pre-cariousness of Jewish existence in that land.

The last diary entry, a passage in Latin and Hebrew from Ovid's *The Metamorphoses*, is a lushly pastoral description of the coming of night to the mouth of a grotto, as Nox sprinkles a flowery soporific on the scene. The exquisitely artificial tranquility of the *tableau* is of course the antithesis of the atrocities that had so recently taken place on the street outside as "foretold" by the Jeremiah prophecy of wrath. In the more local context of structure of *The Way Back*, the passage closes the climactic cycle of diary entries by returning to the starting point of a Latin exercise and by creating a setting of charmed sleepfulness in which the resisting, enterprising will of the individual fades and is forever put to rest.

The death of the will prepares the way for resurrection of the self. Late on the night of Tishri 12 Lilienblum draws the conclusions that had been cryptically implied in the pastiche of passages: the Jews are ultimately and unchangeably alien to European society and rather than emigrating to other countries in which the sad tale will repeat itself, let them go to their ancestral homeland and once again make it their own. The nation may yet transform itself; for Lilienblum his own transformation has happened al-ready.

> The great stone that has pressed down on my heart for such a long time fell off in a moment, my eyes opened, my soul exalted, and I became another person. The dew of resurrection fell anew upon me and melted the "great glacier" that had covered my heart these many years. (2: 198)

The reawakening of the will, which had taken place at the beginning of *The Way Back*, yet which had not affected the longstanding paralysis of emo-tion, is now canceled and fulfilled by the reawakening of the spirit.

The price to be paid for Lilienblum's rebirth is the end of auto-biographical writing. When Lilienblum ceased seekng "great things" for himself, his will became entirely identified with the larger enterprise into which he had been reborn. Lilienblum thenceforth became an institution and his further autobiographical writings, such as *Derekh la'avor ge'ulim (A Way for the Redeemed to Pass Over)*, became institutional history. The space between self and society within which the authentic autobiographical impulse arises was closed forever.

INTO FICTION

*Part
Two*

THREE

Mordecai Ze'ev Feierberg
and the Reveries of Redemption

In the brevity of his life, Mordecai Ze'ev Feierberg resembled nothing so much as an angel created to perform a single task and then promptly disappear. It was only in the two years before his tubercular death at the age of twenty-five that Feierberg began publishing stories about the inner world of children and adolescents coming of age under the star of religious decline and dissolution. The pathos of these tales caught the attention of a generation of readers who had been born too late to be persuaded by the verities of the Haskalah and too early to be consoled for the death of God by the advent of new ideologies. The members of this "twilight generation" had spent the best years of their youth immured in study houses during the last decades of the nineteenth century; yet when they left the beit midrash and emerged "into the light," they felt themselves to be lost rather than liberated. They were men condemned to a lifetime of wandering between a religious tradition to which they could not return and a world transformed beyond recognition. By virtue of his early death, Feierberg saved himself from this grim indeterminacy. His brief life was rigorously coterminous with a single moment and it enacted a single gesture: the failure of belief and the act of apostasy.[1]

Feierberg was born in 1874 and grew up in and around Novograd-Volinsk, a town of some three thousand Jewish souls in the northwestern Ukraine. His mother tended a small grocery store. His father, an especially learned and rigorously pious man, was an adherent of Habad Hasidism who served as a *shoḥet* (ritual slaughterer). Feierberg attended the beit midrash of the Chernobyl Hasidim and devoted himself to Talmud study. His father oversaw his studies and required him to memorize the laws of ritual slaughter in hopes of preparing the boy to succeed him in his office. Impelled by intellectual curiosity, Feierberg's extracurricular readings led him from the Talmud to works of medieval ethics and Kabbalah and then to the line of free rationalist thought opened up by Maimonides. From there to the literature of the Haskalah was a short but crucial jump, and it had the effect of labeling Feierberg as a heretic and making him a target of persecution in the town and in his own family. At the age of twenty, he showed the first signs of being infected by tuberculosis, and a year later he traveled to Warsaw for medical consultations. There he showed his first writings to

Nahum Sokolov and I. L. Peretz, whose encouragement confirmed him in his conviction of a literary vocation. Feierberg returned home, and under conditions of deteriorating health and worsening relations with his family, he devoted himself to writing and to organizing Zionist discussion groups. He managed to produce six short stories, some journalism and criticism, the novella *Whither? (Le'an?)* before he died in the winter of 1899.[2]

The mystique of Feierberg's life and death was enhanced by the charm of his insularity. He was taken by his readers to be the last flower of the beit midrash and the doomed culture it represented. Other Hebrew writers had come from the same origins but had left earlier and gone farther. They traveled to the North to attend the great Lithuanian yeshivot, where it was known that young men made contact with the underground intellectual currents of the Haskalah and Jewish nationalism. They moved to the big cities of Russia and Central Europe where they were thrust into the contest of radical ideologies and social movements. They learned Russian, German, and Polish, and they exposed themselves to the dominant forces in world literature. They left the family circle and mixed in the free ambience of student society. Feierberg, in contrast, was almost entirely homebound and homegrown. (The year he was born Lilienblum had already been living in Odessa for five years.) Whatever knowledge of general culture Feierberg possessed was acquired through translations into Hebrew and Yiddish and through the works of such cultural importers as Ahad Ha-am and Berdichevsky. It was only at the time of his death that Feierberg was struggling with the rudiments of Russian and German grammars. It was, then, largely the resources of Jewish classical literature that Feierberg had available to him as a reservoir of serviceable images and metaphors. Driven by as desperate pressures as other writers, yet provided with fewer cultural models, Feierberg was forced to develop more internally Jewish aesthetic solutions.

For these reasons, Feierberg occupies his own place in the development of Hebrew autobiographical writing. Although he read and was influenced by *Aviezer* and *Sins of Youth*, he was not moved by the same Rousseau-Maimon model that had inspired Guenzburg and Lilienblum. There is here nothing of Guenzburg's belief (*pace* Maimon) in the powers of reason to heal the soul's distress, and none of Lilienblum's admiration for the positivist heroes of Russian literature. The sharpest difference concerns the question of style. Lilienblum's account of his adolescent rebellion against the forces of Orthodoxy is already a parody of the high diction of Haskalah Hebrew. When it comes to describing his grown-up years in Odessa he strives to achieve a plain style, one from which there has been drained the last residue of pathos and self-pity. The ideal is language tethered as closely as possible to the illusionless world of practical thinking and doing. Feierberg's ideal, on the other hand, could not have been more different. By temperament and commitment Feierberg was a romantic, and his romanticism expressed itself in several ways.[3] Reality in Feierberg's writing is imagined reality; his characters do not act in the world so much as they dream and slip into extended reveries that transport them to unseen worlds. Forced back into the here and now, these doomed young men react to their predicament with just the sort of pathetic outcries and anguished ejaculations that Lilienblum would have found unacceptable. The dreams and reveries are constructed almost entirely out of the material of the aggadic tradition of classical Hebrew literature: parables, midrashim, wonder tales, kabbalistic mythology. The use of these sources marks off Feierberg from many of the other figures in the autobiographical tradition and expresses an essentially romantic commitment to the programatic retrieval of national origins.

Feierberg's place in the autobiographical enterprise is assured, in the end, by the fact that in his work the central moment of apostasy receives its fullest articulation. Both Lilienblum and Brenner show little interest in probing the cognitive and emotional determinants that move them or their heroes to break with the tradition. The inevitability of the break is taken for granted, and it appears either as a burlesque of self-importance (Lilienblum) or as an absence in the text, literally an ellipsis, to be filled in by the literary competence of the ordinary reader (Brenner). For Berdichevsky's protagonists, religious crisis has ostensibly been put so far behind them that the event is not even included in the narrative continuum of the text. Yet despite this elusiveness, which on Brenner's part amounts to a tactical evasion, apostasy remains the matrix of the genre's thematics; that is to say that apostasy figures as the fundamental experience without which the present anomic and alienated condition of the characters would not have come about. In Feierberg we are given not only the event but the process leading up to it. When Nahman, the hero of *Wither?*, commits the signal sacrilege of extinguishing a candle in the synagogue on the Day of Atonement, it is a culmination richly prepared for. We have been shown the varieties and stages of dissonance experienced by the child in his encounter with religion. We have followed his attempts to find shelter within the folds of the tradition even as he is impelled toward unwilling rebellion.

Feierberg's works belong to the autobiographical tradition, furthermore, because of the confessional burden they discharge. Hebrew autobiographies are not of the sort written by distinguished figures at the close of their careers. The Hebrew writers who turn to autobiography are invariably young men to whom the most formative, and disastrous, experiences of life have already happened. Their need to tell their story results not from a desire to defend a career and set the record straight but, simply, from pain: the excruciating pressure to disburden the self of feelings of failure and shame. In Feierberg's work the psychological axis and the cultural axis intersect in a particularly affecting way. The adolescent's fear of loneliness, suffocation, and death—the lot of sensitive youths everywhere and always—has the effect of deepening the *other* confessional burden: terror before the loss of God and of the life of holiness. Confession, then, is a *function* of narrative rather than a specific *form* of narrative.

Whither?, Feierberg's major fictional statement, is not written in the first person as are the other works in the autobiographical tradition. But the mere fact that Nahman does not formally narrate his own story does not mean that his story does not manage to get told in his own voice. The internal monologues and the free indirect discourse in which most of his thoughts are rendered—and the narrative is nothing but his thoughts—accomplish this purpose. The choice of the third person is underscored by the fact that a number of the earlier stories, the Hofni tales, are in fact told by their protagonist-narrators. Gershon Shaked is right:

> Apparently Feierberg preferred the third person for his novella because it was precisely here, rather than in the stories, that he felt closest to himself. In order to prevent an identification of the autobiographical "I" with the narrator, he insisted on creating a gap between them which would impose an objective dimension upon the subjective ordeals of the hero.[4]

Feierberg is considerably more sophisticated—and calculating—an artist than most readers have assumed. The mystique and the pathos of his work have led to a conception of him as a kind of primitive who simply transposed into writing the naked pain of the loss of God. Even if this were all it would be a great deal indeed. But it is my intention in this chapter to argue that there is much more. From within Feierberg's romanticism there can be discerned a keen analytic intelligence which addresses the etiology and substance of apostasy: what are the origins of apostasy? how does it develop? how is it experienced? what are its effects? The overriding question in connection with Feierberg's work, I think, is a formal one. It concerns the supposedly simple transposition of ideas and feelings into writing. Feierberg not only found a way to handle the problem of pathos—how so much anguish could be made affecting yet not ridiculous—but also the problem of consciousness. How can a moment of cultural transformation in which a civilization as a whole is in crisis be made intelligible through the experience of a single mind? We shall first take up the solution Feierberg found for the formal problem and then proceed to discuss the analysis of apostasy.

Feierberg's solution came to him as a way of accommodating the tension between two demands: the pressing need to explore the individual's inner world of thoughts and feelings, on the one hand, and a felt responsibility to the collective experience of the Jewish people, on the other. Feierberg's preoccupation with subjective consciousness reflects not only the painful events in his own biography and the spiritual crisis that took hold of East European Jewry as a whole. It reflects as well a larger development in Western literature. The description of the interior space of the self deserving of attention for its own sake, a space generated by rules of its own which evince no clear or necessary connection to the larger social system, constitutes one of the points at which literature can be said to have become modernist. Thereafter, one of the central concerns of fiction is the representation of consciousness itself: memory, reflection, and the manifold operations of the imagination. For Feierberg, it must be stressed, individual consciousness represented not only the sad fate of man after separation from the tradition but also the only possession of his own that man is left with after the break. Individual consciousness is thus an opportunity and a consolation as well as a fate.

At the same time, Feierberg maintained a programatic allegiance to the collective life of the traditional culture he was rejecting. He believed that despite the apparent impoverishment of the ghetto (his term for the culture as a whole), the ghetto is possessed of a richness and integrity of its own. It was the task of the Hebrew writer, he wrote in a letter to Ahad Ha-am, to penetrate the discouraging surfaces of ghetto life and "trace the most inward form of our outwardly manifested world" and thereby reveal the hidden soul of the Jew.[5] He took his own injunctions seriously, for although he had broken with the spirit of the ghetto he returned to that world and its literary heritage as the proper locus of his artistic activity, and he argued vigorously against such writers as Berdichevsky who advocated the "liberation" of Hebrew literature from those confines.[6]

Mediating these demands, the one a personal urgency and the other a felt commitment, presented a most difficult challenge. Radically different varieties of imaginative experience require radically different varieties of textual materials. To represent collective consciousness, Feierburg utilizes material drawn from the aggadic and legendary strand of the Hebrew literary tradition: Lamentations and the Song of Songs, the heroic narratives of the Former Prophets, midrashim, medieval exempla, kabbalistic myth, folk tales and Hasidic stories.[7] To represent individual consciousness Feierberg attempts to reconstruct the reticulated verbal patterns of the individual mind: its meanderings and fantasies, its fears and ambitions, its associative energies, its visionary powers, its alienation from itself, and its reaction to the external world which stands stubbornly opposed to it. The problematic of Feierberg's fiction resides in the fact that each modality of the imagination is by nature not only resistant to the other but also entails aesthetic dangers of the most serious kind. The problems raised by the attempt to treat individual consciousness concern how to avoid the dual dangers of engulfment and discontinuity. Such states of strong feeling as dread, bitterness, and exaltation may submerge writing in a sea of sentiment for which there is no adequate correlative; similarly, the associative circuitry of the mind as it switches from context to context vitiating its own constructions conduces to a discontinuity which may effectively cancel the possibility of the kind of consecutive narrative basic to fiction. The problem presented by aggadic, legendary material, on the other hand, concerns the problem of how to domesticate its inherent alienness, how to take a body of foreign material with its own referential integrity and make it serve the purposes of a new fiction—how, in short, to make it lead *into* the story rather than away from it. At the heart of aggadic material there is the strong logic of narration which has to be broken before consciousness can be assimilated, and conversely, at the heart of individual consciousness there is a lyric fragmentariness and circularity which has to be pulled together and straightened out before narrative can emerge. If the challenge in the treatment of aggadic material is to collapse aesthetic distance, then the challenge in the treatment of consciousness may be said to lie in the attempt to achieve it.

Feierberg's six short stories, all written before the composition of *Whither?*, divide evenly along chronological lines into two groups. The early stories ("Yankev the Watchman," "Shadows," "A Spring Night") are set in lyric mode; they are evidence both of the power of Feierberg's attraction to the expressive individual imagination and of his difficulties in contending with its aesthetic demands. In the later group ("The Calf," "In the Evening," "The Amulet") Feierberg experiments with the creation and manipulation of narrative, either by interpolating it fully formed into a more variegated composition or by perfecting an analogical method of relating different dimensions of the tale. And only in the reverie-form in *Whither?* will an adequate vehicle for the integration of lyric and narrative be found.[8]

"Yankev the Watchman" *(Ya'aqov hashomer)*,[9] Feierberg's first story, is ostensibly about the sufferings of the town watchman who at an early age had been pressed into the Czar's army as a "cantonist"; however, the complications of the narrative frame—the aging narrator recalls, among the memories of his early childhood, stories about an unfortunate youth who was by then an old man—suggest that this is equally the story of the narrator as it is of Yankev himself. Although the Yankev-narrative is skillfully done in parts, focusing effectively on two or three imaginative events in the life of the dazed child, the story bogs down in the bathos of the narrator's rhetorical demands for justice for his case and in a process whereby Yankev himself is gradually dematerialized by the allegorical theme of cosmic exile *(galut hashekhinah)* his fate is made to symbolize. In the treatment of Yankev we feel Feierberg trying too hard with too heavy a hand to make his character embody the national experience, and instead, the result is to call attention away from Yankev and direct it toward the narrator and his overwrought exertions.

The fact that the "I" of the narrator rather than the figure of Yankev is the hidden subject of the story is made clear in the prologue that begins this story as it does the two others of the early period, "The Shadows" and "A Spring Night." The prologue begins in the midst of an attack of existential bile in which the narrator reviews the spectacle of gratuitous suffering which has caused him a kind of spiritual death in which he questions the very worth of existence. Just as he approaches final despair, however, the graves of memory are flung open and the holy souls of the oppressed fly out, reawakening in the narrator the "strength to live on"; there, among the souls, as real as life, is the image of Yankev the watchman. The sense of life restored by the evocation of Yankev is not merely a rhetorical or sentimental gesture: not only is the narrator saved from ultimate metaphysical negation but the story itself is rescued from the bilious rantings of the narrator, and provided, in the form of an account of Yankev's life, with a reason for being told. The dangers inherent in consciousness bereft of narrative are given in the narrator's embittered image of the world as

> this vast rock which lies beneath the eternally hammering sledge that eternally splits it into infinite fragments of stone and sand. . . . This dust which has been scattered and carried to the ends of the earth until not a grain again resembles the pebbles first placed on the pile. (p. 40, 146)[10]

The figure takes its power not only from the concrete image of infinite and irreversible disintegration, but also from its parodic relation to the verse in Jeremiah (23:29) "Is not my word . . . like a hammer which breaks the rock in pieces," a verse the rabbis took as describing the wealth of exegetical possibilities contained by each divinely uttered word, as well as the divine language at the origin of the tongues of the Seventy Nations.[11] Feierberg deftly reverses the value but not the form of the activity in question: what in God's hands is the endless multiplication of meaning from a single source, in man's hands is meaning's endless breakdown and fragmentation. In the second half of the image the parody on a kabbalistic motif makes the point even more sharply: unlike the divine sparks which, though exiled from their divine source, remain recognizably divine and capable of one day being redeemed, the dust of human effort has been pulverized beyond recognition and scattered beyond recall. Thus in addition to reflecting on the futility of human endeavor, the conceit describes the risks involved in the writing of the story itself: the risks of self-cancellation run by wandering within the converging passageways of the mind.

Instead of disappearing in Feierberg's next story, "The Shadows" *(Hatselalim),*[12] those passageways become even more labyrinthine. The rancorous meditations of the aging narrator of the previous tale are exchanged for the adolescent narrator's sweetened embrace of his self-imposed solitude. Hofni, on whom Feierberg hoped to base a series of first-person fictional memoirs, is a child of the ghetto at a time when the fabric of religious culture is fast unraveling.[13] By night in the beit midrash, the beit midrash which has been abandoned by his contemporaries for better pursuits, Hofni sits alone and soliloquizes on his love for the shadows which surround him. Rocking over his Talmud folio as the magnified shadows sway "back and forth interweaving and overlapping" in response to his movements, Hofni ruminates on the moment the shadows first drew him to nocturnal study, on the swarm of doubts and desires he is certain never afflicted his father's vigils in his own day, on the unconscious masses who never trouble themselves about study of the Law, on the great shadowy tomes in the surrounding bookcases, which, in a moment of visionary intensity, Hofni imagines turned into martyred Jews who are swept away weeping and groaning on rivers of blood. And so it goes as Hofni describes "the whirlwind of frighteningly bitter thoughts that lashed at my mind and cast a black cloud over me" (p. 56, 136). The whirlwind, alas, is not just in the lad's mind but on the page before us as well. Not only do reflections on the great themes of isolation, doubt, and theodicy have to be carried by fragmentary utterances whose rapid alternation and obscure transitions give us little to hold onto, but the vortex of thought pulls us down further and further into an embrace with death. Hofni's auto-erotic embrace of the shadow-world of martyrdom and meditation make it perfectly clear that the mind, left in isolation to populate its own world with images and figures, will fashion, like the crumbling beit midrash, its own tomb.

Aware of the tendency of his story toward a death-embrace, Feierberg attempts in its second half to provide Hofni with some egress to the world in the form of two new characters. The first is Reb Shlomo, a poor but learned Jew who often comes to the beit midrash on winter nights to lose himself in study; but Reb Shlomo never in actuality appears in the story, remaining only an imagined presence in Hofni's mind and an occasion for the lad's reflections on the deficiency of his own devotion to study. The representative of the real world who is finally ushered into the beit midrash is a poor village Jew who having lost his way in the snow has arrived hungry and cold after a long journey. Hofni leads him to the only place in town where people are still up at that hour, the social club of the local westernizers, where the youth and the visitor are treated with derision and condescension.[14] This confrontation with the pervasive injustices of ghetto life shakes Hofni from his self-absorption, and, finding himself once again among the shadows of the night, he declares that his love for the darkness has passed, and that he is now ready to make a new life in the daylight of the world.

Although the next effort, "A Spring Night" (Leil 'aviv),[15] does little to make good this declaration, Feierberg takes a determined step forward in a later group of stories ("The Calf," "In the Evening," and "The Amulet") simply by adjusting his narrator's age. In place of the fulminations of old age or the anguished self-absorption of adolescence, Feierberg returns in time to the mind of the child. By taking this simpler and more emotionally integrated point of view as a narrative origin, the writer can make his story re-experience the genesis of those states of consciousness which will later harden into enduring and overwrought metaphysical conditions. There is an economy here and a happy reduction of rhetoric which makes the pathos of the child's wonderment and dread far more acceptable to the reader than an old man's spleen or an adolescent's auto-erotic dilemmas. In "The Calf" (Ha'egel),[16] for example, the outrage of a child over the slaughter of a favorite animal makes an effective and natural vehicle for such a theme as the arbitrary suffering of the innocent which was treated with considerable awkwardness in the early stories. A simple co-ordination of the death of the calf with the death of Hofni's innocence makes it clear enough that this cycle of death will not end when Hofni grows into maturity in the world of men and history.

In the first part of "In the Evening" *(Ba'erev),*[17] written next, Feierberg describes with an even surer hand the impressions made upon the mind of the child by the milieu of the heder: the pitiable anger of the rebbe and his assistants; the fantastic tales swapped by the boys when they are left alone between *minḥah* and *ma'ariv;* the solitary trek home through mud and snow. However, when Hofni's mother submits to his coaxing and tells him a long tale concerning the struggle for the soul of a Jewish child stolen in infancy from his parents by a Polish landowner, Feierberg's story takes off in an entirely new direction. In its "flawless command of narrative pace and mood"[18] the story introduces a sense of movement entirely unattested in his earlier prose. Shuttled across an expanse of years or held hovering over a single scene, the reader knows he is in the grip of a narrator who has discovered how to produce and control the literary illusion of motion and who, one suspects, will not easily do without it. This is a world far different from the self-consuming confusion of the mind in which thoughts collide, pile up, and collapse of their own weight. Moreover, in reworking and combining elements from three separate Hasidic narratives, as S. Werses has shown,[19] Feierberg demonstrates his ability successfully to appropriate legendary materials for his own imaginative purposes—here to represent the struggle between the ghetto and the hostile but alluring world outside—while at the same time maintaining the literary integrity of the materials themselves. The tale thus shows Feierberg not only breaking through to narration but also learning how to neutralize the foreignness of material arising from the collective rather than individual imagination.

Beyond the separate gains of each half of the story, there remains the question of the connection between two very different kinds of fictional materials, between a sketch of heder life and a wonder tale. It can, on the one hand, be argued that the two are integrated by the common theme of initiation. The story takes place on the day Hofni is being graduated from the lower tiers of the heder to the ranks of the older boys who stay on to study at night. The pride which suffuses the moment, however, is disturbed by the experience of listening to his mother's tale, a tale which is frightening not only because it describes the wiles Satan uses to seduce boys away from Judaism but also because of the very fact that the story is left without an ending: the ultimate fate of the stolen child's soul is left for another night's telling. This subversive indeterminacy turns Hofni's innocent celebration of maturity into an initiation of another kind, a foretaste of the world of unremitting temptation and struggle which will soon enough be his. Whereas loss of innocence in "The Calf" resulted from the anguish of direct experience, it should be noted that in "In the Evening" its loss results, more subversively, from the experience of narration itself.

Yet no matter how well-wrought this connection, it remains only a thematic bond; the divergent materials Feierberg was working with could be related by apposition and analogy alone. The "peg" the heder story provides for the telling of the tale is wobbly in the extreme, and once begun, the tale ends by completely consuming its narrative framework. To make this point, however, is not necessarily to devalue the story, but to indicate that the considerable achievement of "In the Evening" is secured at a price: in order to perfect his facility with narrative it was first necessary for Feierberg to split it from consciousness and cultivate it separately in its own autonomous context. Considering his success with the tale-form, Feierberg might well have continued in that direction; but something essential and compelling about the kind of immediate individual consciousness depicted in the early stories forced him, whatever the aesthetic risks, to return to consciousness as a fictional medium into which narrative might be integrated rather than merely implanted.

Before Feierberg proceeded to the work in which he would attempt such an integration, he exacted in his last story "The Amulet" (Hakame'a)[20] the maximum amount of serviceability from the conventions of the short story before putting the genre aside for the novella. The stories, we have seen, are characteristically divided into two moments, marked by two very different compositional textures: a solitary imaginative experience followed by the intrusion, in various forms, of the "real" historical experience of the People as a whole. The ratio of emphasis, we also noted, shifts from story to story: whereas in "The Shadows" the mistreatment of the poor Jew is absorbed by the tortuous historiosophical speculations of the adolescent narrator, the vivid but thin impressions of Hofni's heder experiences in "In the Evening" are subsumed by the expanding vistas of the tale of theft and struggle. By returning to the treatment of consciousness in "The Amulet," Feierberg not only draws these two moments into a tight symmetry but also perfects the analogical bond between them. At the beginning of the story Hofni awakes in the middle of the night seized by the kind of mortifying nameless dread which makes it seem as if his mind had fully grasped the portentous meaning of the tale he had been put to bed with in the previous story. Unable to fall asleep, Hofni experiences a momentary voiding of consciousness during which, not knowing whether he is asleep or awake and unable to recognize his surroundings, he is left to the terrors of pure sensation. Although slowly the sideboard and his parents' bed once again become familiar, unlike Adam at the Creation, he cannot match names with things, and he is left so utterly without will that he cannot bring himself to take his arms out from under the coverlet to perform the ablutions that would make it possible to recite the *Shema'* and thus release himself from this state. Again the next night Hofni awakes in a fright, this time from a dream about the martyrs of the Chmielnicki era based on a story told him by a comrade concerning a heder class, teachers and students, who had offered their throats *en masse* to the Cossacks' knives. Hofni's vigils of dread signify the dual modalities—void and nightmare—which are left the individual imagination after it has been disabused of its childhood élan by exposure to the historical drama of the People. This exposure, which the imagination first seeks as a deliverance from imprisonment within itself, becomes the same experience which is responsible for the reduction and demonization of the mind's imaginative powers.

The irony of the story's second half emerges from the changing valuation of Hofni's dread: what begins as motiveless childhood silliness ends by becoming a symbol for the spiritual situation of the entire generation. The father's tirade about the decline of Hasidism and the spiritual orphaning of the generation is reinforced by the kabbalist to whom Hofni is brought for counseling. In the wake of the Messiah's failure to come, the holy man explains, Jews have lost "the power of expectance . . . the inner mind has shrunk to nothing . . . the Shekhinah refuses to descend . . . and because holiness is departed and left a vacuum behind, Samael has spread his nets and goes forth to stalk souls" (p. 117, 63). As the two men struggle to apply Lurianic theology to the present crisis of the People, which they perceive as unrelated to the inconsequential fears of a small child, the reader who is alive to the analogical method of the story knows that the *historical* situation the men describe is nothing other than that of Hofni's mind as it is first voided and then invaded by nightmare.

Despite refinements in the analogical method, the thematic opposition of individual to collective and the formal opposition of consciousness to narrative still have to be represented separately and consecutively. It will be the achievement of *Whither?* to make the two into one: not only to originate a compositional form which can incorporate the two sets of thematic and formal elements into a single, simultaneous imaginative event, but also to relate these events dynamically one to the other and thereby construct the larger story of the novella.

On the question of the "achievement" of *Whither? (Le'an?)*,[21] there has actually been little agreement in previous critical argument. It is generally agreed that the novella succeeds in describing how the crisis of faith which beset the generation of the nineties was produced from within Judaism rather than from without, as had often been the case in the less tortured conversions of the sixties and seventies.[22] Credit is also given Feierberg for introducing into Hebrew literature a sympathetic depiction of the inner world of the child, which considerably revised the Haskalah model of the child as a learning machine. In less thematic matters, however, there is less appreciation. The last third of the book, from Nahman's betrothal to his proto-Zionistic speech, is thought by many to be an aesthetic failure. The first two-thirds, characterized by Nahman's visions, meditations, and dreams, are generally taken to be impressive in their lyrical impact but highly deficient in their abandonment to emotive expression and visionary origination for which no adequate forms are established. Y. H. Brenner put the case most bluntly when he said that *Whither?* is only about a "young Jew with a sensitive heart whose birth-thoughts and birth-pangs are painful to him and who comes before us to pour out his soul."[23] J. Fichman, in remarking on the promise rather than the maturity of the work, put the case most sympathetically when he said that "more than constituting a literary work, [*Whither?*] expresses the thirst for one,"[24] and I. Rabinowitz most theoretically, in claiming that Feierberg's powers as an artist were simply not strong enough to prevent his giving way to the shadow-world of the overwhelming erotic and demonic forces he summoned up.[25] Since the visionary element called into question here does in fact constitute the basic fabric of the work, any critical effort on behalf of *Whither?*, such as the one I wish now to present, must therefore make *its* case on these terms also.

Far from being an amorphous mass of expression, the visionary materials of *Whither?*, I would argue, are organized into a series of tightly designed units which move the meaning of the story in successful if unconventional ways. Although there are several different varieties of imaginative materials from which *Whither?* is composed—dreams, parables, monologues, quotations, dramatized reasonings[26]—the work's unique and central narrative unit is one I wish to call the "reverie."[27] A reverie is a kind of expanded and portentous literary form of the daydream. The reverie is not properly speaking a dream, because it takes place in a waking state, nor is it a soliloquy or a monologue, because it is neither spoken aloud nor spoken *before* anyone; nor is it entirely a vision, because it contains many elements of meditation and reflective reasoning. In *Whither?* the reverie takes the form of a series of imaginative movements which begin as a meditation on a present object or task and move toward a fantasy of heroism or martyrdom, which in turn evokes threatening questions of eschatology and theodicy which finally burst the reverie and return Nahman to the unredeemed present. These reveries, of which there are about a dozen in the first two-thirds of *Whither?*, are the most significant among the narrative units of the work. One would be hard pressed to find here any of the ordinary "scenes" from which fiction is usually constructed: dramatized conversation, social exchanges or confrontations, changes in external conditions which affect the hero's choices. The only real events in *Whither?* take place within consciousness, and it is largely through the experience of such events of consciousness that the narrative develops. The changes Nahman undergoes result from his imaginative experience *within* the reverie: some option is closed and the remaining ones seized upon in the next reverie with renewed desperation. By thus situating narrative within consciousness, Feierberg was able to integrate the two modalities of imagination whose stubbornly separate careers had limited the possibilities of his earlier work.

Before proceeding further I wish to make clear that despite my intention to deal with *Whither?* from the point of view of the reverie, I am aware of the existence in the novella of several other kinds of technical strategies. Most striking in this connection is the fact that the novella begins (although the device is quickly abandoned) in an entirely different mode, as a tale told *about* Nahman by a mother of a Hofni-like child. At the center of the work stands the great speech of Nahman's father, which is a monologue rather than a reverie. And from the Ninth of Ab scenes and forward, roughly the last third of the book, the narrative *describes* Nahman's meditations rather than attempting, as in the case of the reverie, to constitute them. These sections and their methods, however, are similar to those in the works of many other writers of the period, and in *Whither?* they are simply not the most successful parts of the book. I shall certainly attempt to show how the reverie is related to the father's monologue and why the reverie form disappears in the closing sections of the novella, but I choose to stay close to the reverie as a subject because it is Feierberg's major innovation and a significant aesthetic solution to the dilemmas of the age.

I wish to begin with a synchronic reading of one reverie and then proceed to a diachronic analysis of each of the reverie's constituent elements. The section I quote from comes near the beginning of the novella.

[A.] A sudden ray of light entered from the next room. Through the slightly opened door he saw his father sit down on the floor in a corner. . . . A moment passed and he could be heard as he began to chant the midnight vigil in a slow, drear voice. . . . Nahman eased himself down off his bed and tiptoed to the door to see his father more closely. It was a fearful, an awesomely holy scene. The plaintive chant bore into the recesses of his heart and soul—"How long will there be mourning in Zion and weeping in Jerusalem?"—The old man was secretly weeping. Tear after tear rolled down his white beard; "I have set watchmen upon thy walls, O Jerusalem, they shall never hold their peace day nor night." [B.] He thought of the stories about Jerusalem's walls that he had heard from Jews who had been there. In his mind's eye he saw two large teardrops fall from the Wailing Wall, while a fox ran stealthily in and out of its breaches. He stood among the ruins by the holy wall and watched the crowds of Jews as they wept out loud and threw themselves on the ground. Here were the remnants of Jerusalem's towers, from a crumbled mound of which he heard a voice cry out: "Woe to the father who has sent his children into exile and woe to the children who are banished from their father's table!" A veil of darkness covered Jerusalem. The city lay in mourning. Before a cave by one of its gates sat the aging King David and played a frightfully sad and poignant tune upon his harp. Near him an armed Arab stood guarding the city, his spear in one hand and his sword on his hip. High, far away the heavens split open and there was God himself sitting on His throne and looking down on the world that served as His footstool. Here was Jerusalem lying desolate. [C.] The throne rocked back and forth, and two enormous tears hurtled to the bottom of the great sea. Then all the holy souls who had martyred themselves in His name came forth from paradise surrounded by fire, while a river of blood flowed before them. Their bodies were beaten and torn; their bony hands were held high and in them were the scraps of parchment from the Torah scrolls they had saved from the foe.

Before the mercy seat they flung themselves down, but an awesome voice called out to them from above: "Return to your place of rest, ye holy souls, the time has not yet come!" Then Mother Rachel too fell upon the throne with a heart-rending wail, and the holy fathers prostrated themselves at its feet with a terrible cry. . . . [D.] But the long bitter exile was not yet over. Jerusalem was burned to ashes. The land of Israel lay waste. The Shekhinah was in exile, and the Jews lay scattered and dispersed among the nations. Satan reigned victorious. Samael held sway over all. Mikhael, the angel of Israel, his father had told him, lay bound in chains. Man was ruled by his passions and could not worship God. [E.] Ah, when would the Messiah come? He must come. No, he must be brought. The Messiah wouldn't come by himself, his father had said. Each generation must bring him. And yet so many had tried! Joseph de la Reina. The blessed Ari. The Baal Shem Tov. They couldn't bring him because the time hadn't come. But perhaps it now had. It was time to try again. The Messiah must be brought. He must, no matter what!

. . . .

From that night on—so he remembered—his childhood innocence and animal spirits were taken from him. It was then that he first came to realize that life was a dreadful contest in which he was condemned to struggle and toil for as long as he lived without ever knowing whether he was winning or not. (pp. 134–37, 138–39, 73–75, 76)

The reverie consists of five characteristic moments, whose transitions I have marked in the text with capital letters. The first moment (section A) is the *setting*. Through the crack in the bedroom door Nahman glimpses his father in the outer room sitting on the ground and weeping over Jerusalem in the *tikkun ḥatsot* prayer, and drawn by the plaintiveness of the chant, he comes to the door to observe him.

The reverie proper (section B) opens with a *meditation*, which begins when Nahman's observation of his weeping father gives rise to his own thoughts about Jerusalem destroyed. This is the threshold at which contemplation of the external object (the ostensible occasion for the reverie) is left behind for independent imaginative origination. Nahman paints a tableau of Jerusalem's ruins with colors taken from a range of traditional sources (Lamentations, Lamentations Rabbah, Talmud Berakhot, and others); here the Western Wall with its weeping Jews and the heavenly voice crying out "Woe!" and there King David in the shadow of the armed Arab, with God on his throne above. The tableau exists on a static plane as if Nahman's mind was filling the corners of a canvas; and although the sense is conventionally tragic, very much what we would expect to be the associations of an imaginative heder boy, it nonetheless betrays a kind of unexpected and unspoken delight in the act of conjuring up and filling out a scene.

The scene erupts at the beginning of section C with the rocking of the divine throne and the release of two great tears of mercy. The martyred souls, who have waited for eras for such a sign of God's intention to bring the redemption, rush up from paradise on a river of blood and fling their tortured bodies in supplication before the Almighty. The divine tears, however, have been a sign only of interim compassion and not of ultimate deliverance, and despite the wailing intercession of Mother Rachel and the patriarchs, the battered souls are told to return below, for the end has not yet come. In this moment of *vision*, the static plane of the preceding tableau is shattered by the heavenward flight of the driven souls which describes an infinite chasm between the mercy seat and the great sea below. The violently propelled movements of this scene, with its desperate rush toward the opening of redemption, spring from sources very different from the child's self-gratifying fancy, sources closer in origin to the threatening and chaotic unconscious imagination.

In the fourth moment (section D), the *historical* moment, the deflated tone carried by the repeated hammering rhythm of facts reflects the immobilizing recognition that nothing at all has changed and that the "long, bitter exile" remains in force. The unrelenting pressure of the indefinite present tense gives the sense that the destruction has happened all over again and that the visionary evocation of a redemptive opening has only thrust the world deeper into the hands of demonic forces.

The last moment, divided into two parts, returns to the present and then proceeds to describe Nahman's *response* to the experience he has just undergone. In the first part (E to the ellipsis) the intractable hold of the unredeemed present weakens in the face of speculations about the Messiah. The dispirited aftermath of visionary intensity yields to a determined voice which declares that the Messiah must be brought: the voice gains in authority as it first admits perplexity and speculates on why the great saints of the past have failed, and then asserts that the time is at last at hand, and finally cries out its unconditional commitment to the task. This section is not only a victory over the paralyzing recognitions of the previous one but is also an escape from the present into the future, a future created by an imagination which has inserted itself at the center of the historical drama. Although the second part of the last moment (after the ellipsis) is not part of the reverie proper and here follows a dream I have left out, it nonetheless indicates the completed pattern. After the great imaginative event, the interior space of Nahman's mind is left behind, and the decisive changes which have resulted from the reverie are reported in the discursive voice of the narrator. Here, as is the case following most of the reveries, we are told of the price Nahman has had to pay for the experience. The vision of redemption and unredemption with its concluding pledge to bring the Messiah has disabused Nahman of his "childhood innocence and animal spirits" and placed him directly into "the dreadful contest" for the deliverance of the world.

Among the general features of the reverie it should be first pointed out that the reverie transpires entirely within the imagination, and it is through the operation of successive *varieties* of the imagination that the effective sequence of movements is produced. The reverie begins with Nahman's fascination in the act of observing his father, which in turn gives rise to a pleasurable pictorial meditation concerning the awesome subject of his father's prayers. However, the scene Nahman has conjured up, sentimental and precious in conception, serves almost in spite of itself to trigger a quite different kind of force. An involuntary imaginative impulse surges to the surface and transforms passive rumination into violent vision. When the momentum of vision is then blocked by God's edict, Nahman's mind is returned, not to the ingenuous fascination of the outset, but to a bitter consciousness of the unredeemed state of the world. When Nahman regains control of his mind it is to draw a new map of the future, this time a fantasy of militant action. One of the central moments in this sequence is the one in which the involuntary imagination wrenches control from Nahman's indulgent fantasizing, a moment which signals in substantive terms the shift from an authorized, pious picture of Jerusalem destroyed to an unauthorized vision of a rebellious attempt to coerce the end.

The reverie describes a great unclosed circle. From its starting point in present observation, Nahman's mind rises to hover in the timeless past of the People and then rushes forward toward a future beyond history; the failure of redemption returns Nahman to the present, but it is not the present he left: the spontaneous fascination of childhood has been exchanged for ineradicable historical awareness. The reverie has picked Nahman up and sent him back toward the indefinite past and then forward toward the infinite future and has finally set him down at a place which is slightly but significantly distant from his point of departure. It is this small breach, during which options are closed and others opened, which advances the story of Nahman's progress toward apostasy; it is an advance which takes place during and as a result of Nahman's great imaginative flight. *Whither?*, it may therefore be said, unfolds on two narrative planes and at two narrative rhythms: the cosmic reaches of the reveries with their strong circular movements and the gradual change of Nahman's soul as it alters by small linear steps.

The very presence of both a "cosmic" and an individual meaning in this passage is an important aspect of Feierberg's achievement in *Whither?* The voice which cries out from the ruins "Woe to the father who has sent his children into exile and woe to the children who are banished from their father's table!" (in section B) surely bewails the catastrophic pain of both the exiled Jewish people and their abandoned God, but it *also* bewails the equally catastrophic pain of both Nahman, who is about to descend into the long exile of apostasy, and his father, who is about to be afflicted with an abandonment which he himself, like God, has decreed. The exile of the Jewish People from God and Nahman from his father (and he from his God) represent, however, only the collective and individual dimensions of the tragedy; the dimension which may be said to be truly cosmic is the exile of God from Himself, of the transcendent *'Ein Sof* from the immanent *Shekhinah*—the very theme of the *tikkun ḥatsot* prayer. Individual, collective, cosmic—the dimensions of exile proliferate and interpenetrate: through the crack in the door Nahman, the son, contemplates the exile of the People, as he watches his father bewail the exile of the Father from Himself. Feierberg succeeded in creating a fiction which, as Baruch Kurzweil has written, "collapsed the barriers between subject and object,"[28] between the fate of the writer, his community, and their God.

One cannot read Feierberg's novella without being struck by the sense of longing which permeates its pages. Every object Nahman comes in contact with serves as a touchstone of desire, as an occasion for extended flights of longing in the direction of unseen worlds. Nahman, in fact, can almost be said to have no "character" of "self" in conventional fictional terms but to appear before us solely as a point of desire whose existence is defined not by what it has but by what it longs for. The control and orchestration of this effulgence of desire is one of the functions of the reveries of *Whither?* The reverie is a kind of neutral field whose positive and negative terminals are given changing designations. Whatever the desire, to begin with, certain features are always in play; imaginatively there is always a negative pole of distraction which longs for visionary fullness; metahistorically, a pole of unredemption which longs for redemption; and textually, the constricted world of the Talmud which longs for the free flight of aggadah. As the narrative progresses, the specific poles of presence and absence undergo transformations; passive fantasy *versus* the power of eso-teric knowledge; the present which is poor in opportunities for dramatic self-sacrifice *versus* the passion of historical martyrdom; God's apparent concealment from the world *versus* his intimate rapport with Israel in the exegesis of the Song of Songs. Feierberg's generation, it has been said often enough, was rent by terrible conflicts between the ghetto and the world, the sacred and the secular, the community and the individual, the squalor of the present and the hypostasized glory of the past. In the reverie, with its flexible field of desire, Feierberg found a vehicle capable of representing the dimensions and vicissitudes of the conflicts of an entire generation.

Desire which can never be fulfilled is the propulsive force behind verbal production which can never be at rest. The unrelenting movement of the imagination as it streams across the poles of the reverie is one of the most characteristic features of Feierberg's mature style. The reverie's appropria-tion of narrative energy is, of course, one of the principle sources of this movement. The vision of redemption first at hand and then deferred, for example, is a miniature narrative whose breathless progression from event to event recalls the accomplishments of the interpolated tale in "In the Evening." Whereas in the latter case, however, such movement is carried by a self-contained story, in *Whither?* the same sense of movement has been moved inside the mind and made to serve as part of a larger imaginative event. A less obvious form of movement, one usually present in the nonvisionary moments of the reverie, is produced by a progression, not of events, but of logical or rhetorical statements. Nahman's speculations about the Messiah, (the first part of section E) for example, are actually a series of assertions and refutations, a fact which is easy to see once they are rearranged on the page:

Ah, when would the Messiah come?
He must come.
No, he must be brought.
Each generation must bring him.
.   .   .   .

And yet so many had tried!
.   .   .   .

They couldn't bring him because the time hadn't come.
But perhaps it now had.
It was time to try again.

The movement here is two-directional. In Hofni's mind there is an unhesitating progression from syllogism to syllogism, yet in the mind of the reader there is actually an oscillation between the syllogistic and hortatory, between truths deduced from historical evidence (i.e., from the failure of redemption) and proclamations of the states of reality which "must" (read: "should") come into being. Feierberg's ability to produce both a rhetorical movement and an ironic awareness of its speciousness represents a significant disciplining of the kind of amorphous rumination which swamped his earlier prose.

As important to *Whither?* as the circuit of the imagination within each reverie is its movement from one reverie to the next. This movement provides a significant instance of the interplay of imagination and ideology, for as each episode concludes with a newly arrived at theological-historiosophical position, it decisively conditions the imaginative economy of the next one. I wish to follow this change through a discussion of each of the five moments of the reverie in the central episodes of the novella. In order to take the passage discussed above as a common point of departure, I am putting aside two less developed reveries which precede it (pp. 177–78, 101–2 and 186, 106–7). The seven core reveries and their subjects are as follows:

R_1—The midnight vigil (pp. 134–37, 73–75)
R_2—Bringing the Messiah (pp. 139–47, 76–81)
R_3—Martyrdom (pp. 149–51, 83–84)
R_4—Alter the idler (pp. 163–65, 93)
R_5—Jephthah's daughter (pp. 165–66, 94)

R$_6$—The Song of Songs and the allegory of the scholars (pp. 167–69, 95–96)

R$_7$—Gersonides and apostasy (pp. 172–73, 98–99).

The *setting* for the reverie, to begin with, moves through three symbolic sites: from the home, to nature, and finally to the beit midrash. After the midnight vigil Nahman leaves the intimate space of his father's house and his father's authority for a craggy ledge overlooking the woods and streams at the edge of the town (R$_2$). Here pheasants call, streams whisper, leaves stir—this is a zone of imaginative freedom where, as in Bialik's "The Pool" (*Haberekha*), "another language" (*safah 'aheret*) from that of the heder and the market place is spoken. Although this would seem like the proper place for Nahman to fulfill his vow to bring the Messiah, his repeated efforts fail, and when he approaches the craggy ledge two years later (R$_3$) it has become merely a touchstone of memory, a "journal" of the naïve days when "his will grew bold and expansive" and sought to "soar from the ground to challenge and master all things." The subsequent removal of the remainder of the reveries to the beit midrash signifies confinement in a space in which the originating powers of the imagination are even more severely qualified. The great volumes of Talmud commentaries which surround him there remind Nahman of the authority of the past and of his responsibility to it rather than to himself, and the decrepitness of both the building and its sole other inhabitant, Alter the idler, remind Nahman that by remaining in the beit midrash, rather than "living," he is being buried alive. It is the disclosure of the beit midrash as a tomb which finally supplies the compulsion for Nahman's ambiguous flight to freedom.[29]

The *meditation,* the second moment of the reverie, is usually begun as an unauthorized alternative to a more normative activity. Nahman's observation of his father reciting the *tikkun hatsot* (R$_1$) is an avoidance of going to sleep as he should; the visionary adventures at the craggy ledge are an escape from the prosaic world of the heder (R$_2$, R$_3$); and the reveries in the beit midrash are all in one form or another begun as an illicit glance upward from the Talmud folio Nahman should be studying. Unlike the rich tableau of Jerusalem destroyed, later meditations tend toward greater discursiveness and toward verbal patterns imitative of the kind of processes of conjecture and ratiocination that are evoked by experiences of wonderment and fascination. Although, for example, the first reverie at the craggy ledge (R$_2$) begins with a sword-waving fantasy of heroic action, Nahman soon realizes that despite his bluster he has no real idea of *how* to bring the Messiah, and he then passes over to a meditation on the holy books he has heard spoken of and the esoteric wisdom they are supposed to divulge to those who know how to read them. When he returns to the ledge after the failure of his messianic mission (R$_3$), he is enveloped first in memories of his own failed aspirations and then in reflections on the perennial suffering which has resulted from the deferrals of the past.

A significant shift between the early reveries and Nahman's later enclosure in the beit midrash is brought about by the great monologue of Nahman's father which stands at the center of the novella. Its theme is not the heroic individual and his power to bring redemption but the isolated soldier who must endure every hardship just to maintain his place in God's army. In the image of the soldier there is no moral glamor, no romantic authority, no promise of secret knowledge, and even no enviable martyrdom; in a fallen generation such as Nahman's there is only dread, temptation, and isolation as rewards for fighting God's fight. The fact that the monologue is a speech and not a reverie is significant, because its very purpose is to qualify radically the sense of potency which has until now surrounded Nahman's imaginative flights. Implied in both Nahman's reveries and his father's speech, to be sure, is a distance which intervenes between subject and object; but whereas in the case of the reverie it is a distance of desire filled by imagination, in the father's case it is a distance of resistance filled by dogged struggle. The father's reproach thus elaborates a set of parallel distances with different polarities (Good Impulse/Evil Impulse, *kelipah/tokh*) which counters and eventually consumes the world of Nahman's desires.

The difficulty Nahman experiences in achieving any kind of imaginative flight when he is left alone by his father in the beit midrash (R_4) indicates the deep inroads the monologue has indeed made in the free operation of Nahman's imaginative faculties: "a swarm of confused memories swept through his mind; he was ridden by fragments of feeling that came from and led to nowhere" (p. 164, 93). To escape this debilitating confusion Nahman searches for some textual foothold for the imagination other than the Talmud, which has come to symbolize his captivity, and he finds it first among the vital primitive tales of the Former Prophets (R_5) and then among the enchanting allegories of the midrash to the Song of Songs (R_6). But when these beautiful legends are involuntarily transferred in his mind to tales of bloodshed and victimization, Nahman turns from myth to philosophical speculation as a subject of meditation (R_7). Aware for the first time that the history of Jewish thought has been marked not by uniformity but by violent controversy and mutual accusation, Nahman meditates with special pathos in the moments before his own heresy on the example of Gersonides, whose attractive rationalist doctrine of prophecy has been declared by some authorities a flat denial of revelation.

In the moment of *vision* at the center of the reveries the controlled cerebral speculation of the meditation is usurped by an involuntary imaginative force which creates its own mythos. This mythos is characterized by the same sense of movement associated with narrative, and like Feierberg's previous use of narrative it amplifies and refashions aggadic material. The thematic movement here is from redemption to martyrdom and then from the denial of martyrdom finally to apostasy. Although the souls which rushed up from under the divine mercy seat to demand redemption have been suppressed (R_1), Nahman is left nonetheless with a conviction of the possibility of forcing the end, and at the craggy ledge (R_2) he crosses over from his theosophical meditation on the existence of secret knowledge to a theurgical vision of the magical power invested in the manipulation of Hebrew letters, a power which can "command all the world and bid them to perform his will." When Nahman returns to the ledge after his efforts have come to nothing, he transfers his visionary energy from the glory of the redemption-to-come to the pathos—and also the glory—of the martyrdom of the past, recalling a story from the midrash about

> the magnificent children of Jerusalem, those tender holy babes. Before him stretched the great camp of four hundred boys and girls. They stood on the bank of the broad river contemplating their captive fate; headlong they hurled themselves into the water. . . . His spirit moved freely through the wondrous places where the little heroes had passed. . . . (p. 151, *84*)

The delicious enviability so palpable in this description is decisively squashed by the father's assertion that being a hero in the new generation requires a sacrifice far more chilling and far less dramatic. Since this is a fate which Nahman cannot face directly, he responds by conjuring up visions of sacrifice which are even more desperately romantic. Recalling the tears he had recently shed over the story in the Book of Judges about Jephthah and his daughter, his mind quickens and is soon lost in an extended evocation of that tragic story of mistiming and sacrifice, an evocation which focuses with special pathos on the daughter's valiant acceptance of her fate, in exchange for which she asks only two months in which to wander in the mountains with her companions to bewail her virginity. Next when Nahman manages to force his mind back to the open folio of Bava Qamma long enough to "break" a difficult passage, he begins to revel in the pleasures and pathos of Jewish learning (R_6) and he is soon engrossed in an extended re-evocation of the allegorical interpretation of the Song of Songs, in which the beloved becomes the Daughter of Israel and the vineyards she wanders through the houses of study and the masters of the Law. However, this denial can be perpetuated no longer, and as he meditates on his own attraction to the suspect teachings of Gersonides (R_7), Nahman is terrified by the very idea of heresy, the idea that because of "one single thought he stood to lose all, even his share in the world to come." He tries desperately to suppress these thoughts, but an inner voice makes itself heard despite his efforts. "You fool!" it mocks, "What can you lose? What makes you think that there's a world to come at all? If the Torah doesn't come from God, then neither does anything else, so what is there to be lost?" (p. 178, *98*). In his depiction of Nahman's moment of apostasy as the sudden articulation of a suppressed voice, Feierberg makes clear what has been implicit all along: the roots of heresy lie in the revolt of the imagination, and when the mass of doubts and reasoning reaches a point where faith is possible no longer, the break comes not as a final logical step but, like conversion, as an imaginative leap.

In no reverie can the visionary moment be sustained for long before it is brought up short by the contradictions of Jewish history. In the experience of rupture is the beginning of the fourth, *historical moment* of the reverie. In some instances the recognition is expressed in hushed, dramatic tones as in the picture of redoubled exile and desolation in the lines following the failure of redemption in the *tikkun ḥatsot* episode; however, Feierberg is also effective when he shows, as in the case of Nahman's messianic reverie (R_7), how vision breaks down in the midst of the difficulties of day-to-day life: the constant solicitations of the Evil Impulse, the temptation to go swimming in the river with the other boys on Friday afternoon; the petty provocations of schoolmates at prayers. In Nahman's second reverie at the craggy ledge (R_3) the reality principle is introduced by a kind of natural speculative faculty reacting to the idyllic vision of mass martyrdom. The vision leads to a heavenward gaze at the stars, which Nahman imagines to have twinkled just as brightly and impersonally on the night of that aweful sacrifice. He is seized by an unwished-for rush of thoughts: "Ah, who knew what went on above! Perhaps it was all just a joke. The Bible mocked the customs of the gentiles, but might not the gentiles have a book that mocked the customs of the Jews?" And thus a conjecture about the relativism of historical destinies leads directly to the thought, entertained for the first time, of the absurdity of Jewish history. When left alone in the beit midrash after his father's speech (R_4), Nahman's vague ruminations about the boredom of Talmud study and the decrepitness of the beit midrash are suddenly catalyzed by a glance at Alter the idler which prompts the realization that in contrast to his father's inflated visions of the soldier of God, this man picking at his beard and rocking back and forth in a mindless trance represents in reality what it means to be a model soldier at this moment in Jewish life. As he glides with Jephthah's daughter through hills and hollows (R_5), it is again the image of Alter the Soldier which recalls Nahman to the present. Like the biblical maid, he realizes, he too would be sacrificed by his father, but unlike her, he would be given nothing in exchange except an opportunity to die a slow death in the beit midrash.

The *response* to the reality of history, which constitutes the final moment of the reverie, is characterized by a double movement of acknowledgment and suppression: the threatening revisions of Nahman's notions about the nature of Jewish existence which are necessitated by the confrontation with the reality of that existence drive him to increasingly more desperate attempts to shore up his faith. So, though he knows at the end of his vision of the opening and closing of redemption that he has been ushered into a "dreadful contest between good and evil" (R_1), he rebounds by vowing to dedicate his life to bringing the Messiah, and when his efforts become mired in personal weakness (R_2), he pursues with greater asceticism the instrumental attainment of the holy spirit *(ruaḥ hakodesh)*. Nahman's discovery of the bitter joke at the center of Jewish history (R₃), however, is so dangerous a realization that his only response can be shame and remorse: "He would have liked to tear out his heart together with such thoughts and cast it to the swine . . .—but where could he take refuge from the furies of his own mind?" The monumental speech of Nahman's father sufficiently bolsters his son's conscience to make the scenes in the beit midrash examples of extreme dichotomy: although Nahman's imagination produces one vision after the other of disintegration and entombment, after each he forces his mind back to the text before him with such concentration that he produces new interpretations which challenge the master commentators of the Middle Ages. For a moment, lost in the burning intensity of study, he is even ready once again to be a hero on behalf of the Lord and His Torah. The tension can obviously not hold and it snaps at the point where doubt has become too radical and denial too extreme. Disciplined in rational thought by his readings in the philosophers, Nahman finally realizes that the teachings of Gersonides have only been "an authority on whom to pin his own heretical thoughts" and that now he must face the fact that he has become utterly and ineradicably a heretic.

Feierberg's invention of the reverie is a profound accomplishment, and we have considered it until now as a solution to an aesthetic problem: the integration of individual consciousness with the collective imagination of the tradition. The achievement of the reverie is obviously not exclusively aesthetic, and for the remainder of the chapter we shall probe the reverie and *Whither?* as a whole for its analytic yield: What forces are responsible for the collapse of faith? What variety of orthodoxy is being rebelled against? What is the ironic use made of the Kabbalah in the presentation of apostasy?

It may not be too obvious a point to observe, to begin with, that apostasy, as it is presented in *Whither?*, has little to do with modernity or Western ideas.[30] To be sure, Nahman's recruitment into the army of the faithful takes place against the background of widespread defections from the ranks, and the burden of faithfulness becomes all the more oppressive for its loneliness. Yet the presumption remains that the collapse of religious faith is the result of forces that are entirely immanent within the tradition. Two of these stand out. Most of Feierberg's reveries, especially in their visionary moments, center on a longing for redemption: Nahman brandishing a messianic sword on the craggy ledge, the martyred souls storming the divine mercy-seat, the theurgical maneuvers during the Rosh Hashanah services aimed at "forcing the End." As each of these attempts ends in failure, Nahman is sucked down ever more deeply into the abyss of despair over the unredeemed captivity of his people. This is something more than an initiation into the stern realities of adulthood. Perfect faith in the coming of the Messiah and perfect patience in the indefinite deferral of his coming were the twin doctrines mandated by the rabbis in the after-math of the Destruction. Feierberg implies that there exists within later Jewish piety the tendency to disrupt this balance. By inflaming expecta-tions for redemption, which are destined to be disappointed, damage is done to the very capacity for faithfulness.

Another classical tension subjected to abuse is the relationship between halakhah and aggadah. Nahman's education after the first level of the heder is devoted entirely to the study of Talmud and medieval codes. These legal texts hone the mind and provide the occasion for virtuoso displays of dialectical skill, yet the needs of the soul, it is implied, are left unmet. The study of aggadah is relegated to an extracurricular activity, a sanctioned recreation when the mind is exhausted from worthier labors. In *Whither?*, however, Feierberg stages a drama of the return of the repressed. Nahman reverses the hierarchy by making the aggadah into the secret world of fantasy in which he feels most truly alive. Set free of its tether to the halakhah, the aggadic imagination grows in power until it ends in under-mining the entire enterprise of belief. The faculty of imagination has its own needs for nourishment, and they can be ignored only at a cost.

These tensions within Judaism should caution us to be as accurate as possible in identifying the religious outlook Nahman rebels against. While at times it is convenient to speak generally of the "tradition" and the "sources," Feierberg has been careful to register the precise colorations of the book's milieu. We should first be clear about what the book is not. Despite the hasidic connections in Feierberg's biography (his father's ad-herence to Habad, the son's attendance at the study house of the Cher-nobyl Hasidim), Nahman's spiritual world in *Whither?* is not grounded in Hasidism. The folkloristic frame-story of the novella, which Feierberg drops after the opening, makes Nahman's sufferings the result of a curse placed on the father for his *failure* to believe in the Zaddik from Chernobyl. The hasid's joyous trustfulness in the face of the travails of this world could not be farther from the father's spiritual stance. Nor would it be correct to speak in this context of the mitnagdic culture prevalent in Lithuania, with its esteem for intellectual values and scholarly accomplishments.

More precisely, Nahman's father practices a style of elite piety de-scended from the Lurianic Kabbalah of sixteenth-century Safed. The the-osophical structures of the Kabbalah, as we shall see shortly, are turned into fictional ideas by the novelist, yet this is not the level at which the characterization of the father operates. He is not a mystic or a thinker *per se* but a Jew whose practice reflects the pervasive influence of Kabbalah on Ashkenazic Jewry from the seventeenth century onward. Through the mediation of such works as the *Shenei luḥot habrit* by Isaiah Halevi Horowitz and the *Reshit ḥokhmah* by Eliyahu de Vidas, which are mentioned often in the novella, secret doctrine was converted into a pietistic ethics suitable for widespread adoption. This regime, under which Nahman is raised, is dualist in essence. Reality is composed of fragments of primordial evil

(Samael, *kelipah*) which are entwined with sparks of divine light, just as the human soul is rent by an unremitting conflict between an evil impulse and a good impulse. The effects upon the young child are palpable:

> How many dreadful warnings were written in the holy books about the night-time kingdom of the *kelipah*! . . . He, a weak and lowly boy, was all alone in this dismal world. Thousands of angels and hidden powers lurked all about him . . . the whole world lay in ambush to drag him down to the fiery pit, to hell. . . . He felt desperate; it was hopeless; there was no way out. (pp. 133–34, 71)

To keep from being ensnared, the Jew must live a life of constant vigilance and repentance. The ordeals of the present generation are a punishment not only for its own shortcomings but for ancient iniquities. The destruction of the Temple and the exile of the Shekhinah are to be mourned weekly and monthly on specially ordained fast days, as well as in the ritual of the midnight vigil *(tikkun ḥatsot)*, portrayed so vividly in the first reverie. The utter gravity of every moment in life is nowhere made clearer than when Nahman's father calls him away from play with his friends and informs him that from now on he will pray the afternoon service with the adults in the synagogue: "Every moment of pleasure and enjoyment," the father explains, "is put there by the devil to drag us down into the vanities of this world so as to rob us of our place in the next. We mustn't take pleasure, son, we mustn't ever take pleasure in this world!" (p. 128, 67).

If this is the kind of Judaism that confronted Nahman, then we must think it little wonder indeed that it is thrown over. But what in fact is being rejected? Is this ascetic, otherworldly, fundamentalist religion identical with "Judaism," or is it just one version, a perversion, of a larger and less corrupted entity called Judaism? Is there, then, a vision of the tradition in Feierberg's work which is separable from the oppressive regime that is visited upon his protagonist? The question cannot of course be answered unequivocally, but it remains a crucial issue in understanding Feierberg's analysis of the great crisis in Jewish culture. We are given a clue, I think, by the fact that the story is presented from the point of view of a child-adolescent. This feature of the novella may seem so fundamental as not to represent a choice. But that is not quite so. Feierberg could have kept the child as the subject but chosen, as Brenner did in *In Winter,* to describe the experience of the child largely from the retrospective viewpoint of an adult narrator. In *Whither?* Nahman is the sole "focalizer" of the narrative, which is constituted in good measure by the discourse of the boy's consciousness.

This choice has the effect of making the child's encounter with the ascetic piety of the father especially brutal. When an adult assumes the rigors of such a regime, he presumably accepts the discipline as justified by the spiritual rewards it offers. Or for a man who practiced such piety in his youth and abandoned it as an adult, there are the consolations of retrospective understanding. A child like Nahman, however, remains vulnerable; there is nothing to protect him from the assaults upon his innocence. The worst offense, of course, is the constant dread of sin and punishment. Everyday life is imagined as superabundantly populated by demons and tempters. The believer treads as on the edge of a knife; the slightest misstep leads to damnation. The anxiety is sharpened by the child's difficulty in discriminating between the more important and the less important. The precepts and interdictions of religion are presented as all bearing a life-or-death urgency. As a result the child is overwhelmed by the near impossibility of avoiding the certainty of eternal punishment by virtue of the very fact of being alive. In Feierberg's work, the conception of what, under normal circumstances, it means to be a child is conventionally romantic: innocence, high spirits, love of play, imagination, spontaneity. The imposition of ascetic piety becomes a systematic molestation of the child in everything that makes him a child.

The indictment, then, is unremitting. Judged from the viewpoint of the child, this belated piety is so oppressive that it does in fact seem to stand separately from the sources of classical Judaism experienced by Nahman in his reveries. *Whither?* can therefore be said to offer a differential analysis of the ills of Judaism. The problem lies not in the tradition itself—although there are inherent tensions here as well—so much as in the body of ascetic doctrine and praxis superimposed upon it. Yet in the end this discrimination counts for very little. In the genuinely tragic outlook presented by Feierberg, gone forever is the possibility of disentangling the two. Lilienblum and other reformers may have envisioned a renewed Judaism stripped of its otherworldly excrescences, but this was a dream Feierberg no longer dreamt. The infection had spread too far; there was not enough living tissue to save.

Incredible as it might seem, the aura of tragic pathos touches even the father. He is the exemplar and enforcer of the order that crushes the boy's spirit and fills his life with terror, yet he is himself never portrayed as cruel or sadistic. In a novella made up almost entirely by the internal consciousness of the son, a large and important scene is given over to a monologue by the father. The scene is located critically between Nahman's heder years and his graduation to independent study in the beit midrash, and it has the function of explaining to him the meaning of the passage from boyhood to youth. It is also the chance for the father, who is ironically destined to outlive his son, to deliver his *tsava'ah*, his ethical will, and to describe the boy's spiritual patrimony. This stunning piece of rhetoric, developed and sustained over several pages, is devoted to the elaboration of one obsessive image: the army of the Lord.

> Whoever wants to worship God . . . must certainly be a soldier. . . . He has given us His one true Torah, His commandments and His prohibitions, and we have all sworn to be His army, His holy troops. Have you ever thought, son, that while most men are comfortably asleep on soft beds under familiar roofs, an army must camp in tents in the field and suffer from cold, wind, and rain? A

soldier must get used to a hard life, to wandering and to lack of sleep. . . . Most of his days are spend in homelessness and exile. (pp. 156–57, *86*)

The army image does not belong, to my knowledge, to the world of kabbalistic piety represented by the father. It adds a distinctly modern, nineteenth-century resonance to his pronouncements and links them to the religious strife taking place at that time within European Jewry. In reaction to Haskalah and Reform, the traditional rabbinic leadership was quick to define the religion practiced in their communities as the only proper, and hence "orthodox," expression of Judaism. As tradition is put on the defensive, it assumes a stance of militancy, both theologically and politically: veritably a church militant. The stance becomes exceedingly beleaguered toward the end of the century as large numbers of Jews emigrate or join social movements. It is in the midst of these widespread defections "from the camp" that Nahman is recruited by his father into the army of the faithful. A soldier's life is hard enough in the best of times, but at the present moment, the father declares, the army is at war, and the required sacrifice will be even greater. Nahman is being inducted into a loneliness that knows no end.

Taken as a mortifying initiation ritual, an updated version of the sacrifice of Isaac, the father's speech is vastly effective. It is also overdetermined. The description of children involuntarily conscripted and condemned to military service far from home raises the specter for the Jewish reader of nothing so much as the "cantonists." These were the unfortunate Jewish youngsters who were pressed into the Czar's army during the first half of the nineteenth century and made to serve for twenty-five years. Few survived, and fewer survived as Jews. Feierberg's own literary debut, a story called "Yankev the Watchman," was a moralistic tale about just such a victim. The practice was discontinued after the death of Nicolas I in 1855, but at least in Feierberg's metaphoric arsenal—and not his alone—the horror was still alive. The cantonist outrage becomes a figure for the monstrous act of incarceration perpetrated by the fathers against the sons.

For all this, Nahman's father does not come off as being monstrous. He is a true believer, not a hypocrite, and it is pathos rather than irony and ridicule that informs his portrayal. He is destined to stand by helplessly as the prestige of the Torah is dragged to the ground and the great culture of piety unravels. Sympathy was not generally accorded to the figure of the father by other writers in the genre such as Brenner and Sh. Ben-Zion. Moreover, the biographical witnesses to Feierberg's own life attest to the beatings and persecutions suffered at the hands of the father when the son's "desertion" became known.[31] The absence of vindictiveness in *Whither?* is less a sign of generosity of spirit than an indicator of the kind of writing we are dealing with. This is not the sort of confessional act distinguished by its psychological realism; and Nahman is not the kind of autobiographical hero who is driven to understand how his identity emerged out of conflict with his parents and to settle scores for the price he was made to pay. The figure of the father lies much closer to myth than gritty reality. He is an embodiment of the pietistic tradition and is not differentiated from that tradtion by any noticeable particularity.

In the reality constructed by Feierberg, the nurturing parental functions have been taken over by the tradition itself. That is the womb which has produced Nahman and that is the domain from which he is destined to be banished.[32] The eclipse and appropriation of the biological family by a larger cultural-metaphysical moment—and the unexpected return of biology in the form of erotic need—is a pervasive theme in the Hebrew autobiographical tradition, as we shall see in the case of Berdichevsky's heroes especially. As for Feierberg's characters, their considerable libidinal energy is entirely infused into their longings for redemption and their struggles with the tradition. Between the time Nahman loses his faith and the public display of his apostasy, he is married off by his father to the daughter of a wealthy merchant from another town, and Nahman is fortunate to find in his wife both an object of desire and an ally in his struggles. But these scenes, coming as they do after the imaginative intensity of the reveries has ended, are unconvincing. We well know by this point that Nahman's life is simply not lived at the level of real relations with flesh-and-blood people. His life is lived elsewhere.

The father is left in his pathos because, at this spiritual level, Nahman never ceases being his son. The dramatic structure of *Whither?* is made up of a theme and a counter-theme. For most of the novella we follow the accumulating momentum of apostasy as it moves toward the ultimate break with the tradition and, by extension, with the father. Yet from within the depths of this negation there begins to unfold a surprising movement toward a new kind of kinship. The play of this reversal, which is truly dialectical, dominates the last third of *Whither?*, roughly from the point when the use of the reverie is halted. The complexity of the exchange is already foreshadowed at the outset of the story. The midnight vigil scene (pp. 134–37; 73–75), which was analyzed above as an example of the reverie, manages to fuse the perspectives of the father and the son. Lying in his bed at night, Nahman is tranfixed by the sight of his father sitting on the floor in the next room intoning dirges over the destruction of the Temple. (This was not, incidentally, a special fast day but a daily ritual originated by the practitioners of Lurianic Kabbalah.) As the son contemplates the father, he conjures up a vision of Jerusalem destroyed and hears a voice cry out among the ruins: "Woe to the Father who has sent his children into exile and woe to the sons who are banished from their Father's table!"[33] The complexity of the scene results from a shifting sense of who are the children and who are the fathers. In his mourning for the Temple, Nahman's father identifies himself with the sinful sons of the midrashic parable who have been banished from the table of God, the figurative father. Through a *mise en abyme,* this entire tableau is embedded within the perception of the real son Nahman. What *he* sees is his father mourning his banishment from *the* Father. The sight prefigures a double loss: Nahman, the true son, will be exiled not only from his true father but also from God, whose fatherhood has already long been forfeited by His belated sons.

Not unsurprisingly, it is the figure of the Destruction that Feierberg uses as a hinge in shifting between theme and counter-theme. Feierberg makes Nahman's final realization of his apostasy fall out on the day before the Ninth of Av, the solemn summer fast devoted to the destruction of the temples and other historical calamities. In an extended scene set during the evening service in the synagogue, the meaning of the Destruction undergoes a series of modulations. Nahman begins by simply feeling removed from what is going on around him. The whole town is abustle with preparations for the fast. "Yet Nahman felt remote from it all. He was no longer the person he should be or that others still thought he was. He had become someone else" (p. 175f., 97). Feeling shameful and hypocritical, he cannot look people in the eye. Sitting on the floor bent over their tallow candles, the congregation recite the mournful evening prayer, while Nahman realizes that he is now "cut off from the House of Israel, banished from among his own people."

The desire to achieve otherness resonates throughout *Whither?* From the first stirrings of fantasy as a child to his macabre visions of entombment as an adolescent, Nahman had longed for a world beyond the doorstep of the house of study, whether this was the "other world" with its "other language" *(olam aher, safah aheret)* he found in the woods beyond the town, or the playful ray of light on the wall of the study house which bid him discover "what a big, bright wonderful world" is to be found just beyond its confines—this longing for another world had been the distant pole of desire in all of Nahman's reveries. But when the moment of apostasy finally arrives, like Adam and Eve discovering their nakedness, Nahman realizes he "has become another" *(nehepakh le 'aher),* and later when he sits lost in his thoughts after extinguishing the candle on Yom Kippur, he realizes that "now, at this very moment he had begun another life" *(hayyim aherim).* Though bound by the same word, the Other *(aher)* which Nahman has become is far different from the liberation and novelty *(hayyim aherim)* he had sought. Now as an apostate—like the Tannaite sage Elisha ben Abuya, called the Alien One *(Aher)*—he listens to the chanting of the book of Lamentations, mourning more for his lost faith than for the destruction of Jerusalem.[34]

The awareness of loss rather than removal now comes over Nahman. The next part of the service is the recitation of the Book of Lamentations. Here Feierberg makes brilliant use of the description in chapter three of Lamentations of the anonymous male sufferer who begins by experiencing his persecution at the hands of God as an unexplained ordeal and ends by acknowledging his sinfulness and appealing for forgiveness.[35] The verses chanted by the cantor and interleaved with Nahman's thoughts, and the result is a bitter irony. The sufferer—and by extension the Jewish people—may have been subjected to the most horrible persecutions, so Nahman ponders, but hope could always be retrieved from the memory of earlier happy days in the relationship with God. Since there was a God from whom Israel could become alienated through sin, there was a God to whom Israel could return in repentence. Why should the mourning of the congregation, then, be so deep and abandoned, for do not they, unlike him, believe in God and His mercies? As though by a negative identification with the anonymous sufferer of Lamentations, Nahman finally comes face-to-face with the enormity of his loss. When the numbness of shock and estrangement have worn off, Nahman cries out inside himself:

> Why have they robbed me of the brave, the mighty and terrible Lord who breaketh the cedars of Lebanon and maketh them to dance like sheep, the merciful Lord who restoreth the humbled in spirit . . . ? Give me back my God, the God of the Jews! The God of Aristotle can do nothing for me. He is a figurehead, a king without a kingdom, not a God who lives. (p. 179, 100)

From within the immediacy of the experience, apostasy is presented by Feierberg not as a choice or as the rebellious outcome of a search for meaning but as a swindle. By following the rationalist Jewish philosophers in their efforts to refine the idea of God, Nahman thought he was joining the quest for the greater truth. Now he has awakened too late and found himself the loser, for there is no going back.

Just as the Temple was destroyed, so Nahman's spiritual world has been destroyed. Thus father and son, the fate of the collective and the experience of the individual, are brought together under the sign of the Destruction. Yet this analogy, like so many features of the novella, is not left its plain meaning. There exists an *esoteric* understanding of the Destruction, and it is at this level that father and son are most truly joined. When Nahman's father notices the boy's agitated condition during the Tisha B'Av service, he assumes that it is a result of an overzealous mourning for the Temple. Such grief is based, to his mind, on a mistaken *exoteric* understanding of the significance of the fast. It is not for the destruction of Jerusalem we mourn, explains the father. "Son, son, the Land of Israel is nothing but earth and dust. Jerusalem is just a city of houses, markets, and towers. The Temple itself was only a large building, with great slabs of marble and much silver and gold" (p. 182). When Nahman logically asks, "But for what are you mourning tonight, then, Papa?" the father proceeds to reveal the "secret" meaning of the Destruction. It is based on the kabbalistic notion that the earthly calamity that befell Israel was the mirror of a cosmic calamity in which the immanent aspect of the Godhead, the Shekhinah, was exiled from the transcendent aspect. Since "holiness itself is in exile," the father explains, man is lost except for his memories of the ancient age of unity.

So we too are ruined in the Exile, because Samael has stopped up all the channels that lead to holiness, so that we would have died a spiritual death, God forbid, or nourished ourselves from the *kelipah* (for the spirit must nourish itself just like the body), if it weren't that by recalling the divine flow from the days when the Temple still stood, we can manage to survive the Exile until the Redemption has been wakened. Yet until then we are helpless, because our spiritual powers are in exile and in thrall to Samael. (p. 183, *102–3*)

Now, Nahman may rail against the quietism enjoined by his father's outlook, and he may make a valiant appeal for the this-worldly, self-initiated reawakening of the nation. But on the most essential point he accepts the father's analysis. Just as the uninitiated traditionalists underestimate the true consequences of the Destruction, so the contemporary proponents of national renewal miss the true nature of the present historical moment. Because they see only the persecution and economic wretchedness of the people, they assume that such practical measures as political organization, productive training, and settlement in Palestine will be sufficient to renew the nation. His father's son, Nahman knows the crisis goes much deeper, deeper still than merely the adding of the cultural perspective of an Ahad Ha-am would allow. For Nahman, what has happened is a cosmic dislocation parallel to and no less than the exile of holiness that, according to the Kabbalah, took place at the time of the Destruction. It is a rent at the root of being which no practical measure can ameliorate.

Both father and son await an *it'aruta' dila'ela'*, a spiritual awakening. For the father this can come only through God's grace. For the son the stirrings of such an awakening can be discerned in the current excitement about Jewish settlement in Palestine, the Hibbat Zion movement. Feierberg focuses the final scenes of the novella on his hero's connection to this new possibility. "Mad" Nahman rouses himself from his ghostlike withdrawal and, before he dies, delivers an impassioned public speech foreseeing the rebirth of the Jewish people in the East. Yet however glorious Nahman's rhetoric, its failure as writing oddly confirms the father's faithful despair.[36]

For what characterizes the entire final third of *Whither?* is an unmolding of the imaginative intensity we have come to expect from such passages. The visionary moment at the center of the reverie has been collapsed by an historical illusionlessness which can authorize neither images of romantic martyrdom nor fantasies of supernatural redemption. In place of vision Feierberg introduced affirmation, affirmation of the vaguely defined rebirth of the People. This change, noted among others by Gershon Shaked,[37] determines the ruling irony of the final sections of the novella: The great ideological-spiritual leap into the future proclaimed with cries of "Forward! Forward!" is presented in language which, in its discursive statement or enthusiastic exhortation, takes us very much in the opposite direction, back to a language barren of the extraordinary movement which embodied the reveries of destruction and imprisonment.

What remains genuine in the last section, however, is the sense of personal loss, the horizonless anguish at the theft of a faith in exchange for which there is nothing worth having, expecially the cheap positivism of the Haskalah. In once again locating authenticity within the situation of the individual, the writing in the last third of *Whither?* vitiates the fusion of subjective and collective consciousness which had been the achievement of the reverie form and returns to the isolation—though not temperament—of the individual mind in Feierberg's earliest stories.

After the great and incomprehensible outburst of his final speech, Nahman lapses into silence for what remains of his life. In Nahman's silence lies Feierberg's integrity: the admission that in the absence of the originating imagination silence is preferable to rhetoric. Aphasia is the unnegotiable outcome (and inevitable meaning) of apostasy. The awesome realization Feierberg came to grips with at the end of his novella—and his life—was the paradox that the Jewish imagination lives only through negation. In its struggle to break free of the past, the imagination draws its authenticity of sentiment—and the very materials of its vision—from that which it is opposing. Whether conceived of as a contest with an angel or as a necrophiliac embrace, the exchange of blessings and powers which streams between the writer and his opposing past ceases to flow once the beast is finally dead. It would be left to Hebrew writers who, unlike Feierberg, were allowed if only for a little to defer their own deaths, to struggle in the void to create an autonomous aesthetic freedom.

FOUR

Berdichevsky and Erotic Shame

The erotic problem in Hebrew literature is an outgrowth of the transformation of sex and the family in Jewish society in the nineteenth century. This is a social history which is yet to be written, and in its absence one can point only to the largest social patterns.[1] If for the moment we take Emancipation as a term for the modernization of political and social institutions and Enlightenment as a term for the modernization of mental attitudes and literary opinions, then we may make this generalization: Whereas in France and Germany these two processes often proceeded at the same pace, among the intellegentsia in Eastern Europe Enlightenment often far outstripped Emancipation. This is to state a commonplace, but one worth underscoring when it comes to the issue of relations between the sexes. The *consciousness* of the "Enlightened" Hebrew reader in Russia and Poland was infused with substantially new ideas about the nature of men and women and the relations possible between them, while the *realities* of courtship, marriage, and family remained largely traditional. What were these new ideas? They derived from a redefined conception of the self as the locus for the twin functions of reasoning and feeling. As quintessentially human faculties, according to this new conception, ideas and sentiments are the possession of women as well as men (although feminine nature may be endowed with a greater capacity for sympathy and a correspondingly lesser one for rational activity). Since men and women are made from the same stuff, as it were, their relations at their most refined take the form of a communion between like beings. Men and women are drawn to one another not by social duty, religious obligation, or even sexual need alone, but by spiritual affinities and invisible bonds of sympathy. Marriage represents the union of body and spirit, serving man's higher faculties as well as his lower ones. A man's wife is his spiritual helpmeet with whom he shares a living current of sentiments.

Now, whatever can be said in praise of the Jewish family in the Eastern Europe of this period, in all its variegated complexity, it must be admitted that the reality and the ideal did not go hand in hand. The new notions I have presented are a digest of midcentury attitudes from the period of what is called the Romantic Haskalah. The radical tension between these attitudes and the untransformed social institutions of courtship and marriage is evident, as we have seen, in the works of Guenzberg and Lilienblum, whose autobiographical narratives belong to a more realist strain in

Haskalah literature. Guenzberg's *Aviezer* (written in 1828, published in 1864) is a critique of the practice of arranged early marriage, which forces early adolescents to enact their sexuality prematurely and which removes boys from their parents' homes at a tender age. The premature demand for sexual performance divorced from a life of shared sentiments runs the risk, it is charged, of precipitating a developmental calamity at once social (impotence) and cognitive (apostasy). Lilienblum's *Sins of Youth* (1876 and 1899) presents a contrast between two kinds of relationships: the traditional arranged early marriage, which dehumanizes the spirit by reducing con- jugal love to a series of housekeeping and childrearing arrangements, and a relationship based on an affinity of spirit between the maskilic rebel and a young women of similar sympathies. In the end, Lilienblum never in fact abandons his wife and children, nor does he violate the chaste idealization of his rapport with the anonymous Miss N. Nevertheless, Lilienblum's resistance to both possibilities is profound. It is the very experience of relationship in itself that is put in question. For the fragile self wounded by the tradition and the struggle against it, any deep entanglement with a woman of any sort can compromise the aspiration toward either remaking the self or contributing to the renewal of the people.

The tension becomes even sharper when the boundary is crossed between autobiography-writing and novel-writing. At the level of dis- course in itself, this distinction may now seem to us less than crucial; yet in the late nineteenth century the decision to write long fiction involved a peculiar confrontation with the received conventions of genre. The very idea of the novel as an enterprise was perceived by these writers to carry with it the specific subject matter implied by the European term for the form: *roman*.[2] The relations between the sexes had to figure in the con- struction of the novel, if not as a central axis then at least as a crucial component. How seriously this requirement was taken—and how impossi- ble its fulfillment—can be seen in the works of such Haskalah novelists as Mapu and Abramowitsch; "romance" is always present in the structure of the novel, yet it is a component which is most often comically detachable from the main thematic business of the novel, and bears no mimetic relationship to social reality. From the perspective of the generation of Berdichevsky and Brenner, then, the allegiance to these generic con- ventions on the part of Haskalah literature perpetrated a lie. In the social and educational system of East European Jewry, the romance of the novel hardly existed; indeed, it was a conspicuous absence. In his allegiance to *this* truth, the truth of Haskalah autobiography rather than the novel, Lilienblum was indeed the precursor of the innovative psychological real- ism in the fiction of the new generation.

The fiction of Mica Yosef Berdichevsky (1865–1921) constitutes a new stage in the representation of the erotic problem. Feierberg never left his town deep in the Ukraine; Lilienblum got only as far as Odessa. It was

Berdichevsky who succeeded in breaking out of the orbit of East European Jewish society, making his way to the West, and receiving a doctorate in philosophy from the University of Berne in 1896. With its mixed company of Jews and gentiles, men and women, student life in the university towns of Germany and Switzerland (where women were formally allowed to matriculate) was hardly conducted without conventions and restraints. Yet compared with the way life was lived in the Jewish towns of the Pale, this society of young people separated from their families was truly a liberated environment—at least, as we shall see, as regards external constraints. The ideological climate changed as well. Berdichevsky's polemical writings had called for the reawakening of the vital energies of the "young Hebrew." Although sexual and domestic arrangements were not specifically addressed (this is true of all social and political institutions, as distinguished from religious and cultural ones), nonetheless the momentum of Berdichevsky's critique carried a strong implication in this area as well. Break the stranglehold of tradition! Restore the life of the senses! Release the instinctual powers of the individual! The force of these slogans could not easily be restricted only to certain sectors of the lived life. There was, then, a philosophical urgency to student society in the university towns. If nothing changed in the romantic lives of these new Jews, it could not be laid to a want of either opportunity or sanction.

For these young people things in fact did not go well. The confrontation with eros on the part of the yeshivah students-turned–university students in Berdichevsky's fiction turns out to be a pitiful and painful failure. Although these heroes distinguish themselves in their seminars and master advanced philosophical thinking, they break down badly in their relations with women. This is the dilemma explored in *Two Camps (Maḥanayyim)* and *A Raven Flies ('Urva paraḥ)*. Both these texts are absolutely critical for the history of Hebrew literature because they present a new language for the description of experience, and because they represent a new dimension in the representation of significant psychic and emotional forces. In the context of Berdichevsky's career, these stories constitute an important yet brief moment in which the author's fiction focuses on contemporary problems of identity before moving back in time and place to reimagine traditional society. But there is a broader framework as well. Changed attitudes toward sexuality—the very weight it displaces in culture—are an essential component of modernity. To understand the role of sexuality in the emergence of the modern Jewish mind, especially the force of its invasion of the world recently vacated by religious values, little intelligence can be gleaned from history and philosophy. It is with Hebrew literature, particularly the stories of Berdichevsky, that one must begin.

Two Camps and *A Raven Flies* were published within months of each other in 1899–1900, a year of extraordinary creativity for Berdichevsky in many fields.[3] It is in *A Raven Flies* (whose enigmatic title will be explained later on), the story published second, that the erotic problem is central, and it is on that work that this chapter will focus. A brief look at the earlier story will help in understanding how the erotic theme moved to the center in passing from one text to the other. *Two Camps* tells the story (in the third person) of Michael, an ex-yeshivah student who has made a complete break with his religious past and now studies advanced subjects at the University of Breslau in Silesia. Absorbed in his studies yet terribly lonely, Michael gradually falls in love with Hedwig, the young adopted daughter of his gentile neighbors. Once aroused, his erotic feelings, of which he remains entirely unaware, cannot be stilled, and in a paroxysm of need Michael sleeps with a poor laundress. The woman turns out to be Hedwig's natural mother, who had been reduced to her pitiable state after being seduced and abandoned by a corrupt Jewish businessman. Appalled at his transgression, Michael breaks down and seeks, Oedipus-like, to put out his eyes before moving far away.

Dan Miron, in his seminal work on the story, argues that *Two Camps* turns ironically on the theme of blindness.[4] The hero's determined pursuit of *haskalah* (literally, enlightenment), as detailed in his progress from the natural sciences to philosophy, is so entangled in the delusions of rationalism that he remains totally blind to the existence of nonrational life forces, to which, in the form of eros, he falls victim. Contrary to critics who have read *Two Camps* as a story about the discovery of sexuality, Miron acutely observes that the story's theme is in fact the *failure* of that discovery; rather than being itself the focus, sexuality functions as a metonymy for all those dimensions of life ignored by the Enlightenment worldview. Michael's is the story of the unmaking of a maskil, who is undone by forces he never succeeds in bringing to consciousness. His self-consciousness is in truth quite restricted. Although Michael's experience remains the chief focus, we see him only from the outside because of the omniscient third-person mode of narration, which allows much attention to the feelings and histories of other characters as well.

Of the many comparisons that can be made between these twin narratives, several points are immediately useful. The point of departure in *A Raven Flies* is the confrontation with eros, not the hero's intellectual delusions. It begins with the search for female companionship; love, not enlightenment, is the declared project. The mode of telling, moreover, is significantly different. *A Raven Flies* is written in the first-person form of the autobiographical confession; the text is constituted entirely of the narrator's mind, with all its obsessive self-consciousness and repetitiveness. It is a narcissistic narrative in which the experience of others possesses little differentiated reality. Finally, *Two Camps* is a story that turns on guilt, and *A Raven Flies* is a story that turns on shame. In *Two Camps* unsanctioned sexual impulses are tragically released, while in the later story the *failure* to enact these impulses and the experience of their insufficiency become sources of pathetic humiliation. Where the first ends with a gesture of self-castration, the second ends with a wish for the suffering and death of the other.

A Raven Flies is a particularly rich text; it will provide an opportunity to discuss the following issues: (1) the experience of, and resistance to, sexuality as a form of nonrationality that poses a threat to identity; (2) how, in the throes of sexual obsession, the adored "other" replaces traditional religious structures as a source of meaning; (3) clinical narcissism as a condition of the self in the world after faith, as expressed in grandiosity and in the will to power both in the pursuit of knowledge and in social relations; (4) the narrative materials (reverie, nightmare, neurotic repetition, and others) used in the innovative representation of self-consciousness and such questions of autobiographical form as the motives for narration and the reader's expectations of some kind of learning; (5) the function of fictional truth in *A Raven Flies* as a self-critique of Berdichevsky's polemical stance prior to 1899.

It is by virtue of the hero's fall into sexual desire that these issues come to light. Yet only by first understanding the "heights" the hero falls *from* can we appreciate the novelty of his breakdown. His consciousness at the outset of the story is in fact a complex amalgam of attitudes from a number of different literary and cultural sources. They define a sensibility, and it is this sensibility—with all its idealism and blindness—that is systematically dismantled as the narrative unfolds.

To feel the texture of this consciousness I shall take the first of the nineteen brief chapters of *A Raven Flies* and read it in its entirety before going on to take up the themes listed above. Because the novella does not exist in translation, this procedure will also allow the English reader to hear something of the text. A brief summary of the plot concludes this section. The short commentary aims at identifying the elements of false consciousness, especially as regards attitudes about women, which will later be exposed and undermined. The reader already familiar with the text may wish to proceed to the next section, in which the analysis of the thematic issues begins. (The quoted text that follows is taken continuously and consecutively from the beginning of chapter 1. This corresponds to pages 3–7 in the first edition and pages 36–37 in the Devir edition.)

[A Chapter]

As it remains fixed in my memory, I had already glimpsed her three times before we spoke . . . I was then still attending a university in a German city.

As a Jewish student who had recently quit the beit midrash for the university, I long remained an abashed ingenue *[bayyshan]*, untutored in manners and immersed only in books and their shadows.

Although the books had changed, I, their reader, had not. My thoughts may have taken a different shape but the abstract habit of intellectualizing and dreaming had not altered a whit.

Yet soon after I really began to change.[5]

The first sentence is a false start. The proper exposition begins with the narrator's introducing himself and setting the stage for the story about to be told. Preceding the exposition, this irrelevant piece of information about an unidentified woman has the effect of an unintended utterance, a fragment of repressed material ungovernably reasserting itself. Although the sentence hints generally at some erotic entanglement, the specific segment of the relationship "fixed" *(shamur)* in his memory is its prehistory: a moment of unilateral possession in which the speaker has the woman in his sights without her knowledge (not once but three times, a detail which seems to be savored). By its grammatical markings, the text is recognizable from the first sentence as a narrative which is both retrospective and autobiographical (i.e., one in which the first-person speaker is also the subject).[6] As readers of such a narrative we expect to be told in the course of the story how the narrator developed into who he is *now* (at the time of the writing) from who he was *then* (at the time of the earliest events in the story). Connecting these two selves, then, we expect the record of some change, whether violent or evolutionary, incomplete or total. Another possibility, however, is enacted by the way in which the first sentence involuntarily preempts the exposition and inserts the obsessive memory of an earlier event. Here, then, at the very outset of the story, the possibility is raised of an alternative narrative shape: repetition rather than change, breakdown rather than development.

The introduction, when it comes, presents a picture already very familiar to readers of the Hebrew literature of the eighteen-seventies and -eighties: the ex-yeshivah student who breaks with his past and makes his way to the university yet remains unchanged in his mentality. (*Bayyshan,* literally, one who is easily shamed, is a portentous marker of the role to be played by shame and humiliation.) Mired in the abstraction of books and ideas, the student has merely exchanged one beit midrash for another. This is a topos taken directly from Lilienblum, and the narrator uses it to identify his difference: *that* is the way I started out, like all the rest, but afterwards I truly underwent a change. The adumbration of these changes (the discovery and pursuit of love) would seem to anticipate the opening of a new chapter—a higher chapter—in the sentimental education of the Jewish hero. We already know, however, that this controlled beginning has been usurped by an earlier beginning, one which anticipates a very different kind of story.

> Sitting alone in my room in a corner of the bustling city, I then learned to experience and to feel. I keep going over and over in my mind all the emotions that were stirred in me then for the first time. . . . Stirrings of love were among them, but only in theory. I had not yet found a real embodiment for these feelings in an intimacy with a woman to whom I could reveal myself, a woman whom I could love and who would love me in return.
>
> In my stunted maturity I lacked a natural prompting that would tell me that *this* is the woman made for me. . . . The fact is that *all* the attractive women who

came across my path seemed the same to me, and I could have fallen in love with any one of them if I only knew in advance that she would return my affections.

The discovery of the life of feelings separates the narrator from the previous heroes of Haskalah literature and puts him beyond their crabbed positivism. True, he has yet to connect his feelings to a specific object, but the essential breakthrough has still been made. How compromised this claim is in fact begins to be revealed by the way in which he rationalizes his difficulties. They turn, he explains, on the difference between the potential and the actual: he loves, but the world has not afforded an opportunity for the love to be realized. This pseudo-Aristotelian logic shows him to be far less removed from the mental world of the Haskalah than he would have us imagine; it also calls attention to the vastness of the gap between the potential and the actual, a gap which quickly becomes a comic space. For falling in love, the narrator pathetically admits, *any* girl will do, as long as he can be guaranteed in advance that he will be accepted.

> This is a duality held over from my Jewish education in my father's house. . . . Inwardly I am proud and assertive; outwardly I am timid and meek [*bayyshan*].
>
> When I look in the mirror, I see an attractive man with whom on the whole I am quite satisfied. Yet when it comes to approaching a woman, I do not have a shred of faith in myself.
>
> Day in and day out I see friends who cannot hold a candle to me being successful at love; even simple folk find love. But that a woman should love me too, *me*, Elimelekh, the son of Yonah—this was something I thought next to impossible.
>
> I was already over twenty years old, and it had not yet happened. Several times I was ready and willing, but nothing came of it. Whenever I met an attractive woman I would already be brimming with thoughts of love, and even before I got close enough to speak with her, I would already be asking myself: is she the one who will love me?

By invoking the role of his early education and family in creating his present dilemma, the narrator introduces the question of responsibility, an issue which is central to any confessional narrative.[7] How much responsibility for his failures must the narrator accept himself? How much can be assigned elsewhere? He has just left off taking credit for making the major step of discovering love, while blaming the world for frustrating his achievement. Now he points a finger at his upbringing. The dialectic between blame and stipulation, between rationalization and admission, shifts back and forth throughout *A Raven Flies*, creating the text's knotty rhetoric. In a first-person autobiographical narrative there can be no external sources of authority to umpire the narrator's statements. The reader is provided only with the internal ironic markers of tone and topos. Here, for example, the time frame offers such an indication. The ridiculous blaming of others for one's failures at love (even while trumpeting the capacity for love) makes sense only as self-mockery. The narrator's willingness to draw a picture of himself as a bumpkin caught in the toils of bad faith depends upon the later arrival of a more developed self, an achieved self from the safety of which he now speaks.

The inside/outside dichotomy also introduces an important thematic opposition. In the Hebrew literature of the time "inside/outside" would automatically be taken as relating to the conflict between Jewish values and secular European values, between what lay inside the "camp" or the "home" and what lay beyond it; and it is these two realms and their conflicting perceptions of self that the narrator adduces here. As the story progresses, however, the frame of reference changes. In Berdichevsky's psychological technique the opposition between inside and outside ceases to be cultural and instead comes to refer, phenomenologically and existentially, to the experience of self and world. The national, the cultural, and the religious undergo a psychological reduction. The theme of *A Raven Flies* is in part the sudden, vertiginous opening up of a vast inner space and the implications of this new development for the transactions between the individual and the others who surround him. In the face of an ever more hurtful sense of insufficiency in the world, the narrator will increasingly inflate the value of his self. What begins here as self-esteem based on past history will be replaced first by a grandiosity fabricated as a compensatory defense and eventually by the *Resentiment* of the insulted and the humiliated.

> It will happen effortlessly. Lovely in looks and manners, possessed of beautiful eyes and hands and hair, she will naturally appeal to me. Why should she not be the one I have dreamt of loving all this time?
>
> Talking for hours, opening my heart to her, walking the woods at sunset or sitting by ourselves indoors as the sun rises—this is all it would take to sow the seeds of love. For love to be firmly planted I would just have to take her hand in mine or caress her hair. . . . Then I could love her with all my heart and share with her all my dreams. When I would go away for a short time, I would pour out my thoughts in letters, and on my return there would be tears of joy in my eyes when she came to greet me and I kissed her. . . .
>
> The idea of the kiss was in general the zenith of all my fantasies and longings. To kiss a woman I love and fondle her tender hand was my soul's great desire.
>
> The meeting of two beings through an intimacy of both flesh and spirit constitutes the ennoblement of man and his exalted awareness that he is not *alone*. . . .

Abruptly the narrative turns into a reverie; the tense changes to the present and a little tableau unfolds. The reverie does not serve as the major structuring device in Berdichevsky as it does in Feierberg, but its presence here should not be surprising. When desire has no outlet in the world and must remain internal to the self, the reverie makes a kind of narrative "action" possible. Although the reverie here is a simple fantasy, it performs the same narrative function as it did in *Whither?*: the ballooning of desire in a moment of imagined fulfillment, followed by a deflated fall into undefended reality. As a glimpse into the narrator's vision of fulfillment and redemption, the content of the reverie can tell us a number of things about Elimelekh's (his proper name has already been introduced) unspoken attitudes. The face of the woman, to begin with, is a blank. The female other in his eyes is an interchangeable object, possessing no characteristics or substance of her own. She is literally an invention and projection of desire. She is also passive and receptive. The activation of love waits entirely upon his initiative, and the steps to be taken are very few: a touch of the hand, a caress of the hair. It is as if there were simply a switch to be thrown; he has merely to muster his courage to take this first step and the rest will be taken care of. This metaphor, sowing seeds which then grow on their own, is conspicuous for its asexuality, given its employment in an erotic context. The metaphor underscores the reassuring passivity of a process, which once put into motion, needs no attention.

At the center of the imagined experience of love lies self-revelation. The "opening" *(hitgalut)* of his heart will plant the seeds of love, which will then guarantee him a setting in which he can "share with her all his dreams." At times the woman is conceived of as merely a receptacle for the narrator's desperate need for self-disclosure, and at times she is a privileged recipient of his overflowing spiritual wealth. In both cases the woman is a solution to the narrator's condition: he suffers under an enormous burden of interiority, which can be relieved only through finding a redemptive outlet. (The narrator wants to picture this interiority as a richness of spirit, while the ironic perspective of the narrative puts it in the light of a desperate emptiness.) It is this opportunity for disburdening himself which seems central to the encounter, despite the rapturous description of The Kiss. The erotic component of the reverie is altogether remarkable for its low threshold of sexuality. The kiss on the lips and the fondling of the hand are not metonymical pointers to darker genital mysteries, nor do they represent a self-imposed restraint against the writing of such things openly. Rather, the kiss represents an adolescent level of sexuality in which sexual feelings in the form of chaste playful arousal are allowed, while the surge of nonrational drives, with their potential for destruction, is contained. Finally, there is the rhetoric in which these sentiments are couched. The narrator's declaration that the "meeting" of two souls through an intimacy of flesh and spirit constitutes the ennoblement *(hitromemut)* of man, sounds like it is taken directly from an Enlightenment chapbook. In this formulation, the flesh is sanctioned by virtue of its conjunction with the spirit. The narrator's desire is not only saved from suspicion of carnality but transformed (literally, elevated) into a positve duty toward the furtherance of civilization.

Being constantly *alone* was a great affliction to me. I used to sit in my little room lost in longings and dreams of love, while outside there were women beyond number. Why shouldn't one of them love me? Why shouldn't one of them become close to me? Why won't they find out what is inside of me, my thoughts, my musings? Why won't they realize on their own that I am capable of loving all of them, if only they would take the first step? Why don't they choose me? Why aren't they sensitive to *my* aspirations instead of pursuing those whose spirits are not so rich as mine by half? Why can't they sense the flame of passion that burns in my soul? Why can't at least one of them acknowledge that I am the man of spirit who can enrich and embrace them forever? Why do they pass me by, seeing nothing in me? Why?

The reverie collapses because the narrator finds himself overextended semantically. The reverie had risen to its height with the pronouncement that the proper union with a woman exalts man to an "awareness that he is not *alone* [*levado*]." The gap between "alone" as part of a slogan and "alone" as a description of a pitiful reality, with which this next paragraph opens (the emphases are in the texts), is enough to make the reverie crash of its own weight. The inside/outside opposition returns to underscore the entrenchment of the narrator and to indicate how great a pressure of deprivation it will take to dislodge him. The paragraph consists of an anaphoric reiteration of rhetorical questions with very little development of meaning. This loss of control suggests nothing so much as a childish tantrum. The repeated demand that women acknowledge his worth and bestow their love upon him brings the theme of blaming others to comic absurdity: Since he will not even show himself outside, he expects the women to go in and take him out! The question of the responsibility of others for his suffering is not a small point. As the demands pile up, a note of nastiness can be discerned—and not just as regards these uncooperative women but as regards the men who, though inferior to him, are chosen in his place. Experiencing loneliness and humiliation as an insult rather than as an existential condition sets the stage for aggression against those imagined as responsible. In the novella this possibility does not go unactualized.

On Sunday mornings when my secret yearnings forced me from my room and my books into the throng, and stunned I made my solitary way among the crowds of men and women promenading through the gay boulevards, most of them couples arm-in-arm and exuding a sense of togetherness—it was then that I conceived a great envy of all those complacent souls. . . . Alone and disoriented, I move like a mourner among revellers; a melancholy I've never known permeates me.

Sometimes I peer into the faces of the women who pass by, and I am stupefied that no one of them has the pity to love me or at least draw close to me, for I know that I am no less worthy than the ones they will choose.

The innumerable books I read about women and the secrets of their ways fail me the moment I meet them face to face. The romances and love poetry I read to sublimate my desires only serve to fan the smouldering embers into a blaze. . . . My incomprehension refuses to go away: Why don't I get to live as do the characters in the books? Why can't my life be like theirs, at least once? After all, is not my capacity for love even greater than theirs? . . . I understand the exaltation of love better than all of them. To any woman willing to love me I can sing a new Song of Songs, a song of love magnified and heightened, a song of spirit and yearning.

This is the nadir of the depression that follows the reverie's collapse. Yet the depression lasts only a brief time, for by the end of the passage the engine of fantasy is already again being revved up ("I can sing a new Song of Songs"!). This return of reverie (and its subsequent deflation) means that we are encountering not a one-time structure but a recurrent pattern, whose rise and fall determines the syntactic rhythm of the novella. That this is the low point in the cycle is evinced by the narrator's finally being driven from his room. The disparity between inside and outside becomes too great; the internal pressure of need can no longer be borne. He is *forced out*. What he sees on the outside only redoubles his depression. The scene in the streets is the classic spectacle of a middle-European city at play on a Sunday, a world in which everyone seems happily and contentedly coupled. Between this world and the narrator stretches a curtain of unreality, through which he can peer with only a stunned sense of disbelief. The many terms for cognitive disorientation used here refer to a crisis of a peculiar kind: The narrator has long viewed the world as indeed divided between himself and others, a division whose basis lies in *his* spiritual and intellectual superiority, and thus in *his* deserving of reward. What has happened now is that the division remains, but the reward has gone to the wrong side. The narrator is forced to make the difficult admission of his envy for those whom, in his grandiosity, he despises. His discomfiture, however, remains at the level of a painful contradiction rather than as a spur to a revision of his values. His conviction that spiritual-intellectual aptitude and achievement constitute virtue and that virtue deserves love, remains fundamentally unchanged.

Like many other heroes in modern fiction the narrator looks to literature of romance both as a source of "how-to" information and as an escape from the experience of unfulfillment. The theme has a special resonance in nineteenth-century Hebrew literature because of the Haskalah critique (especially in Abramowitsch) of the medieval scholastic habit of looking for truth about the world in books rather than in the world itself, that is, rather than through empirical observation. (This is not to mention Berdichevsky's own diatribes on the subject of the tradition's preference for bookishness over vitality.) Here, at any rate, the resort to books fails, and produces instead the opposite of instruction and sublimation. Coming up against the wall of reality, the narrator again begins to ascend into the space of reverie.

I recalled that in my father's world inside the Pale love comes only after solemnizing a marriage under the four poles of the hupah. . . . I also recalled

> from what my friends tell me that it is possible to purchase love for money as one would any other commodity. Yet both of these ways were equally distant from me, and equally incomprehensible. . . . Intimacy with a woman with an exalted soul is the only thing I understand and seek, a perfect soul whom I could love with all my heart, and with whom I could share all my dreams and ambitions. . . .
>
> There are hundreds of women in this big city. On every avenue there are houses whose masters have daughters. Some of them must want love, and some must be as lonely as I am. Some must have it in their power to love me and to understand my struggles and my inner world. And for some how easy it would be to find me in my room and, like a sister from birth, claim a share in all that is mine. To such a one I would give away all my wealth of spirit. I would take care of her like the apple of my eye and venerate her like a goddess. She would always know that our love was superior to the love of ordinary people because it would be rooted in a transcendent spirit. Together we would dream the future of man and nations and seek paths for the coming generations.

The narrator makes much of his principled rejection both of the arranged marriage common in the shtetl and of the prostitution available in the city. The lumping together of the two institutions as equally abased perversions of love displays an extraordinarily cavalier attitude toward traditional Jewish society. In his high-minded dissociation from his benighted past, the narrator wishes to present himself as a man who is wholly his own creation, a man liberated from the least traces of nostalgia, sentimentality, or misplaced loyalty. He will choose his own kind of love, and it will be based on an affinity of ideas and feelings rather than on parental wishes or a cash nexus.

The irony, of course, is that his greatest wish, as expressed in the next paragraph, is to be chosen rather than to choose. As the energies of fantasy are again stirred, the essential passivity of his desire becomes transparent. The vision of relationship he presents is ostensibly one of bestowal and donation; he will unlock the treasure house of his spirit and share its abundance with the favored partner. The language of the passage, however, suggests a transaction that moves in the opposite direction. What he most longs for, and the prerequisite for everything else, is for her to take the initiative in redeeming *him*. The natural claims of a sister on a brother and the veneration of a worshipper for his goddess are two modalities of relationship used here as hyperboles for the narrator's supposed generosity of spirit. Later on in the story both of these rhetorical gestures, in the form of sexual exploitation and obsessive dependence, will become demonically realized. But for the moment, as the reverie reaches its zenith, these untoward possibilities are lost in the transport of a love both lofty and forward-looking.

> But the coming generations have not come, nor has the girl in the dream. Alone I sit in my room and fantasize alone. . . .
>
> I am indeed alone, and my dreams are mostly about myself as an individual

who is seeking a role in life. All I wanted at the time was to alleviate the "sacred" burden imposed on me by my parents and to regain the vigor of the "human" side of myself. By contrast, my friends were immersed in the affairs of the community and preoccupied with the plight of the collective at the expense of their individuality.

For them, the community takes precedence over the individual, while for me, the individual comes first. They do their thinking together and try out their ideas on each other; I think on my own and have no need for the collective.

They spend their nights at meetings deliberating about the fortunes of the people. I sit alone in my room day and night reading books.

Even today I still can't decide whether it was a gift from God or a divine calamity. My friends tried to coax me into attending a student gathering about some communal issue or other, and for once I gave in. The real inducement, in fact, was the knowledge that among those attending would be a certain female student. Since in those days the university was still closed to women, the prospect of getting to meet one was no small matter.

So I went.

The collapse of the reverie from its own grandiloquence is again triggered by a gap between slogan and reality, one which this time is implicit in the cliché, "the generations to come." And again, at the end of a new down-cycle of rationalizations, the narrator will be sufficiently impelled by his needs to leave his room and venture outside. This second, involuntary, self-violation of the threshold places the opposition between inside and outside into a more specific framework: the difference now is between participation in the public space of the Jewish people and maintaining the private domain of the self. The passage suggests something of the milieu of Jewish student life at German universities at the end of the century. Though they are happily emancipated from the world of their fathers, many students retain a strong identification with the people and take active roles in the debates on the Jewish question. As part of an enlightened vanguard, they view themselves as responsible to the people, and in a spirit of high seriousness debate various Zionist and socialist proposals and form emergency committees on behalf of distressed Jewish communities. From all this activity the narrator holds himself aloof, applying himself day and night only to the acquisition of knowledge and to his own enlighten-ment. His nonparticipation, he claims, is neither temperamental nor mis-anthropic; it is a principled stance rooted in a Nietzschean affirmation of the superiority of the gifted individual spirit over against the mass of men. The narrator regards himself as one of the chosen, or at least aspires to be one, by committing himself to a program that requires effacing the par-ticularity of his personal history and recovering those parts of him that participate in the human-universal. His isolation, then, is nobly conceived. The repeating sentence couplets contrasting "they" and "I" further ascribe credit to the narrator by recalling (through inversion, of course) the medita-tion recited upon concluding a talmudic tractate, in which the merit of scholars who remain faithful to the study house is contrasted to the wantonness of those who rush about in the world only for the sake of profit.[8]

The conclusion of the chapter returns us to the chapter's first sentence, its "false start": not the longing for The Woman and love in the abstract but the pull of a specific woman, the one glimpsed from afar those three times. The narrator puts down his books, leaves his room, and attends the meeting, thereby crossing the threshold he has invested with so much importance. It is this act that constitutes the enabling condition of the plot; it makes the relationship with the woman possible, and thus the story. The narrator also acknowledges this as a moment of high destiny. Yet the act is presented as being, from the beginning, deeply compromised. It is by force of a seduction by his friends (*haverai hisituni*) and the pressure of his own needs that he crosses a line which, according to his convictions, should not be crossed.

What we have learned from the first chapter can now be summarized. The narrator presents himself as a young man of twenty-five who has completely broken with his traditional upbringing and devoted himself to university studies and who is now ready to complete his emancipation by seeking a mate. The florid ideas he entertains about love are drawn from the sentimental literature of an earlier age; he imagines a relationship, barely sexual, based on high-minded sharing of ideals and feelings. The loftiness of these motives is undercut by the narrator's revealing, despite himself, a deep and desperate sense of loneliness. He is prevented from fulfilling his needs by an extreme shyness and a radical lack of self-confidence in social relations, which he attributes to the unworldliness of his education and early training, and from which the wisdom of no amount of books can save him. That others of his companions, whom he holds to be hardly his equals intellectually, are easily successful in love poses a bitter contradiction; it forces him into the humiliating position of envying those he regards as inferior to himself, especially in their preoccupation with public causes as contrasted to his dedication to self-cultivation through enlightenment. The impasse caused by the intersection of pride and passivity is finally overcome by the prospect of meeting a woman he has seen from a distance.

Eventually, Elimelekh gets his chance. After some indeterminate contacts with Rachel (the woman he has sought to meet), Elimelekh leaves Breslau to continue his studies at the University of Berne. Though struck by the physical beauty of Switzerland and encouraged by the presence of women in his classes, his loneliness persists. Suddenly, he receives a letter from Rachel announcing her plans to come to Berne to study and requesting his aid in getting settled. When she arrives they quickly fall in with one another; he arranges food and lodging, lends her money, and gives her private lessons in university subjects. Although they spend all their time together, their relationship remains "pure," and they act toward one another as brother and sister. This contentedness, however, does not last.

Unawares, Elimelekh becomes gradually drawn to her sexually, and when she rejects a small overture, he is crestfallen. His hurt takes the form of a righteous accusation against her for foreclosing the possibility of love. The academic year has ended, and the students, including Rachel, go off to the mountains for the summer holiday. Remaining behind in the city, Elimelekh endures waves of rage and jealousy and redoubled loneliness, all the while resisting admitting what has happened to him. He revisits the places they frequented together and perceives all external nature as suffused with his grief. Unable to go on, he finally gives in and goes off to the mountain village to join her.

This is the first of several capitulations. Each time Elimelekh feels compelled to return to her, and although he makes do for a while with their old, nonsexual companionability, he cannot abide the situation and confronts her with an ultimatum. Each time he is turned down he feels more desperately lost; his fate, his being, is in her hands. Eventually there is a turnabout. Some time during the next academic year, Rachel declares that she has changed and that she may now be able to look on him in a new way. Elimelekh cuts her off with a speech about how she has irrevocably ruined everything and now it is too late. He begins to treat her with callous cynicism and misogynistic diatribes; two months pass and he drops her totally. She suffers terribly. One day she faints in class in his presence and he affects disinterest. Seriously ill, she calls to him from her bed; after refusing several times, he finally comes to her, but he feels nothing. His heart is dead. His studies completed, Elimelekh plans to depart for Germany. The past year and a half, he concludes, have been like a bad dream— a waste of time.

After fantasizing lavishly about the love of a woman, the first thing Elimelekh does when Rachel arrives is to switch off his sexual feelings: "My thoughts and dreams about love disappeared the moment she became part of my life; in my naïveté I thought our intimacy was of the purest sort and would remain so forever" (p. 18). The possibility of actual sexual experience (even in the broadest sense) is so disturbing to Elimelekh that he de-eroticizes Rachel; he shifts the norms of his behavior to a model governed by ideas about friendship and brother-sister sympathy, a model which incidentally grants him the role of mentor and allows him to retain his position of strength. This unconscious tactic ends by having the opposite effect. With the relationship safely categorized, Elimelekh is left undefended before the subtle effects of daily contact with a sympathetic woman. Despite himself, he becomes deeply drawn to her physical presence.

> There were times I simply wanted [*homed*] her. When we used to sit reading together, our souls enmeshed, I knew that all I had to do would be to take her in my arms and kiss her and then perhaps everything would be different. . . . But my hands would not perform the commission of my heart, so I would sit there reading, reading and wanting, wanting and reading. (p. 21)

This indeterminate swing between intellection and desire ("reading and wanting, wanting and reading"), with the implication of their functional interchangeability, is a nice emblem of the narrator's situation at this early point in the story. Elimelekh never succeeds in getting his hands to do the bidding of his heart. But not this alone: It is only in the hindsight of retrospective narration that he is even able to accept the reality of the presence in him of physical desire. Properly speaking, then, A Raven Flies is not a story about the discovery and expression of sexuality. The sexuality is indeed there, but no discovery or expression ever takes place; it is repressed.

Even the several times Elimelekh belatedly tries to shift the terms of the relationship, the approach is made through ridiculously florid and hackneyed speeches and letters, none of which ever comes around to saying what is really wanted. (The non-release of instinctual feeling distinguishes A Raven Flies from its twin text, Two Camps. Sexual need, experienced as absence and insufficiency rather than as power, is linked to the structure of narcissistic shame which, I shall argue, stands at the center of the novella.)

This act of repression is the spring of the narrative; the events of the story become intelligible insofar as they are read as unconscious efforts at denial. These attempts are of two sorts: cognitive rationalizations, which offer ideological explanations for the withdrawal from sexuality, and displaced behavior, in which the narrator, in violation of his cerebral self-conception, undertakes increasingly nonrational forms of action.

Chief among the defenses is the fantasy of Elimelekh and Rachel as brother and sister. "The more she pushed me away, the closer I drew to her as a loyal brother" (p. 22). It is easy to see what in this conception is pleasing to him: it simply adopts the consoling components of the great reverie of love, while keeping the more deeply troubling forces of sexuality at bay. As a brother, Elimelekh enjoys tender exchanges of solicitude, and as the older sibling, he retains his role as bestower of wisdom and spiritual instruction. The anxiety of choosing and risking are bypassed as well. As brother and sister (in the terms of the fantasy), Elimelekh and Rachel have *always already* been bonded to each other. The problem, of course, is that this is not what their relationship is in fact, and there are no incest taboos to prevent the inevitable from happening. And it happens all the more quickly because the fantasy allows Elimelekh, who believes himself to be immune, to be close to her and therefore be caught unawares.

The brother-sister fantasy has special poignancy if it is taken not as an avoidance but as the fulfillment of a longing. Like many of his generation, and like Berdichevsky himself, the narrator has cut his ties to his family by rejecting their way of life and moving to the West. For this loss and all it implies, he betrays no sign of need or nostalgia; on the contrary, his family connection is effaced (another contrast with Two Camps), and he presents himself as a man self-conceived, a man whose patrimony is the history of reason. If life in the void must be lived bereft of blood ties, then let it be cheered by the solidarity of rebellion, the companionship of comrades working toward the new future, or at least the comfort of fellow orphaned spirits. Yet for Elimelekh this path is barred. Echoing Berdichevsky's own pronouncements from earlier years, the narrator has declared his belief in the sovereignty of the individual and, except in that one crucial instance, he has rejected the appeals of friends to join in organizational gatherings whose function is as much social as anything else. Community, as a mediating term between family with its discontents and the self in its aloneness, is thus rendered unavailable. Since Elimelekh has made the individual—and individuated—self the only reality, redemption by another individual self can be the only solution: the lover, or alternatively, even preferably, the other-as-sister.

The other significant defense against sexuality might be called the Reverie of the Romantic Soul. Left alone in town after his first rejection by Rachel, Elimelekh wanders about grief-stricken. Against his will, he is drawn back to the places which had been the scenes of their relationship, places which in her absence now present a gravelike aspect. The trees and the hills, not just he, seem to mourn her loss; and with this experience comes the insight that "just as the nature around us affects us, so we affect it, such that there is a reciprocal sympathy of action between the inanimate and the animate" (p. 27). As his reverie about the *anima mundi* begins to spiral upwards, he transmutes his homely grief into a neoplatonic religious ecstasy. His longing for his lost beloved is in fact, he reasons, "the yearning of every individual soul to reunite with the All, from which it was separated at birth" (p. 27). The woman and our yearning for her must therefore be understood "as a symbol of our interwovenness into eternal being" (p. 28). The reverie soon collapses into some rather grisly nightmares (of which more in a moment), and the narrator retrospectively acknowledges the sophistry of this escape *(kakhah hayyiti mitpalsef)*. What remains notable is the romantic tenor of the escape. Elimelekh, the man of reason, is forced by the disorienting strength of his grief to reach out to a new, romantic worldview to make sense of his experience.

At one point the romantic reverie turns foul and plunges into nightmare. Elimelekh dreams that he is a "disembodied golem with no hands or feet, eyes or mouth" (p. 28). Another time he dreams that "he is walking among the tree tops above the roofs of the houses, but the trees are upside down, with their roots in the air and their branches down below" (p. 28). It takes little analytic acumen to recognize these dreams as expressive of the fear, indeed the reality, of impotence and deracination, an unconscious registering of the psychic punishment Elimelekh is undergoing. The availability of these dreams to interpretation, their utter transparency, is in fact just the point. The narrator records the dreams and the terror they instil, and it is clear that it is this fear that breaks the back of his resolve to stay away from Rachel and makes him join her in the mountains. Yet the *meanings* of the dreams, as obvious as they are, remain entirely unintelligible to him; he is oblivious to these truth-telling messages from his unconscious and takes them as signs of incipient madness. Throughout *A Raven Flies* the unconscious never becomes conscious; this is not a story about insight. The closest one gets to the unconscious is these uninterpreted nightmares. Like sexuality, which is embedded in it, the unconscious becomes known only by the evasions of it, the reveries of bad faith and the increasingly desperate forms of behavior.

Erotic obsession is one of the signal forms of nonrationality explored in the novella. Although Rachel rejects him, not once but several times, Elimelekh comes back to her, and each time at greater cost to his meager stock of self-esteem. He cannot help it, but also he derives a perverse nourishment from his helpless situation. In this analysis of the seemingly contradictory structures of obsession and compulsion, Berdichevsky breaks new fictional ground. An example is the perception of the other as seen from within the obsession. From the scraps of "reliable" information concerning Rachel's character, a rather predatory portrait emerges. She seems essentially to live *off* of Elimelekh, taking money from him well after rebuffing his approaches. She benefits greatly from his academic tuition, and uses him extensively as a source of emotional support. Exploiting the pretense of the brother-sister relationship, she even comes crying to Elimelekh when her affairs with other men go sour. Despite all this, in the phenomenology of Elimelekh's experience of her, she is the apotheosis of radiance, a source of perfection and life. (There is, of course, a psychological grain of truth in this: because he cannot confront sexuality but needs relief from his loneliness, he in a sense does live off of his obsession with her, as she in fact lives off of him.) In obsession, the other is transformed and transfigured without reference to reality. The achievement of *A Raven Flies* lies in its making the enormity of this distortion poignant and believable. This is accomplished by the skillful use of first-person narrative in such a way that we have virtually no channels of knowledge other that the perspective in which objects present themselves immanently to the consciousness of the narrator.

Possession by the other is part of the ordeal. Elimelekh is so preoccupied with Rachel's sexual presence that the flux of his emotional life becomes regulated by her every physical gesture. "My feelings changed as she changed dresses" (p. 34), he admits, and then proceeds to describe the various degrees of arousal occasioned by her white outfits as opposed to her black outfits, not to mention her dressing gown, or the effect of the rustle of her breast beneath her tunic. In the love note in which Elimelekh finally declares himself, he writes: "You are the light of my world. You possess the power to restore the crown of my youth. Your love has the capacity to sustain whatever is in me, to make of me what I need to become" (p. 35). These hyperboles are the banal currency of literary love—especially epistolary love—everywhere and always. Here, however, the clichés are put to ironic use insofar as, contrary to their rhetorical intent, they represent a literal truth: Elimelekh *has* put her in a position of complete sway over his life. She is in fact his only light, his only hope.

The last stage in the narrator's encounter with sexuality is sadism. As long as the other remains enthroned at the center of the universe, the self can explain the failure to perceive love as a sign of his own unworthiness and take out his deprivation on himself. But when the illusion falters under too great a weight of reality, the other may be deposed, and what was once dependence turns into aggression, payment exacted for humiliations endured. When this happens to Elimelekh the rebellion begins on the border. He first dreams of homicide-suicide; he wounds himself and her, but "she refuses to die, and he [must] violently strangle her until her arms fall limp at her sides" (p. 40). Next come misogynistic diatribes. In an attempt to get distance from his situation by identifying the irritant and assigning blame to it, Elimelekh undertakes a series of philosophical expositions in which Woman is presented as God's curse upon the emancipation of man (pp. 44–45). This high-minded disquisition soon degenerates into pathetic invective, a mean-spirited parody of the expulsion from the Garden of Eden and God's curse upon women, with Elimelekh appropriating God's role as the curse-giver. All this still takes place in Elimelekh's imagination. When the tables turn and Rachel decides she wants him, he is in a position to make her truly suffer. And he does very so very skillfully, affecting apathy when she faints in class and withholding his presence from her sickbed. (He makes it much worse for her then she did for him, for at least he had her companionship and esteem if not affection.) This is not stylized sadism *à la* Havelock Ellis, but a psychological sadism, all the more plausible for its ordinary occurrence than for its clinical perversion.

The link between religious experience and the turmoil of sexuality is not immediately apparent. On the face of things, religion would appear to be absent altogether. In contrast in Feierberg and Lilienblum, Elimelekh presents himself as someone for whom the calamity of apostasy and the drama of rebellion remain far in the past. Family seems not to exist for him. No letters arrive from or are dispatched to brothers or sisters left back in the East; there is not even an appearance put in by the figure of the orthodox father, whose threatened visit was a comic vestige in *Two Camps*. So total is Elimelekh's liberation that his stance hardly betrays a trace of negation; unlike the many characters that people contemporary Hebrew literature whose identity is defined by what they reject, Elimelekh has ostensibly left all that behind him and securely installed himself within the order of the new. The "new" in this case is rather vague. It is not the Deism of his Haskalah precursors, nor the ideologies (Zionism and socialism) of his comrades. Rather than these sets of systematic beliefs, which are in many ways homologous to traditional religion, Elimelekh seems committed to the general humanistic ideals of knowledge and progress. *Ru'ah,* in the

Goethean sense of *Geist*, is the spiritual medium which he believes himself to be living in and nourished by, and to which he might one day make a contribution.

Most of all, he views himself as reborn, or at least a candidate for rebirth. At the age of twenty-five, he has lost some of his best years to early oppressions and struggles, and now, after effecting a complete separation from his past, he is ready to be remade. For this Switzerland is the right setting. The lushness and exhorbitance of the country's physical beauty move the narrator to compare it to the Garden of Eden (p. 11). The comparison does not rest on nature alone. The opening of Swiss universities to women means that this is a paradise in which the two sexes, each released from the debilities of its origins, can freely mingle. (Temptation and fall, the sinister possibilities of the Garden, will not be left unexploited either.) The quaint medieval beauty of the city of Berne leads the narrator to invoke another myth of restoration. Berne, with its antique perfection intact, suggests what Jerusalem would have been like had it not been destroyed. At first Elimelekh is saddened by the tragic discrepancy between the fates of the two cities, "but soon afterward, my thoughts abandoned the Judaean Hills in order to dwell here in this land of joy and youthfulness" (p. 13). This "here and now" is a time imagined as if prior to both the Fall and the Destruction.

This fabricated innocence turns out to be something quite different. The violent stirrings of sexual need—unacknowledged, unmet, unfulfilled—sweep away Elimelekh's new identity like a house of cards. What is left is the abyss of the self. This is the space that was once densely packed with the thick stuff of tradition: not just belief but family, texts, and sacred time, all as transmuted by individual experience into the substance of personal history. Through an act of will, Elimelekh has successfully managed to extirpate these contents. Although he believes he has thereby restored a primal innocence, the reader sees the cavernous interior of an abyss newly vacated. Spatial metaphors are indeed helpful in understanding his situation: Elimelekh conceives of his life two-dimensionally as a slate wiped clean, now freshly available to new impressions. Irony furnishes the reader with a third dimension of perspective, which exposes the depth beneath the surface and thus the tenuousness of Elimelekh's constructions.

Depths do not remain vacant for long. What happens in *A Raven Flies* underscores a larger truth expressed by the literature of the generation as a whole: When its plausibility collapses, religion does not simply pass away but creates a titanic vacuum in its wake. Living in this void is painful and anguished. Few can endure it; many seek secular substitutes which, like religion, function to supply the needs of meaning and community. To ignore the existence of the void and to act as if it does not exist, however—which is what Elimelekh does—means to relinquish any control of what "fills" the void. In Elimelekh's case the void is invaded and taken over by erotic feeling. While he is indulging in lofty reveries of love imagined as an emanation of spiritual abundance, erotic need floods the unacknowledged interior space of his being. Elimelekh's situation, I wish to assert, needs to be described in religious terms. There is a dimension of what Rachel means to him that is not adequately described by sexual dependence or possession. Immediately after delivering the letter declaring his love for Rachel ("You are the light of my world"), Elimelekh is literally convulsed by the realization that "*in her hands* lie my life and my future; all I have is in her hands, everything is in her hands" (p. 36, emphasis in the text). Rachel has in fact become the source of all meaning in his life, the ultimate ground of his being. The violence of his reaction comes from the sudden awareness of the loss of his autonomy and the fact of his ontological absorption into the field of her being.

The depth and quality of this shift are registered in a passage describing Elimelekh's thoughts as he travels by boat to receive Rachel's reply to his letter.

> Like a mourner I sat in a corner and felt as if something separated me from all the other passengers. They are strangers to me and I see their faces for the first time. But one thing I know for certain: what happened to me did not happen to them. My soul is different, my spirit is different, my people is different.
>
> A slight smile passed over my lips as I realized that I was probably the only one here whose ancestors had stood at Mt. Sinai. I thought, too, that Mt. Sinai is lower than all the mountains that border the river we are now sailing. . . . A great sadness stills my thoughts as I suddenly remember Rachel there on the mountain top and that in an hour I shall know my fate [*aharit devari*]. (p. 37)

Elimelekh perceives his anxious spiritual desperation as his lot not by virtue of his being a man among men who has loved and lost, but because he is a Jew. Being chosen to suffer the terrors of impotence and unreality is the meaning of the election of Israel; and the revelation of this destiny was given at a mountain whose supposed awesomeness is dwarfed by the real mountains at hand. The drift of these meditations is toward the stigmatizing and belittling of the meaning of Jewish history, over which Elimelekh exercises his sardonic judgment. But suddenly this *hauteur* is collapsed by the thought of Rachel, who has replaced God and the Jewish people as the inescapable ground of meaning in his life. When he admits a moment later that the "immortality of my soul I see in *her*" (p. 38, emphasis in the text), he is admitting the functional continuity between the old dispensation and the new. The difference is that the new one is not kinder. In the void created by the withdrawal of traditional religion, religion *of a sort* rushes back in. Enchantment, disenchantment, reenchantment—this is a series which does not spiral upwards. The place where God once ruled becomes a demonic space.

Not all psychological narratives invite clinical investigation. The danger of reductionism is substantial and the ultimate yield in insight often slight.

Criticism is usually on firmer ground when it makes intuitive use of psychological models that have become part of the general discourse of the culture rather than when it reaches "out of its system" to apply clinical models. In the course of *A Raven Flies,* however, there is reason to act contrary to this wisdom. There is no readily available term in the critical lexicon about fictional character to naturalize the sequence of mental states assigned to Elimelekh in the narrative. My intention is to introduce such a term in the hope that its explanatory power will be proved by providing a coherent way to understand the figure of the narrator.

This is the concept of narcissism as a personality disorder developed in the last twenty years by Heinz Kohut and Otto Kernberg. In the small child, according to Kohut, narcissism is a normal stage of development. The child is possessed of a "grandiose sense of self" in which it views itself and its needs as being located at the center of the world. Other people do not exist for the child as truly differentiated identities ("objects"), but are rather experienced narcissistically as extensions of the self ("self-objects"); the kind of control the child expects to have over these self-objects "is closer to the control a grown-up expects to have over his own body and mind than . . . the control which he expects to have over others."[9] In normal development the child gradually recognizes the imperfections and limitations of the self, with a resulting diminution of the domain and power of grandiose fantasy. Exhibitionism and grandiosity are eventually tamed and integrated into the adult personality, while providing the libidinal fuel for self-esteem, the achievement of ambitions, and the enjoyment of activity. Others become recognized as separate beings with separate needs with whom pleasure and nourishment can be exchanged on a reciprocal basis.

Narcissism becomes a disorder when, because of trauma, the adult carries the childhood stage into later life. The trauma is usually the premature removal of the primary providers of the child's nurturing; the child suffers the sudden termination of the blissful state in which its needs are met by the world. In reaction to this disturbance, the grandiose self is retained in its archaic form and strives for fulfillment of archaic aims. "The child attempts to save the originally all-embracing narcissism by concentrating perfection and power upon the self . . . and by turning away disdainfully from an outside to which all imperfections have been assigned."[10] The adult becomes marked by the exhibitionism and grandiosity that were appropriate to the child. Others retain the status of self-objects rather than becoming loved and admired for their own attributes. The psyche moves to save a segment of the "global narcissistic perfection" that once existed and assigns it to the self-object, which is invested with power. The grandiose self attempts to maintain continuous union with the self-object and to exert control over it, while the object of narcissistic love feels oppressed and enslaved by these expectations and demands.

The concept of clinical narcissism was not put forward by its formulators merely as a theoretical revision of psychoanalytic doctrine, but as a way of accounting for historical and social change. The nature of family life in Viennese society in the high bourgeois era, they argue, had a great deal to do with Freud's conception of the organization of the psyche. Freud placed the issue of impulse regulation—together with guilt and castration anxiety—at the center of the drama played out between a repressive social order and the instinctually-motivated individual. The theorists of narcissism assert that the transformation of society in the twentieth century, with all the attendant changes in the nature of the family, created a type of personality whose characteristic disorder is narcissistic and which turns on questions of shame and "object loss." Now, without assessing the validity of these claims, I wish to use the concept of narcissism to approach Elimelekh's character. I do so on the assumption that in *A Raven Flies* the figure of Elimelekh performs a representative function in relation to his cultural generation. I use "representative" not in the sense of a "type" that stands for a group or class but rather in the Lukácsian sense of a hero who contains within himself the contradictions of a historical moment. It would be a mistake, then, to diagnose Elimelekh's erotic obsessions and delusions of grandeur as a private complaint, the symptoms of an idiosyncratic weakness. Instead, the story presents Elimelekh's narcissism as a symbolic wound inflicted by larger social and historical forces.

Take, for example, the question of personal origins. For the etiology of clinical narcissism Kohut points to the traumatic early withdrawal of love from the small child, who must then compensate for this sudden deprivation. This is the case as well with Elimelekh, although we find out only, as it were, despite himself. Elimelekh presents himself as a man who is entirely self-made and whose childhood history is of no account, being merely the common record of imposed folly. The personal past erupts into the narrative only at one point: Elimelekh is left so vulnerable by the shattering news of Rachel's rejection of his written profession of love that his pose is momentarily breached (p. 42). In the misery of his long night on the mountain his mind is invaded by an unbidden train of childhood memories. Chief among them is the recollection of the early death of a loving mother and her immediate replacement by a cold step-mother.[11] (The significance of this datum is underscored by its correspondence to the biography of Berdichevsky and to the history of Michael, the protagonist of *Two Camps*.) The massive sense of loss in the present involuntarily yet naturally connects itself to the massive deprivation of childhood.

Now, to the degree to which the figure of Elimelekh is representative, the loss of the mother is also not just the loss of the mother. It is a metonymy for the situation of a generation. This was the loss, to put it in a simplified way, of the world of tradition. The complex of beliefs, values, texts, and family relations which had long provided a rich and nurturing medium for the development of the self was suddenly and traumatically withdrawn, and in its place had come the "cold mother" of the world after faith. Although this idea of the maternal function of the tradition is an interesting one, the real usefulness of this correspondence between the individual figure and the generation lies less in the past than in the present. The disorders of *maturity,* that is to say, how early loss is compensated for in later life—this is the subject of *A Raven Flies.* Elimelekh's narcissism is not trivially pathological. It is a mode of existence in the void.

Significant are the particular vehicles for Elimelekh's grandiosity. He sits alone in his room (not in attendance at lectures) and systematically consumes the resources of the university library with the intensity of the autodidact who has come late to learning. His thirst is total and universal; he wants to know everything. "I forgot all the components and boundaries of my own life; I forgot myself and my ways and went in search of the thoughts and deeds of humankind" (p. 10). As he watches the spectacle of the march of Western thought, he forgets himself, his background, his nation, and merges himself into the cavalcade of universal history, onto which he has transferred his affective life and in which his spirit now directly participates. Yet what first presents itself as self-effacement soon becomes a pathway to power. Elimelekh's studies follow a certain progression: He begins with the history of civilization, and then moves to the philosophical contemplation of history and human nature, and finally arrives at metaphysics and the critique of thinking. Elimelekh has "transcended" the "components and boundaries" of individuals and nations by moving from particulars to universals, from the content of thought to an examination of the very ground and possibility of thought. This rapid ascent into the rarefied reaches of theory is not intellectual progress so much as the achievement of a stance of judgment: "Like an angelic procession, all of mankind passes before me, and I acquit them or condemn them according to their beliefs. All are judged. Nothing escapes my scrutiny" (p. 10). The Hebrew reader will not fail to appreciate the ironic allusion to the *Unetaneh tokef* prayer in the High Holyday liturgy in which God is pictured as passing all creation under the scepter of judgment and designating who shall live and who shall die.

Elimelekh gives his grandiosity an ideological cover taken from the quasi-Nietzschean ideas of the time. To his fellow students he makes the case for the priority of beauty and poetry over the alleviation of human misery, and of the spiritually endowed individual over the mass of men (p. 14). The flimsiness of these rationalizations, however, is quickly exposed. It is not Nietzscheanism which is dismissed but the bad faith of Elimelekh's misuse of it. Elimelekh's swagger turns out to be generated not by a genuine endowment of will and mind but by a driven sense of loneliness and deprivation, which is only worsened by his aloof manner. Elimelekh must therefore be counted as one of the weak and the insulted of the earth whose motives are rooted in *Resentiment* and who can only dream of being an *Übermensch.* Dreams and reveries, in fact, can be the only medium for Elimelekh's exalted thoughts about himself, and it is the direction and destination of these thoughts that give him away:

On my way home from the university I used to walk along the bridge that separated the quarters of the town. . . . Then my soul would soar to the heavens and I would experience a sense of fullness of spirit that could prevail over all. . . . My place is the whole world. . . . Had I lived in any generation I would have had something to contribute. . . . I see conjured before me a new idea, a new theory of man, a philosophy that consumes [*habola'at*] all other views and explains to humankind the meaning of things. (pp. 14–15)

Berdichevsky's Elimelekh on the bridge bears a close resemblance to Feierberg's Nahman on the craggy ledge, brandishing his imaginary sword in an attempt to bring the Messiah. Both passages exploit the technique of the reverie to move the narrative along a sequence of moments of consciousness toward a climax in which the hero exercises imaginary power as an escape from a constricted reality. Yet, whereas Nahman aspires to hasten redemption for the Jewish people as a whole (though, to be sure, he delights in the prospect of this being accomplished through his own actions), Elimelekh's aims are far more self-regarding. The vague universalism of his ideas is displaced by imperial ambitions. The ends they accomplish are less important than the fact that they will prevail over and consume all other ideas.

Nowhere is Elimelekh's narcissism more conspicuous than in his relationship to Rachel. Even before she enters the scene, he has constructed an elaborate fantasy of the woman he seeks. Even though the fantasy ostensibly envisions an exchange in which he enriches her spirit in return for her relieving his loneliness, the woman in fact serves only as a mechanism for confirming and fulfilling himself. When Rachel materializes, Elimelekh moves to absorb her into the fantasy in utter obliviousness of her own nature. But his attempts to exert exhaustive control over her are resisted by her contrary desires, and he ends up instead as the one controlled, a pathetic figure caught in the toils of obsessive love. In the constricted consciousness of the narrator, Rachel is and always was a narcissistic extension of himself: a self-object.

The following incident takes place soon after Elimelekh gives in to his need to be with Rachel and joins her and the other students in the mountains. The group has gone boating, but Elimelekh stays behind because he is afraid of the water and because he cannot bear to see Rachel in the company of Uriel, a young man with whom she has been keeping company. Midnight comes and Elimelekh impatiently awaits their return. Finally one of the group arrives, barefoot and sodden, to announce that the boat capsized and all were saved except for Rachel and Uriel. Elimelekh collapses with palpitations from the news, only to be told a few minutes later that the report of the drowning is false and that the whole incident was a hoax. The next morning Rachel condemns the prank but is more upset at discovering the true extent of Elimelekh's dependence on her.

The false drowning has the force of inducing a deep sense of shame in

Elimelekh by suddenly revealing his weakness both to himself and to others, and not just to Rachel but to the whole community. The experience of shame intensifies as Elimelekh, having failed to obtain Rachel's love, cannot manage to break with her and continues to return to her after each threatened ultimatum. After treating his friends to an elaborate lecture on the evils of womankind, Elimelekh openly capitulates by taking her back. He shows up at the train station to meet Rachel when she returns from the mountains, helps her find an apartment, and returns to playing the role of her loyal friend. This cycle continues until the shame becomes too great to bear, and Elimelekh turns his pain outward in the form of sadistic rage against Rachel. Shame suffuses the second half of the novella. Like narcissism, to which it is closely linked, shame is not a simple pathology but a modal existential state. It is an unavoidable condition of life in the void.

The English "shame" and the Hebrew "bushah" both contain two different senses, which are differentiated in other languages: *discretion-shame* (French, "pudeur"), as in "having a sense of shame," designates the innate reluctance to violate moral boundaries and interdictions; *disgrace-shame* (French, "honte"), as in "being shamed," is the feeling of unworthiness and exposure that comes after the act, after the transgression.[12] For Nietzsche the usurpation of the first meaning by the second is a critical feature of modernity. Shame-as-discretion belongs to the era of religion. A sense of shame and modesty was the proper stance before the mystery of the universe and the great forces of the cosmos. Indecency consists of the attempt to uncover all things. Truth, Nietzsche writes in *The Gay Science*, is a "woman before whom one exercises a sense of shame."[13] Elimelekh's assaults on the fortress of theoretical knowledge clearly place him among the new men of science and rationality who inhabit a supposedly disenchanted universe. His efforts are successful in an ironic sense: His uncovering of the mysteries of the world inevitably leads to revealing the nonrationalities of the private self. Public and private spheres are exchanged, and the workings of Elimelekh's inner life lay exposed.

Central to shame-as-disgrace is the experience of forced revelation. A disturbing aspect of the self is suddenly uncovered and made visible; the bubble of narcissistic grandiosity bursts. In the case of the false drowning, what is exposed is an absence rather than a presence at the core of Elimelekh's being. Until his discomfiture, he experienced his feelings for Rachel first as a sympathetic overflow of fraternal solidarity and then as a grand passion in which his soul fused with the life of the universe. In both of these defensive reveries Elimelekh conceives of his plight as the result of an excess of spirit; he simply *has* too much. The drowning incident reveals to him the involuntary nature of his situation; he is embroiled in compulsion rather than donation. From then on, as the frequency of his capitulations increases, the meaningfulness of the relationship is progressively emptied out to reveal an absence of substance rather than a presence. Laid bare are states of dependence, obsession, and compulsion, which no redeeming content can transfigure.

Sartre recognizes not only the revelatory nature of shame but also the role of the other in triggering the revelation: Shame occurs when one becomes conscious of being observed by others in a moment of weakness. "It is a shameful apprehension *of* something, and this something is *me*. I am ashamed of what I *am*. Shame therefore realizes an intimate relation of myself to myself. Through shame I have discovered an aspect of *my* being. . . . I recognize that I *am* as the other sees me."[14] What is most painful in Elimelekh's humiliation in the false drowning or his embarrassment over going back to Rachel after his diatribes against women is not, then, the slings and arrows of ridicule but what he has found out about himself.

In this unhappy self-discovery the gaze of the Other has a critical role. The identity of the Other in this narrative is significantly, *not* Rachel, the object of his obsession, whose real existence he is hardly aware of, but Elimelekh's peers, his fellow Jewish students who are self-imposed exiles like himself. It is from this student community—really only an emancipated version of the *kehilah* of the shtetl—that Elimelekh holds himself aloof as a gifted individual spirit. But what he has rejected returns to possess him. The same community ends up by serving as the reflector of his shame and the revelatory catalyst of his impotence.

Pudenda, Scham, mevushim—the terms for genitals make the linkage between shame and sexuality unavoidable. The distinction made in psychoanalytic literature between shame and guilt is much to the point in *A Raven Flies*. Guilt, in this framework, is understood as the painful internal tension generated when the inhibitive barriers erected by the superego are touched or transgressed by id impulses, especially in the form of taboo sexual desires. The retributive punishment for this transgression is the mutilation of the offending organ as the carrier of the forbidden impulses, and this unconscious threat is the basis of the castration anxiety. Shame, on the other hand, is rooted in feelings of inferiority and failure.[15] Shame in psychoanalytic thinking originates in the painful tension between the ego and the ego-ideal (the sum of the psyche's positive identifications and potentialities) and results from the self's failure to attain goals set by the ego-ideal. In contrast to the conviction of transgression in guilt, shame is produced by a sense of noncommission and shortcoming.[16] The unconscious threat behind shame is not castration but the fear of abandonment, the fear that because of our disappointing unworthiness we shall incur the contempt of others and be cut off and left to die by emotional starvation.[17]

Elimelekh's great failure lies in his inability to act sexually and to fulfill the high romantic goals he has set for himself. His failure results less from Rachel's unavailability than from his own evasions. He begins by acting toward her as a brother, and when he wishes to shift the terms of the relationship, he can put forward only grandiose rhetoric rather than changed behavior. Elimelekh's is a double shame: the inability to enact an erotic relationship with Rachel and the inability to sever his tie with her once the futility of his purpose becomes certain. Now it is the second failure, the humiliation of obsessive attachment, which on the face of things is the most difficult to account for. Why does he not just remove himself from the relationship? His motives become clearer if we invoke the psycho-analytic premise concerning the fear that lies beneath shame: the fear of abandonment. Elimelekh's actions demonstrate that he is willing to main-tain the relationship no matter on what basis and no matter what the private and public costs. To put it in technical terms: the fear of object loss takes precedence over the release of impulse. It is far more important for Elim-elekh to maintain continuous union with the object in which he has invested so much narcissistic energy than for him to fulfill his romantic ambitions.

This returns us to the vicissitudes of life in the void. That Elimelekh and the generation he represents bear an inescapable wound is a given of the story. It is the origins of this wound that are the subject for ironic treatment. Elimelekh complains that he is the victim of the repressive religion of the fathers which functioned systematically to deny life. The narrative, how-ever, indicates that the genesis of the problem is just the opposite: the sudden removal of the religion of the fathers, the aching absence of the world of tradition as a source of emotional and cognitive nourishment. The collapsed plausibility of this world induces a state of chronic deprivation, a vacuous need which no substitutes can easily or quickly fill up. Need precedes fulfillment. An Elimelekh can never attain the erotic fulfillment he longs for while he is empty inside, and he can never fill up that void because he can never acknowledge the conditions that created it.

As an autobiographical narrative, *A Raven Flies* poses two perplexing questions: What are the narrator's motives for telling the story? And what is the narrator's retrospective point of view, that is, what is the final "wisdom" that shapes the way the past is presented? The question of the motives is sharpened by the absence in the text of a narratee, a visible or implied listener or recipient of Elimelekh's narrative. We are left to posit some vague notion of the contemporary Hebrew reader, peers of Berdichevsky's on the radical side of the Hebrew national revival, younger admirers who published his works under the Tushiyah imprint. The vagueness is signifi-cant, and it blunts the sense in which *A Raven Flies* can be considered a confessional narrative, despite all the admissions and self-exposures it delivers. Terrence Doody usefully insists that in fiction a

> confession is a deliberate, self-conscious attempt of an individual to explain his nature to an audience who represents the kind of community he needs to exist in and to confirm him. Confession is always an act of community, and the speaker's intention to realize himself in community is the formal purpose that

distinguishes confession from other modes of autobiography or self-expression.[18]

Elimelekh is an isolato whose only identification is with an invisible company of enlightened spirits to whom little would be gained by confessing his record of weakness and folly. There is no perceptible community in which the narrator seeks participation and confirmation.

To whom, then, does he speak? One answer is that the narrator speaks to himself in an act of self-exorcism. Despite Elimelekh's avowed rejection of Rachel—and because of his sadistic treatment of her—he clearly continues to be mired in his obsession. The narrative is a failed attempt on the part of the narrator to persuade himself that he is now free of his disability and capable of resuming his life. The digressive rationalizations for his weakness, which continually retard the narrative, are integral to the apologetic motive. These modulated repetitions and circularities indeed represent the technical achievement of *A Raven Flies:* the first representation in Hebrew of the consciousness of bad faith and neurotic compulsion.

A second approach to the question "To whom does the narrator speak?" would invoke the theme of narcissistic shame. Why does the narrator need to expose the humiliating record of his repeated failures to live up to his own values? Beneath shame, it has been argued, lies a fear of losing the loved object, a fear so powerful that it overrides the pain of self-exposure. Yet despite all of Elimelekh's capitulations and self-abasements, the loss still takes place. But if the object is lost, the need for it is not—and hence the motive for enduring the ordeal of shame. This is a need which is produced by a bottomless deprivation, and it knows no end or resting place. In this sense, the narrative is not reflexive but open-ended. The will toward self-exposure represents a continuing need, intensified after redoubled loss, to make contact with an object. This is a desire for connection that does not abate. Despite the disappearance or betrayal of the love-object, the reaching out to an invisible and unimaginable narratee continues.[19]

Autobiographical narratives stimulate the expectation that some form of retrospective learning or wisdom will be delivered in the course of the telling. Even if the wisdom consists of a painful baring of illusions, it represents a credible gain in awareness. Something of this kind of expectation is encouraged in the first half of *A Raven Flies* when Elimelekh makes statements like the following: "In my naïveté I said to myself that in one leap I had bypassed all the generations of my ancestors and that my spirit was now completely open to new worlds and new ideas" (p. 10). Or: "Then I was mistaken in believing that intimacy between two people is an invariable outgrowth of companionship sustained over time, and that companionship is a function of one's worth and the value of one's deeds" (p. 20). Such statements imply that in the course of the events described in the story the narrator was disabused of these mistaken convictions and granted a truer view of things. So we might expect, for example, that he now acknowledge that it is impossible to leap over the past, or that he now understand that the existence of nonrational factors makes the progress from companionship to erotic love not necessarily automatic.

The promise of wisdom, however, is never realized. Obsession and the shame of dependence overwhelm the narrator and eliminate the possibility of an accession to knowledge. Instead, the narrator moves to take back whatever kernels of insight were implied in his early reflections. Burrowing even more deeply into the trough of bad faith, he denies that the narrated events have had any meaning whatever. The declaration is made in the closing lines of the novella, and it is here that we find the phrase that serves as the enigmatic title for the work as a whole, a phrase whose reference requires a gloss: "And so all the anguish of that year-and-a-half was only a passing shadow, a thing of no account. Only '*urva parah*, only '*urva parah.*" (p. 55). '*Urva parah* was undoubtedly an idiom commonly used by yeshiva students of the time to indicate something purposeless, insubstantial, and of no importance. The phrase appears as the *pointe* to a talmudic anecdote (Beitsah 21a and parallel in Hulin 124b) whose connections to Berdichevsky's text are extremely interesting. It is worth noting that such a complex allusion to classical sources is a rare occurrence in *A Raven Flies*; this is not a text in the manner of Abramowitsch or Bialik in which every phrase yields to revealing its biblical or rabbinic provenance. So when we come across a reference like this it deserves close scrutiny, all the more since the phrase serves both as the work's title and as its closing utterance.

Here is the talmudic source:

> R. Avia the Elder asked R. Huna: Is it permissible to slaughter on a festival an animal half of which belongs to a heathen and half to an Israelite?
>
> He said to him: It is permissible.
>
> The other [R. Avia] said: What difference is there between this case and the case of vows and freewill offerings?
>
> A raven flies ['*urva parah*], he [R. Huna] retorted.
>
> When he [R. Avia] left, his son said to him: Was this not R. Avia the Elder, whom you, sir, have praised as a great man?
>
> What was I to do with him? he answered; I am today [in the condition of a lover who says] 'Sustain me with cakes, refresh me with apples, for I am faint' [Song of Songs 2.4], and he asked me things which require reasoning!
>
> And what *is* the reason [in the case of the animal slaughtered on a festival]?

According to Rashi, this story concerns Rava's father, R. Huna, who was returning from having given the homily in the synagogue on a festival morning. R. Avia importuned him with two legal questions. R. Huna answered the first but put off the second by distracting the asker and pointing to a bird in flight. The son then inquires why the father behaved rudely to elder R. Avia, about whom he always spoken with respect. R. Huna justifies himself by saying that he was being asked a complex and demanding question just at the moment when he was weak and exhausted from his service to the community.

What are the links between Elimelekh and R. Huna—except perhaps for the fact that Elimelekh, like the animal to be slaughtered, is also a creature who belongs half to the Jews and half to the gentiles? Both figures, to begin with, use the phrase '*urva parah* to distract the attention of the one being addressed (R. Avia/the reader), and the play is accompanied in both instances by an act of humiliation (R. Avia/Rachel). There is a further similarity in the way both figures rationalize their actions by pointing to their mental states. R. Huna justifies his weakness by invoking a verse from the Song of Songs in which the lovesick speaker begs for delicacies to still her passion. Elimelekh, too, is hungry, but his hunger more literally resembles the lovesick Shulamith from the Song of Songs, although it is hardly of the pastoral variety. The absence of love has turned his life on its head. Just as R. Huna is forced to forego a legal discussion because of his physical faintness, so must Elimelekh give up his great intellectual ambitions because of the very non-spiritual needs that will not leave him alone.

Yet here the similarity ends. To be sure, R. Huna's behavior does not conform to the ideal of scholarly comportment, but his tactlessness is viewed in the story as one of those lapses that are sometimes allowed an overworked public servant. Besides, the evaded question is put off only for a moment; the Gemarra returns directly to take up the issue of the jointly owned animal slaughtered on a festival. For Elimelekh, however, this lapse or interval becomes the main drama of his life. The only truly significant experience he has ever undergone is the "sentimental education" he has received in his relations with Rachel. And it is precisely this "main thing" that Elimelekh seeks to dismiss as trivial. He avers that his affair was merely a diversion from the main business of his life, when in fact he now has no other life to return to. R. Huna's '*urva parah* was intended to give the exhausted sage a respite in which to refresh himself for continued struggling with life's problems. Elimelekh's '*urva parah* signifies a gesture of perpetual evasion of existential responsibility.

There is very little left of Elimelekh by the end of *A Raven Flies*. In the beginning of the story, the grandiose edifice of illusion that he inhabits makes Elimelekh a fascinating figure, and it is the precise nature of his folly that is significant and interesting. When the edifice collapses, Elimelekh is bereft. No authentic knowledge born of experience is given him in compensation for his ordeal. He ends up clinging to a new set of illusions, which are mean-spirited where the first were high-minded, impoverished instead of grandiose.

Yet if the narrator persists in his blindness, not so the author who has created him. The narrator's efforts to persuade us to see the world as he does do not succeed; on the contrary, his perceptions are submitted to scrutiny and exposed as illusions. We *know* that Elimelekh is wrong. This knowledge is engendered by the authority that puts the narrator before us: the implied author. It is the implied author who urges us to see among the reasons for Elimelekh's downfall the chief "sin" of willed aloofness from others, the sovereign isolation of the self, the glorification of the solitary spirit cut off from past, family, and people.

This author is none other than the Berdichevsky who only a year earlier had written the following words.

> A man must forget much and begin all anew as if nothing had been done before him. Then he suddenly awakens from his long sleep to abolish just those institutions to which until this point he has devoted such care and which now must be torn down in order to be built up again.[20]

With these words Berdichevsky brought to a climax the rebellion against the values of Judaism that he had begun some fifteen years earlier. We stand, then, squarely before a contradiction between ideological assertion and artistic truth. The critique of total negation implied in A Raven Flies simply does not square with the polemical pronouncements of the essays. The disparity calls into question the common conception of Berdichevsky as the supreme individualist of modern Hebrew literature. This contradiction is only one among many that characterize the multiple genres in which Berdichevsky wrote over his long career. Against this background, 1899–1900 stands out as the year marked by both the greatest creativity and the greatest polarity.[21] Comprehending this complexity will be accomplished only by an integrative approach that encompasses all of the dimensions of Berdichevsky's work, and in that effort the testimony rendered by A Raven Flies will be crucial.

BRENNER'S *IN WINTER* AND THE AUTOBIOGRAPHICAL TRADITION: THE PLAY OF CODES

Part Three

The Revision of Childhood

In the following passage the narrator-hero of *In Winter (Baḥoref)* registers the moment in which he realizes that his faith is irretrievably lost. Because this scene is the heir to a by-then venerable tradition of loss-of-faith scenes in Hebrew literature, it will give us a starting point for understanding the place of Brenner's novel in this tradition.

> The final crisis was at last upon me. The sanctuary was destroyed, the walls pulled down, the sacred precincts emptied. The smouldering fire had blazed forth. My youth came to an end. . . .
>
> My dilemma was solved: Come what may, I must make a complete break with the beit midrash, never return and make my way to N., the provincial capital, to begin secular studies.
>
> Z., my hometown, is located on the road to N., and I was obliged to stop at my parents' house on the way.
>
> It was exceedingly hard to bear the mask I was obliged to put on when I was at home. I justified it to myself by reasoning that I was not playing the hypocrite for my own pleasure but for my parents' peace of mind; even though they were "rebels against the Light," I hadn't the right to upset them and poison their life. My plan worked well enough for a while. I was then not yet accustomed to behaving irreligiously, sitting bareheaded or eating without a blessing, and similar matters relating to *practice*. Yet like a "yawning chasm," the great change inside of me soon gave itself away despite all my precautions. (ch. 10, pp. 41–42)[1]

What is most striking in this passage is what is absent from it. The word for crisis in the Hebrew text is the transcription of the European term *Krisis*. It was already used by Lilienblum in the 1870s to designate the final descent into apostasy, that moment in which the crumbling house of faith sustains its final blow and collapses. In Feierberg this moment is rendered with high drama and high seriousness: Nahman committing the public sacrilege of snuffing out the candle on Yom Kippur, Nahman mourning the destruction of his private world of faith on Tisha B'Av while the rest of the congregation mourns the destruction of the Temple. Brenner's narrator prepares us—indeed sets us up—for just this sort of a scene and even invokes the distinctly Feierbergian image of the profaned and ruined sanctuary as a metonymy for the soul of the young unbeliever. Yet we are not given this event in the text, nor do we find even the sort of ironic reworking of the scene that we might have indeed expected. Instead there is nothing. The moment of apostasy is rendered as an ellipsis. The three dots at the end of the sentence, "my youth came to an end . . ." (*kalu yemei shaḥaruti . . .*) constitute an orthographic pointer to a tear in the text, a blank which the literate reader of the period can be depended upon to fill in with passages recalled from other, earlier writers. Note the number of terms set off in quotation marks. A few stock phrases about profaned sanctuaries and destroyed temples—the equivalent to evoking in English those famous bare ruined choirs—and one has done enough to record the passing of this moment. The *Krisis,* which had once been invested with great danger and which had served as the climax of earlier narratives, has now become a conventional rite-of-passage in the life of the young Jewish intellectual, as it has become a stale topos in the literary telling of that life.

Instead, what becomes relevant is the stage of life *after* the loss of faith, that stage in which the young man is supposed to break with his family, leave his benighted hometown, and begin a new life in the enlightened atmosphere of the metropolis. In Brenner's *In Winter,* however, this outward journey never takes place as planned. The visit to Z., the home town on the way from the yeshivah to the big city, is only one in a series of greater and lesser "returns" home.[2] This is a pattern which in fact organizes the novel and suggests its theme, which might tentatively be put as follows: the difficulty in making this break *because of* the self's knotted entanglement with its origins. In the passage quoted above there is an almost comic sense of inappropriateness in the way that concern is shifted from the grave issue of religious crisis to worries about how to handle one's parents on a visit home. Yet it is just this kind of displacement that the novel is about. The narrator describes the double life he led on this visit as undertaken out of consideration for the feelings of his parents. Yet the obvious need for self-justification implies the existence of motives more internal to the self, and it calls attention to the difficulty in conducting oneself in accord with new convictions. For however decisively religious belief may have been repudiated, there is no easy or automatic accession to a new way of being in the world, a new *ma'aseh* (or practice), as our passage would have it. The compulsion to wear masks, then, is not necessarily imposed from the outside. This gap between belief and being, the one transformed and the other as yet unrealized, defines the human and historical moment in *In Winter.* The novel asks the question: What does it mean to live authentically in the immediate aftermath of faith? It returns the answer: Life in this interval must of necessity be double—the embroiled business of at the same time disowning the past and being owned by it.

Under such conditions, consciousness is submitted to special pressures. If one desires to be authentic at a time when existence can be but double, then consciousness is enlisted as the chief means of policing and interrogating the many temptations to evasion and bad faith. Writing about one's past becomes a scrutinizing of motives, a repeated putting of the question, as in the passage above: Was I true to myself? Was I justified in my hypocrisy? The fate of consciousness in the void after faith is one of the central themes of *In Winter*. What happens to the highly charged energies of mind which were once occupied in religious introspection and in the interpreting of sacred texts but have now been disemployed and set free? The novel presents two possibilities, both of which are realized, explored, and played off one against the other. On the one hand, consciousness can serve as an analytical tool for providing insight into the great cataclysm of modernity and in so doing offer compensatory if partial consolation for its afflictions. On the other hand, the severity of consciousness can make the crisis worse by relentlessly dissecting the contradictions of behavior and feeling and by exposing the self's nakedness in the extremity of its dispossession.

These are large issues indeed for any work of art but particularly astonishing for a first novel written at the age of twenty-one. *In Winter* was written—rewritten, actually, after the loss of the manuscript—during the first year of Brenner's conscription into the Czarist army in 1902–1903 and published the next year in the periodical *Hashiloah*.[3] More astonishing still is the fact that the novel is not merely ambitious but accomplished. Many of the autobiographical materials for the novel are taken from the years of late adolescence that closely approach the actual time of the writing, and this is not to mention the turbulence of those years and the conditions under which the writer wrote. Yet where we would expect to find a groping after adequate form and a struggling to resist the press of immediate experience—the signs, in short, of a fledgling literary talent—we find instead a novel that is fully realized, proportionate in structure, and disciplined in expression. In the context of literary history, moreover, *In Winter* is the central document in the development of a particular genre tradition. A novel written in the form of an autobiography, *In Winter* is supremely conscious of the achievements of nineteenth-century autobiographical writing to which it is the heir. And the relationship of this first novel of Brenner's to this patrimony is hardly a humble one. The autobiographical tradition, both in fiction and outside fiction, is marked as a whole by what can be called a kind of evolving division of labor, in which individual works deal with certain moments and themes in the life of the subject and leave to other works other moments and themes. So Lilienblum explicitly states that he cedes to Guenzburg's *Aviezer* "coverage," as it were, of the years of childhood and begins his narrative later in the life cycle. Feierberg returns to childhood in order to trace a different line of development, which culminates in the tragic experience of apostasy in adolescence. For his part, Berdichevsky, in such works as *Two Camps* and *A Raven Flies,* separates out the component of troubled sexuality and explores it at the stage of early adulthood.

In Winter, by contrast, takes on this span as a whole. Brenner returns to the early years covered by Guenzburg and Feierberg *and* the later years covered by Lilienblum and Berdichevsky. Moreover, Brenner encompasses in one narrative the themes of loss of faith and the subsequent struggle of ideologies, on the one hand, and the themes of erotic and existential crisis, on the other. Yet in the end what distinguishes *In Winter* is not simply its breadth and inclusiveness. The operation it performs on these earlier instances of autobiographical writing is an act of incorporation. Brenner appropriates these materials and reorders their inner codes as well as their outward relations. The result is a novel that not only sums up a genre but rewrites it. And exhausts it as well, at least for certain purposes. After the publication of *In Winter* the confessional autobiographical genre ceases to be used—and in effect ceases to exist—as a vehicle for exploring the loss of faith and the dilemmas of existence in the void after faith. (See my conclusion.) This thematic does not disappear but lives on only in other literary forms.

In order to understand this act of incorporation and rewriting it is useful to analyze the way in which *In Winter* organizes the confessional-auto-biographical materials which it inherits and to which it adds. I would like to use the concept of thematic codes and speak about the novel as breaking down into three basic codes, whose action one upon the other creates the novel's drama. The first is the *cognitive-cultural code.* The cognitive code presents reality at the level of ideas and values: the religious and intellectual development of the narrator as he passes through stages of belief, disbelief, and new ideologies, and in addition the analysis and critique of such institutions as the family, the school, student society, and Zionist politics. The second code is the *psychological-existential code.* The psychological code takes the same beliefs and institutions and examines them from the point of view of their role in the development of the self; religious, national, and ideological issues are translated into such categories as autonomy/dependence, confidence/shame, self-acceptance/self-loathing. The third code is the *erotic code.* The erotic code presents behavior motivated at the level of the unconscious drives and records the expressions, displacements, and compensations for sexual desire.

Now, I have introduced the codes of *In Winter* not for the purpose of identifying the narrative poetics of the novel but in order to provide the tools for uncovering the twin acts of violent transformation that lie at the work's center. These transformations are constituted by the aggressive take-over of one code by another code. In the first of these transformations, the cognitive-cultural code is absorbed by the psychological code. The long-used and epic account of the young man's ordeal of apostasy is told by Brenner from a different angle of vision. The changed perspective performs a thoroughgoing psychological reduction upon the received materials. Religious tradition, the family, and the school, these agencies which were once examined for their influence upon the development of the mind and imagination, are reevaluated for their role in forming a more fundamental level of the child's life: the self. This shift is all the sharper for the fact that the former criteria, the cognitive criteria, are not refuted on their own terms, as one belief or idea contends with others, but they are simply pushed aside as irrelevant, for it is no longer beliefs and ideas that describe the ground of reality. (Because the old criteria have been moved away from this newly felt center of existence, they lose some of the overdetermined charge they formerly possessed, and ironically the institutions of traditional Jewish life become newly susceptible to the kind of sympathetic depiction that was never possible when they were conceived of largely as agents of repression.) The psychological reduction that is programatically carried out in the novel, it should be stressed, is a project of the "mature" narrator, Yirmiah Feuerman, as he looks back over his young life and seeks to reunderstand his experience in terms of the new values, the values of psychological authenticity, that he has in the meantime acquired.

The second transformation in *In Winter* involves the absorption of the psychological code by the erotic code. The psychological code is predicated upon a clear standard of self-knowledge and self-acceptance; through his recourse to the past, the narrator discovers his true nature, which is frail and flawed, and he endeavors to accept it and live in the world without false illusions and expectations. This, however, is in fact not what happens. For all his analysis and resignation, the narrator conceives a ridiculous and unrequited attraction to a shallow, half-assimilated woman named Rahil. The attraction turns into a powerful obsession which systematically dismantles the achievements of the psychological program, neutralizing its insights by encouraging reveries of evasion and escape. The narrator had previously forbidden himself the experience of desire, because it carries within it the irrepressible expectation that life might be other than it is. Yet desire not only persists but balloons, and in its assertion are revealed dimensions of the self for which there was little real provision in the narrator's view of the world.

The reading of *In Winter* which I shall present in the following pages will seek to demonstrate how the cognitive, psychological, and erotic codes are placed in a different mix in each of the three equal sections into which the novel is rigorously divided. The emotional valence of each of the codes will also be an important feature, that is, how each of the codes is charged or uncharged, hot or cold relative to the narrator's investment in his self-conceived identity, and how in turn this valence determines whether the narrative materials are presented in the analytic mode or the scenic mode, and why this should matter. But let us now turn to the first of the three parts that comprise the novel in order to examine more closely the conventions of authenticity and autobiographical writing by which *In Winter* presents itself to us.

In Winter: Part One

In Winter rewrites many works: Guenzburg on childhood, Feierberg on apostasy, Berdichevsky on erotic obsession. But it is in Lilienblum that Brenner met his most formidable precursor. Lilienblum's *Sins of Youth* (published in 1876 and 1899) was indisputably the model in Hebrew literature for telling the story of a young man's break with the tradition and the ordeal of his entry into the modern world. As autobiography, moreover, Lilienblum's work became the example of what it means to tell the truth about oneself and to craft the shape of that telling. It should come as no surprise, then, that the prologue to Brenner's first novel is closely modeled on the set of claims and disclaimers that open Lilienblum's autobiography. The following passage opens *In Winter:*

> I've put together a little book of blank paper and I intend to put down some impressions and sketches from "my life."
>
> "My life"—such as it is. I have no present or future; only the past remains.
>
> The Past! If someone overheard me saying this he might well think that I have terrible tales to tell about this past of mine, or some heart-rending tragedy.
>
> But this is far from the case. My past contains no interesting events: no enthralling facts or high tragedy, no murders or romantic entanglements, and no great strokes of fortune or sudden inheritances. Only human shades, vague specters, hidden tears, and sighs.
>
> My past is not the past of a hero because I myself am simply not a hero. (p. 1)

Like Lilienblum, who at the age of twenty-nine states that he is already an old man beyond tears and despair, Brenner's narrator, a good ten years younger, presents his life as essentially over. In both cases the justification for a young man's presuming to write his autobiography lies in the assumption that whatever might be of interest in his life already *has been.* His only possession and therefore his only literary capital is his past. From such a past, the narrator hastens to caution the reader, very little should be expected, especially of the sort of sensational events that enliven popular literature. The autobiographical premise requires telling the truth, and the truth about Jewish life is that, as Lilienblum had put it, "Hebrew drama can have no effect other than sorrow."[4] For Brenner's narrator, any resemblance between himself and a fictional hero is laughable, and so the story he can write about himself can only be a story about a non-hero who passes through the world like the other specters and shades from his past.

The break with Lilienblum comes in two areas that may at first seem incidental. The little book of blank paper [*pinkas*] in which Brenner's narrator means to record some notes and sketches [*reshimot usirtutim*] stands in sharp contrast to Lilienblum's rather grand autobiographical project with its formal organization into officially labeled periods of ideological and emotional development (e.g., "Days of Confusion," "Days of Crisis and Renunciation," etc.). Of course *In Winter* is a far more sophisticated work than merely a collection of impressions. Yet the booklet, this minimalist image for the project of writing about the self, is a good marker of the differences between Brenner's short novel and Lilienblum's substantive autobiography. The scale of the two prologues makes the point as well. Lilienblum's comes replete with epigrams, a formal heading, an excursus on the history of the biographical genre and the author's place in it, and introductions to the four major sections of the book. For Brenner's narrator, on the other hand, half a page is enough to make his claims, to identify himself as a village teacher, and then to break off what is evidently an uncomfortable responsibility with the remark, "Even such an introduction as this one is plenty." It is not just a matter of proportions. The notion of a text made up of "impressions and sketches," even if its realization is much more than that, indicates a wish for fragmentariness and for an escape from the well-wrought forms of narrative expected of the Hebrew writer.[5]

There is also a fundamental divergence on the question of audience. Lilienblum continues something of the tradition of the Hebrew ethical will [*tsava'ah*] still evident in Guenzburg's *Aviezer*. Addressing an hypostasized reader, Lilienblum expresses the hope that the cautionary tale of his shortcomings will prevent younger people from blindly repeating those same errors. "If my tears and my despair have brought me no benefit," he opines, "might they not be of use to others? That is the reason I am writing this account of my life."[6] In the final lines of the prologue the narrator of *In Winter*, by contrast, rejects the very notion of an addressee: "Even though I am not a hero, I wish to record this past of mine, a non-heroic past. As for heroes, their past is written down for the world to read. . . . My past, the past of a non-hero, I write in seclusion for myself alone" (p. 1). Now the claim that a writer is writing only for himself is a familiar topos, and one which is undercut in part by the very fact that in reading these words we complete the communicative transaction and provide the writer with an audience—whether he wanted us or not. Beyond the protest that he is not a hero, the narrator gives us no reasons for making his writing secret and self-reflexive. Placed at the opening of the work, this juxtaposition of the desire for privacy with the desire to write produces an enigma of sorts, and the reader embarking upon the novel is summoned to imagine a set of conditions under which the coexistence of the two desires can make sense. Does the narrator believe that there exist no readers, or no suitable readers, for his work?[7] Does he simply wish to dissociate himself from Lilienblum's didactic self-confidence and his readiness to present his life as a moral exemplum? Does he demur because the project of self-understanding has failed or imperfectly succeeded and he thus has no explanation of himself to offer? Or has he discovered truths about himself that are too difficult to reveal to others or perhaps even to himself?

This last possibility, that there exists knowledge about himself to which the narrator does not and cannot have access, constitutes in the end the most telling difference between *In Winter* and *Sins of Youth*. For if it were not for the scale of the writing and the identity of the audience, the factors already mentioned, there would be little reason for not viewing these two works as fundamentally allied. Are they not, after all, both first-person, confessional accounts of young men coming of age amidst the breakdown of Jewish society in Eastern Europe? True, but at bottom the two works are separated by a fundamental fact of genre: one is an autobiography and the other is a novel. One purports to be a true story, no matter how artfully crafted, told by the author about himself in his own words; the other, though written in the first person and based on personal history, is a fiction about a protagonist who is not identical with the author. In late nineteenth-century Hebrew literature, however, these are distinctions that are hard to maintain. Brenner, for example, was unhappy about the editor's insistence on labeling *In Winter* a novel when it first appeared in the journal *Hashiloah* in 1903.[8]

The instability of assumptions about the nature of novels and auto-biographies created a situation Brenner could use to his advantage. He positioned his first novel in such a way that it could benefit from the generic expectations for authenticity and truthfulness that surrounded autobiography, while at the same time he could preserve the zone of imaginative freedom and invention afforded by the novel. *In Winter*, in short, *is a novel masquerading as an autobiography.* The freedom gained by *In Winter*'s status as a novel, by its fictionality, is realized in two ways. On the simplest level, fictional facts and real-world facts need not correspond. The experiences of the novel's protagonist Yirmiah Feuerman and the experience of its author Yosef Hayyim Brenner are in actuality not identical. The degree of corre-spondence falls somewhere in the range of what popular reviewers call "thinly veiled" on the one hand and "loosely based" on the other. In autobiography such divergence is thought a fault; in *Sins of Youth*, however-much the events of Lilienblum's life may be selected, patterned, and crafted, the presumption remains—certainly on the part of Lilienblum himself—that the facts adduced are actually true.[9] The novelist may well argue that the truth he reaches for is deeper and even more auto-biographically authentic than the literal-minded adherences of biographical writing, and indeed the canons of the novel genre leave him free to work unencumbered in the space between biographical facts and fictional repre-sentations. The study of how life is transformed into art, the quality of the alteration, not the quantity, properly belongs to the practice of biographical criticism. This is a difficult and speculative enterprise, whose starting point is not the discovery of the biographical facts but a clear understanding of the use made of them, their structuration, in the novel itself.[10]

This second kind of freedom—how the divergences between the author and his narrator can be structured *within* the novel rather than *between* life and fiction—presents a more interesting issue, and one we can know something about because the text lies before us. The significance of this structure becomes evident if we take it away for a moment and view *In Winter* as if it were a "straight" autobiography of Yirmiah Feuerman. As such, *In Winter* is already a powerful revision of *Sins of Youth;* the pathos of Lilienblum's intellectual odyssey is deflated, scrutinized, and reduced to its psychological essentials, while at the same time the animus against the traditional religious background is neutralized and the material put at a sympathetic distance. This is already a great deal, to be sure, but it is not all. Because *In Winter* is in fact not a straight autobiography but a narrative in which the narrator is a fictive creation of the author, another possibility is actualized. There exists a dimension of knowledge about the motives of the narrator to which we as readers *can* have access but to which the narrator himself *cannot*, for the reason that those motives are either unconscious or threatening to his hard-won commitment to the values of authenticity. What is acted out but unacknowledged by Feuerman is the entanglement in erotic desire, which plays havoc with his attempt to live by an illusionless existential code. We the readers can see this, by contrast, because Brenner the author shows it to us; he shows us the self-compromising behavior *and* the blindness to it on the part of his otherwise intelligent narrator.

It is this structure of doing and undoing, making and unmaking, which is so impressive in Brenner's first novel. *In Winter* presents an entirely new way of thinking about life in the aftermath of faith, a way based on a new understanding of the primary needs of the self in the shadow of beliefs and ideologies; yet at the same time the novel includes a deconstructive movement which undermines the new regime of knowledge and hints at the existence of more powerful and ungovernable forces. This usurpation is an effect of the second transformation described above: the takeover of the psychological code by the erotic code. This event comes in the last third of the novel, and its force cannot be understood unless we first appreciate the depth and immensity of the revision that is itself subverted. It is this revision, despite its vulnerability to subversion, which represents the great intellectual achievement of *In Winter.* It is therefore to this process, the process through which Brenner translates and reduces the received materials of the autobiographical tradition into psychological understanding, that we now turn.

Establishing the Psychological Code

Because of the novel's autobiographical format, the first order of business in *In Winter* is for the narrator to give an account of his family origins. But how indeed to speak of one's parents? From what point of view? In what voice? The thorny issues of narrative mode nearly overwhelm the narrator at the very moment he undertakes to discharge this responsibility. He is aware that had he attempted to describe his mother at an earlier remove in time, in the "idealistic days of his youth," he would have "loved to melt into a lyric reverie on the subject of her travails, her patience, and the constrictions of her world," and he would have sought "to see in her the emblem of Jewish Womanhood, as the writers of a well-known school would be wont to do" (ch. 1, p. 3). Yet in the maturity of his retrospective point of view—and we must remember that maturity here means all of twenty or twenty-one years of age—there remains no temptation to idealize. The mother cannot be represented as the embodiment of a collective type, nor should that type be infused with sentimentality and nobility and be made to serve other ends.

What the narrator offers instead is not a spree of demythologizing but a conscientious attempt to present the particulars of his mother's world in terms that are social and psychological.[11] His mother Judith, he relates, grew up as an orphan in the house of a relative, where her status was somewhere between a ward and a servant. A disfiguring attack of smallpox at the age of seventeen further lowered her worth as a bride, and she was eventually given to an itinerant Lithuanian whose veneer of scholarship disguised an unfeeling and spiteful disposition. The choice made on her behalf was ostensibly a benevolent one, because the social ethos of the time held that a husband with the appurtenances of learning should on all accounts be favored over a tradesman or a worker. Marriage locked her into a life of abasement. Although she toiled to bring some income into the family and to create a home worthy of a householder, a *ba'al habayit*, her husband ignored her labors and instead praised the accomplishments of other women to whom life had been kinder. It is a humiliation which was repeated continually and which continues in the present. The mother never ceases to seek her husband's recognition, and he never ceases to withhold it.

The father's origins are no less difficult. Deprived of his father as a boy and then driven from home by his mother, Shalom-Getsl learned to fend for himself in the educational institutions of Lithuania, where learning was prized above all else. There he cultivated the trappings of a serious student and acquired the skill of ingratiating himself with his teachers and any others whose good opinion could be of use to him. After five years of suffering the indignities of life as a rural schoolteacher, he decided to try his luck in the more prosperous Jewish settlements in the South, where a Lithuanian lad, though regarded suspiciously as an outsider, was nonetheless a valued commodity because of his learning. By marrying Judith, Shalom-Getsl aspired to escape his penury and enter the middle classes, but his hopes were dashed when the dowry turned out to be nonexistent. To eke out a living he was forced, again, to become a schoolteacher, a melamed, and it was his wife who was in turn made to pay emotionally for his bitterly frustrated social ambitions. As an occupation, the office of melamed perpetuated and fixed for a lifetime Shalom-Getsl's dependence on others. To compete with the town's other teachers and to keep his schoolroom full of paying pupils, he had to bow and scrape before the local householders. "He loved himself and was fastidious on behalf of his honor, yet he was easily capable of humbling, accomodating, and adjusting himself [to the desires of others]. His most serious aspiration was to be a man among men, . . . a voice among the assembled" (ch. 1, p. 5). As his wife strove continually and unsuccessfully to gain the recognition of her husband, he strove with the same futile results to gain the recognition of the "world," that is, the respectable merchants of the town. Yet while her strivings at least led to good works which could have and should have been rewarded, his strivings led to nothing more than a renewed round of groveling and a redoubled sense of resentment.[12]

There is, to be sure, much acute social observation in the narrator's presentation of his parent's lives. He is keenly aware of the impact of social class on domestic relations: which factors, for example, determine the value of a bride, or what is the exact position of the melamed with reference to income and social status. Yet the description of these conditions is not what truly matters to Brenner, nor is this new ground. Within the autobiographical tradition, Guenzburg had long before reflected an even more jaundiced view of his own worth as a bridegroom in the chattel transactions of arranged marriage, and Abramowitsch had undertaken a systematic critique of the mercantilization of family relations. Instead, what is important to Brenner is the *psychological* states created by social conditions and not the *fact* of their creation or the mechanism whereby they were created. This is what sets him apart from others. Psychological reality as understood by the narrator of *In Winter* is everywhere and always the same: the exigent needs of the self for recognition and worth under permanent conditions of denial[13] and the inevitability of shame and humiliation in the clamor to evade these conditions. Despite the differences of circumstances and temperament, and despite the noble and ignoble qualities of their responses, both of the narrator's parents are impelled by forces of deprivation that are essentially the same. The mother's reaching after confirmation from the father and the father's sycophantic posturing before the town cover up the same aching absence at the core of the self. It is this reality which is the narrator's *yerushah*, the sum total of the patrimony that is passed on to him. Feuerman does in fact inherit his mother's conviction of ugliness and physical shame and his father's disadvantaged place in society, but the real inheritance is something which is anterior to these conditions and which stands in relationship to them as reality stands in relationship to circumstance. Because this reality belongs to the world and inheres in it, the deprivations visited upon the narrator by his parents are not taken as idiosyncratic cruelties and personal wounds. Although the father is depicted as unfeeling and the tone taken toward him is hardly neutral, the portrayal of him is analytical and distanced and contains little of the Freudian agon and of the son's struggles to wrest identity and freedom from the crushing authority of the father.

To invoke Freud, however incidentally, is to become aware of what the narrator's psychology is *not*. The discovery made by the narrator—it is in fact an event that takes place before the story begins—is a discovery not of the unconscious but of the self. He knows little of erotic impulses and unconscious drives; he knows much, however, of the effacements of the ego and the deprivations of the self. This is a psychology, moreover, which can be said in the end not to be properly located within the psyche so much as within the world. The world may be perceived psychologically and experienced psychologically, yet the source of pain is not a dysfunction at some level of the psychic structure of the individual but a flaw in existence itself. It is, for want of a better term and for all the dangers of anachronistic misconstrual, an *existential* psychology, and it brings with it, as we shall see, an existential ethics concerning how one should and should not live in such a world. Now, this conception does not go unqualified in the novel, and I have been careful to speak of the *narrator's* psychology rather than that of the work as a whole. Here the distinction between narrator and author is much to the point. Because the narrator's understanding is embedded within a larger epistemological authority, that understanding is contingent. The effect of the authorial perspective is to open it up and deepen it. By showing us the real and undisplaceable workings of erotic needs and impulses, the author exposes the insufficiencies of the narrator's psychology, if he in fact does not overturn it.

In the rethinking of Jewish childhood carried out by *In Winter* the part of the child's world that is submitted to the most thoroughgoing psychological reduction is the area of intellectual function. The works that comprise the autobiographical tradition in Hebrew literature are all written by men who were regarded at an early age as *illuyyim,* Torah prodigies, and because this was the highest status that could be attained by a child in traditional Jewish society, the break with the tradition that came later in life was all the more wrenching. Yet the meaning of this experience for different writers, especially its intellectual component, was not uniform. In Guenzburg's *Aviezer* correct and false intellection remains the key to physical and mental health. For Lilienblum the long years of Torah story represent a sad waste of spirit which set him back half a lifetime in his struggle to acquire useful knowledge. In Feierberg, Torah study is experienced as a slow death through the starvation of the imagination, which in turn uses the texts of the tradition as fuel for reveries of escape and redemption. Although Berdichevsky's university students have left the yeshiva far behind them, they have carried into their new lives the old habit of prideful intellectualism, and they stand woefully undefended before the nonrational forces of life. In *In Winter* all of these traditions are evoked; but Brenner has his narrator make use of them in such a way that the great spiritual and philosophical themes of the earlier literature—reason, intellect, imagination, and emotion—are all drained of their substantive meaning. What is left is a portrayal of mind as a psychological commodity in the social construction of the self.

In the mother's case, the use made of the boy's talent for learning is relatively benign; his accomplishment is the only source of pleasure and consolation in a domestic life filled with humiliation. When it comes to the father, however, the situation is far more insidious. Being the father of the town's prodigy opens up the possibility of escape from his dependent and igominious status as a melamed. "His whole life was concentrated in me; I mean to say that in his eyes I was the one means he possessed to achieve the social ideal" (ch. 3, p. 12). By virtue of his son's distinction the father regards himself as being "not like the rest of the melamdim; he is a melamed only in his schoolroom, but a householder, a *ba'al habayit*, everywhere else" (ch. 3, p. 13). Raising Yirmiah comes to resemble the training of a prize racehorse in which the whole of the owner's capital is invested. To the chastisement and correction of Yirmiah's manners the father devotes himself with special zeal, because the boy's behavior reflects on him and on the claims he has staked out for himself. Yirmiah is required to comport himself with the seriousness and piety of a boy beyond his years, a sage-in-the-making, and he thereby exposes himself to the taunts of the boorish and to the jealousy of other gifted sons and *their* fathers. Most of all, the father tries to accelerate the son's intellectual development so that the prodigiousness of the town's prodigy could be confirmed and kept in the public eye. So Yirmiah is started early on an ambitious talmudic curriculum, pushed prematurely into higher grades to study with older children, and obligated to master and recite setpieces of erudition.

Yet where this sequence in the novel might have read like the Binding of Yirmiah, an updated story of child sacrifice, it is saved from pathos by the narrator's self-scrutiny. One must look elsewhere in Hebrew literature, to Sh. Ben-Zion's contemporary novel *A Broken Soul* [*Nefesh retsutsah*, 1903] or to Lilienblum's own *Sins of Youth*, in order to find exposés in which the "horrors" of the heder system are laid fully at the doorstep of the fathers and teachers. For his part, the narrator of *In Winter* takes a measure of responsibility for complicity in his miseducation. "To be sure, my passion for study was to a certain degree innate and flowed from a temperament that was serious and spiritual, but the principal cause was the pursuit of praise and the striving to make a name for myself" (ch. 4, p. 15). This grandiosity is not in itself inborn but a secondary effect, and the narrator explains it as a response to a deeper distress. In his relations with the other boys of the town, Yirmiah is set apart and ridiculed; whether because of the role his father has cast him in or because of his own endowments of mind and seriousness of temperament, he experiences himself as a stranger among his fellows and an outsider to their games and pranks. As a defense, the boy accepts a view of the world as divided between "him" and "them" but evolves a self-myth in which he is triumphant.

> There was born within me then an arrogance that is hidden, buried, sickly, torturing, and tinctured of infernal envy: "To be sure! They are 'goyim,' and they will be stuck here forever and be simple pathetic souls like their fathers. . . . As for me? . . . I'll travel to Lithuania, to yeshiva. . . , I'll rise above them all." (ch. 4, p. 15)

This prideful aloofness which is in reality a cover for a desperate loneliness, will not be easily shaken off by the narrator later in life, when people will fail to discriminate between the pose and the genuine feelings it is misguidedly meant to conceal. The irony is that the narrator's honest exploration of his own motives ends in discovering that his father is impelled by a similar set of needs; at the deepest springs of behavior, victim and victimizer, as it were, are one. Yirmiah wants to show himself off as much as his father wants to show him off, and in both cases the primary need fueling this grandiosity is a sense of shame over the smallness of the self and a groping for confirmation by others. (Although their deepest motives may be the same, the moral responsibility is of course not equal; what the son does to himself in seeking to resolve his own conflicts is something very different from what the father, in search of his own solutions, does to him. Besides, the father remains fixed in this gesture of exploitation throughout the novel; when a grown-up Yirmiah returns home later on, the father is willing to overlook the son's loss of faith so long as he can now take advantage for his own purposes of the young man's secular proficiencies.) Yet however deep the motives or elaborate the defenses, it should be clear that learning has been relegated to the status of a cultural prop in the real, psychological drama of life.

There remains, however, one component of study which is broken off from the general theme and moved to the center of the novel. A distinctive feature of the narrator's mind as expressed in his style of telling his story— and this holds true for both the mature narrator and his younger dramatized self—is the habit of analysis. He makes generalizations and offers examples; he divides particulars into categories and takes them up one by one; he searches out a single underlying cause and then considers alternative explanations. This is a habit, so it is implied by the narrative, whose origins go back to the boy's schooling. Great parental and communal pressures were brought to bear on the child to develop his capacity for abstract reasoning, textual analysis, and the dialectical manipulation of concepts and principles. At the same time, his imagination was left underdeveloped, and it managed to find nourishment only through his own surreptitious reading. The result was a hypertrophy of the analytic faculty. Severed from its natural balance with imagination and feeling, the analytic faculty grows monstrous and runs amok in the mental life of the young man who has been so unfortunately educated.

This is a familiar theme in nineteenth-century Hebrew literature, and it reflects the dissatisfaction with the traditional Jewish curriculum as the critique shifts from the Haskalah to the period beyond it. But nowhere does this critique become structuralized as in Brenner's novel, that is, turned into a formal principle by which the narrative syntax of the work is constructed. Much in the organization of the story's materials and in the selection of its rhetorical forms gives evidence of a mind in which a cognitive content rejected long ago has been transformed into a mode of perception. What was once a body of thought has become a way of thinking. Some brief examples taken from part one of *In Winter* will indicate some of the more evident markers of this mode. The account of the narrator's father begins thus: "Inscribed in his philosophy of life is [the motto]: 'All according to the prevailing ethos—among hasidim act like a hasid and among maskilim act like a maskil' " (ch. 1, p. 5). This is a generalization that will be illustrated and elaborated in the exposition to follow; its purpose is to present at the outset a conceptual key to the general topic condensed into nearly epigramatic form. Later when the narrator undertakes his first serious attempt to describe the origins of his difficulty with women, he begins with a similar heading: "In general, my relations with the opposite sex were always unspontaneous and reluctant" (ch. 5, p. 16). In attempting to understand his conflicted and ambivalent attitudes to other children his age, the narrator is capable of splitting the issue and entertaining both propositions: "One child in me envied them, always laughing and happy and good-looking, while the other child in me, reinforced in his pride, looked down at them" (ch. 4, p. 15). Introducing his years in yeshiva, the narrator sets to work by organizing the time into two periods: "In the first I was an innocent yeshiva student, suffering, satisfied, an awkward and withdrawn lad but one who knew his own worth. . . . In the second period I was already suspended between heaven and earth" (ch. 9, p. 33). These are instances in which the apparatus of scrutiny and dialectic is bared. Yet the workings of analysis are pervasive throughout the novel. The premise of the narrative enterprise itself rests on a ceaseless desire to make sense of the past, to identify underlying motives and strands of development, and accordingly divide time into psychologically meaningful units.

The Interplay of Analytic and Scenic Discourse

This is a structure which in turn becomes thematized; that is to say that what begins as a mode of perception is itself raised as an issue and made into one of the novel's thematic preoccupations. The question is put as follows. This habit of analysis, which began in the childhood study of Talmud and was carried into later life as a way of understanding oneself and the world, what is its status? Is it good or bad, helpful or unhelpful, healthy or diseased? What, for Jews, is the fate of mind and consciousness once these structures have been uprooted from their native grounds and set free in a world barren of their traditional contents? This inquiry, which is conducted with vague awareness on the part of the narrator and with clear intent on the part of the author, turns in an equivocal but interesting answer. On the one hand, analytic consciousness has the capacity to offer a measure of consolation for the past afflictions of childhood and the present loneliness of an existence without God. By understanding one's fate as part of a larger social and religious transformation, by exposing the bad faith of others who evade the truth of existence, and by tracing the genesis and development of current conflicts—by these applications of the analytic intelligence it is possible to lessen some of the terrors of life. On the other hand, as a compulsion rather than as a tool, analysis may persist in the form of hypercritical judgment. Generalization does violence to particulars, and oversubtlety in probing causes and motives provides a ready basis for rationalization and evasion. Most of all, when analysis becomes the relentless scrutinizing and assessing of behavior, the object of judgment is invariably put at a distance. And when that object is oneself rather than others, the consequences can be unhappy indeed. Later the narrator will give a name to this quality, calling it *nakranut*. The term is derived from the verb whose meanings evoke a set of metonymic gestures for the narrator's compulsion: to peck and scratch at something like a chicken its feed, to pick carrion from the bone, to pluck out the eyes.

I have until now underscored the pervasiveness of analytic discourse in *In Winter* because its presence is rather unexpected in a novel, even one exploiting the conventions of the autobiography, and because the activity of analysis is problematized and placed on the novel's thematic agenda. It would be a gross error, however, to suggest that the analytic mode, even in all its forms, comprises the bulk of the novel's discourse, or even half of it; and if this were the case, who, after all, would want to read such a work? An accurate accounting of the disposition of discourse in the novel would indicate that most of it is made up of the sort of dramatized scenes that we conventionally associate with the genre. For convenience, I shall call this *scenic discourse* in distinction to the *analytic discourse*, which has just been described. Scenic discourse encompasses directly represented events, dialogues, tableaux (descriptive settings), and internal speech rendered in the form of free indirect discourse. The criterion for discriminating between these two types of discourse is often a function of narrative tense and the framing speech-events in the narrative. The novel, we have seen, is constituted entirely by a single act of telling which takes place as the narrator, a young man of some twenty years serving as a teacher in a remote village, writes the story of his life. To the degree to which the narrator, within this act of telling, reevokes and recreates events, conversations, thoughts, and feeling of the past *as if they were taking place in the present,* and often using the present tense, the narrator thereby employs scenic discourse. This is a dramatic representation of the past embedded within the present and the ongoing act of narration that makes up the novel. Analytic discourse, on the other hand, is that which properly belongs to this present act of narration. Part of the time the narrator is engaged in reimagining the past; the rest of the time he reflects, discursively and cognitively, *upon* it. Analytic discourse represents the narrator's ongoing grappling with the specter of his earlier selves—as products of his present consciousness—by describing his motives, identifying the influences on him, and dividing his development into meaningful segments.[14]

The discrimination between these two forms of discourse, which properly belongs to the field of literary theory called narratology, are significant here for several reasons. What interests us in *In Winter* is less the identity the narrator ends up with—in this he is typical of many of his generation— than his relationship to the identity he has broken away from. It is easy to pass beyond the follies of childhood and adolescence; it is more difficult to look back, and more difficult still to look back in a way which admits the persistences of the past. Scenic discourse and analytic discourse are literary representations of the two modal forms of consciousness through which this retrospective grappling is carried out. The interaction of these two modes and their distribution throughout the novel constitute some of the most important, and the most complex, issues in the poetics of *In Winter.* There exists an evident linkage between these modes of presentation and the cognitive, psychological, and erotic thematic codes of the novel. The employment of scene or analysis depends on which of the thematic codes is in play at a given moment and the degree of emotional control the narrator can exert over it. Analytic discourse offers the distance of judgment and critical assessment and is most readily employed in dealing with those experiences that have been most permanently left behind. Scenic discourse is generally employed when there exist grounds for an empathetic identification with the subject, or when it is still unpleasantly alive for the narrator in such a way that self-knowledge and self-consciousness have to be kept at a distance. There are sections of the novel in which one or the other of these modes predominates because of the force of one of the thematic codes carrying a particular charge. Most often, however, there is a frequent shifting back and forth between the two, with a few lines of dialogue inserted within an explanatory excursus, or a brief paragraph of analysis ushering in a vivid tableau. What throws these modal switches is the question we shall now want to explore.

The example of chapter two of *In Winter* provides a good opportunity for examining close up the nature and the import of the shift from analysis to scene. I shall first summarize the four units that comprise the chapter and describe their mode of discourse and then reflect on the differential gains of this method of organization and the energies that move it from one point to another.

First the summary. (A) Continuing the subject begun in the preceding chapter, the first unit describes the relations between the narrator's parents. In order to bring in some little income to the family, the mother undertakes the kind of odd jobs open to women (taking in laundry, teaching girls to read their prayers, plucking and cleaning geese). Yet for all of these labors she manages to win from her husband none of the recognition she so desperately desires. When she is occasionally emboldened to call attention to her husband's hypocrisy, his resentment is expressed by staying away from home, especially on holidays. The unit is written in the style of an exposition; although these are emotionally sensitive matters touched with an evident hostility toward the father, irony provides the distance to accomplish the job of description. (B) What comes next is a polemical aside on the subject of writers who romanticize childhood. "Over time the pain they suffered is forgotten and the pleasant impressions, now amplified and elaborated, pour forth from their hearts like an elixir of paradise" (p. 7). Not so the narrator, for whom there are no angels fluttering at the gates of a lost Eden. For him memories of the past remain muddied and indistinct and all that persists in memory are anguish and deprivation. The unit veers away from the past to the present time of the writing and moves from the specific case of the parents to a general declaration, in which the narrator's truth-telling is contrasted with the inauthenticity of other writers. This substantial analytic distance is lessened somewhat when the narrator seems to reconnect with the "dull and soiled misery" he experienced as a child. (C) When the narrator resumes his story, the focus briefly shifts from the mother to the son. When she goes off to her odd jobs, he would be consigned, already barefoot and dirty, to the neglect of a neighbor. Though ragged in appearance and awkward in body, the boy would mimic adults at prayer in hopes of winning attention. While the language of this section is still descriptive, the style is more pictorial than conceptual. The aim is to render "the image of my likeness when I was four years old" (p. 8), and because that image is repulsive to him, the narrative tone remains caught between self-pity and self-disgust.[15]

Nothing quite prepares us for the fourth unit (D), which is twice as long as the first three combined and runs until the end of the chapter (pp. 8–12): "A holiday morning. Light. The autumn sun breaks across the sash of the one window in my parents' room. The floor has been swept clean with yellow straw and the stove whitewashed. Sparks of tranquility seem to shimmer in the air" (p. 8). Suddenly we are in the absolute present. Physical objects are fixed in their concreteness. A particular hour of a particular morning is being recreated; a stage is being set. The scene that now unfolds is in fact the residue of an incident, reported but not depicted, which took place earlier in the morning. Shalom-Getsl, preening before the mirror in preparation for his attendance at the synagogue on this festival morning, had rejected his son's entreaties to be taken along, and his refusal had entailed the mother's staying at home with the child and missing one of the few occasions during the year when women were encouraged to be present in the synagogue. The scene of the mother and son at home by themselves is told at an unhurried pace. The mother finds consolation by reading a work of popular ethical literature which extols the merit of women who sacrifice themselves on behalf of scholarly sons. Yirmiah recovers his spirits by turning the room into a make-believe synagogue and dancing around and around with a scarf in his hands wrapped up in the form of a Torah scroll. There is a moment of harmony and fulfillment, the mother lost in a reverie of appreciation and value, the son lost in a reverie of grown-up spirituality. The moment begins to ebb when the synagogue lets out and the mother goes to the window at intervals in anticipation of her husband's return. The procession of Jews passes by, the last stragglers have gone, but no sign of Shalom-Getsl. Chatting on her return home, the next-door neighbor cattily lets the mother know that her husband has gone off to the home of a wealthy businessman, where he will be sure to be well fed. The mother is humiliated, the boy ashamed of his father's abuse. The house stands silent, the table set with white cloth, the dishes laid out. The chapter ends as the boy is suddenly engulfed by kisses: "My Yirmiah, my son, my sage, my scholar. . . . You will light up my eyes. . . . With you I need nothing else. . . . My child. . . ." (p. 11).

Viewing the chapter as a whole, we can now ask what is gained by the holiday (Yom Tov) scene. On one level the scene would seem to function merely as an illustration, vivid and concrete, of the generalized observations made earlier in the chapter about the relations between the narrator's parents. It has been stated at the end of the first unit that the father would at times stay away from home on holidays as a way of getting back at his wife for her just criticism of his behavior. Here, then, is a dramatic embodiment of that reprisal and its sad consequences. The pattern of generalization-plus-example recalls the more primitive rationalistic method of Guenzburg in *Aviezer*. It might further be said that the scene, in addition to making things vivid, actually deepens the thrust of the analysis in the way that dramatic showing enlarges discursive telling. A number of nuanced insights about the family dynamics becomes available only through the scene. We learn, for example, about the deeply compensatory nature of the mother's investment in her child, about the role of community and neighbor in exposing her dispossession, about the way in which the boy's perception of his father is mediated through his sensitivity to his mother's humiliation.

Yet taken as a whole, I would argue that the chief contribution made by this scene is knowledge of a different kind. The issue is not the greater effectiveness of dramatic means in communicating what the narrator already knows but the new quality of the knowledge he discovers after, and as a result of, those dramatic means being put into motion. What he discovers, in short, is an experience of empathy for the mother that was hitherto absent from his discussion of his parents. That analysis had evinced a clear understanding of his mother's plight but had nonetheless absorbed it into the larger nexus of human frailty and class envy into which he was born. All this belongs to an earlier time in the narrator's life. It remains a painful memory, but the overlay of irony in his analysis, especially in the opening unit of the chapter, works to keep it in the past. Now, although the Yom Tov scene may have initially been undertaken for the purposes of documenting and even probing this analysis, the accumulating effect of the scene is to break up the reification of the mother as an object of explanation and to break through to a newly felt empathic identification with her. For a moment the narrative point of view is transformed and we see the mother *from the inside*. Even though the focus is the mother, the import of the scene returns, finally, to the narrator and enacts a critical moment in the narrational process. The mature narrator's success in recovering his past selves and overcoming his alienation from them depends in large measure on his ability to accept the unwanted persistences of the past in the present. To identify with his mother's shame means, if only for the moment, to accept the persistence of his own shame, to forego the need to ironize it, and in so doing to restore something of himself.

Why does this shift take place? The effects of the movement from analysis to scene are clear enough, but the motives for it are less evident. A glimpse of an answer is given in the second section of the chapter (unit B above) in which the narrator dissociates himself from the sentimentalizers of childhood. This passage is an instance of a "return to the time of the writing" in which the speaker of a retrospective narrative interrupts his account of the past to reflect on his state of mind in the present act of the telling. As such, it stands at an opposite remove from the Yom Tov scene, in which the narrator's consciousness is momentarily dissolved into the past. After denigrating the romanticizers, the narrator describes his own situation:

> The shape of my past is hidden from the eyes of my memory by a mountain of sand that is dense and muddied and suspended like a sieve. As for the occasional facts that escape from the chaos [*hahafekhah*], I *know* them more than I *remember* them. Even so, they do not take on flesh and knit themselves into a single body. They remain very dark and heavy. (p. 8, emphases in text)

Against the pellucid memories of the romanticizers, the narrator counterposes an image of opacity that draws up just short of blindness. The sand mountain is itself not the past but a turgid and viscous barrier between the past and the narrator's memory. Even in the case of the few facts that make it through to him, he cannot, as some other writers claim to do, summon them up [*zokhran*] in rich and abundant detail; he can only "know them" [*yode'an*], that is, reexperience something of the emotional states emanating from these facts but not recollect their vivid and specific presence. Even these memories remain isolated and fragmentary and resist integration into a coherent shape.[16]

The image of the sand mountain lends itself to being read as something of an *ars poetica* if we attend to its two important classical allusions. The description of the mountain as suspended like a sieve [*kafui kegigit*] evokes a well-known midrash concerning the revelation at Sinai.[17] The midrash relates that in order to overcome the reluctance of the Israelites to accept the Torah, God uprooted Mt. Sinai and suspended it threateningly over their heads and *then* asked for their assent in receiving the Law. The reference to Sinai links the sand mountain to an experience which is both revelatory *and* coerced. Like the commandments, the memories the narrator receives are given to him from, and darkly inspired by, a reality beyond his own, but, also like the commandments, what is given is not necessarily what is asked for. Arriving unbidden, the memories carry imperatives and a burden of undischarged emotion. The second allusion draws on the vision of the dry bones in Ezekiel 37, in which the rehabilitation of Israel is symbolized by the knitting together of bones into skeletons which take on flesh and then return to life. While in the prophet's vision the process of reconstitution takes place spontaneously and miraculously—the skeletons put *themselves* back together—in the case of the narrator no such thing happens. If there is to be a reembodiment of the past, so it is implied, it will only come about through exertion and toil.

The twin themes of coercion and labor allow us to speculate about the logic of composition in the chapter we have been reading. The analysis of his mother's situation that opens the chapter is conducted with expositional balance and ironic acuity. The composure of the argument, however, is at odds with its deeper subject. The description of the mother's humiliation, a humiliation that continues to this day, must trigger in the narrator a set of painful feelings. Analysis, then, subverts itself. The presentation of difficult material, no matter how well thought out, generates feelings which cannot be handled in the analytic medium. First the narrator evades these feelings by generalizing them into his aside about writers who pretty up the anguish of childhood. But eventually he returns to the past and narrates the Yom Tov scene, and thereby makes a connection with feelings to which, so to speak, he has been impelled. The theme of toil comes into play when the scene is compared to what precedes it *as writing*. The use of the dramatic present tense and the concreteness of observation have already been mentioned. The scene is further distinguished by the structuring of the mother's disappointment as a series of worsening moments, the atten- tiveness to her inner life, and the general expansiveness of the scene and the controlled pacing of its discoveries. Now, we may be tempted to account for this phenomenon by simply saying that the font of memory has been unstoppered—perhaps because of the pain recalled in the analysis— and it now flows unstintingly. The sand mountain image, however, would seem to interdict that option and propose in its stead another explanation. The genesis of the scene may lie in one of those heavy, dark, solitary grains of fact that penetrate the barrier closing off the past. All that may be remembered is the feeling of the mother's shame, and around this kernel a finely imagined dramatic event is constructed. The scene, then, is an invention rather than a transcription, however much enhanced, of mem- ory. The narrator has labored with the tools of artifice, in terms of our original figure, to put living tissue on the dry bones of memory and make of them one body. This is a marker of the narrator's commitment to a self- ascribed aesthetic of authenticity. Others may encourage the illusion of childhood scenes vividly and effortlessly recalled. But as for the narrator, we are told, he tells the truth, and in so doing bares the motives that push him to undertake this hard work of the imagination.

The Cognitive Code Redefined: Religion at a Distance

If the Yom Tov scene represents a breakthrough to the inner world of the mother, is this a feat that the narrator can perform in relation to his own past inner life? Who can be more in need of empathy than he?[18] In other words, can what is done for the other be done for the self? Chapter 4, whose theme is the religious world of the child, presents a by-now familiar structure: a severe analysis of the behavior in question, a generalizing aside, and then a plunge into a series of scenic reevocations. The aside is particularly revealing. After dissecting the need for recognition and praise that animated the narrator's will to excel in his studies, and after poking fun at the dryness and irrelevancy of those studies for a young mind (laws of sacrifice, leprosy, and impurity), he looks up and remarks:

> Now, of course, it is impossible for me to understand my state of mind at that time. It seems to me now that my zeal for learning was outward only, something put on for others: my lips moved but my thoughts were far from [the issues of] leprosy and defilement. It is possible, however, that I make this judgment because of a present inability to comprehend the possibility of dutifully consuming such dry stuff and because of a tendency to forget the force exerted by habit . . . upon a young child. (ch. 4, p. 15)

The narrator is forced to entertain this option—and he offers it skeptically—because of an analytical contradiction. There must, logically, have been some real nourishment in his studies if he applied himself to them so single-mindedly. Yet when he immediately afterwards goes back to the past to resume his story, he begins with the admission: "Yes, in truth, not everything was devoid of feeling and knowledge; there was in addition some spiritual nourishment." What follows is a vivid, and at times lyrical, reconstruction of the inner religious experience of a child, experience which is made to seem not only plausible but richly sustaining of both spirit and imagination.[19] The mode of discourse in which these many pages are presented (pp. 16–18, 22–31) is largely scenic but in a way often different from the Yom Tov scene. Instead of dramatizing dialogue and events, these sections excel in the use of the free indirect discourse to evoke in condensed form the succession of perceptions and associations in the child's inner life. Again, we encounter the dialectical and self-transcending quality of the writing in *In Winter.* The narrator's examination of his past leads him into an impasse of painful alienation in which he can view his earlier self only with shame and incomprehension. As a way out he somehow manages to reimagine scenes from his past and thereby break through to a measure of empathy and comprehension. The passage quoted above offers some insight as to how this overcoming takes place. Inherent in the act of analysis is the capacity to hypothesize alternative explanations, and not simply the practice of dissecting and examining. The narrator reasons that he *must have had* some genuine connection to an experience in which he was so deeply immersed, and it is that speculation which makes possible the pages that follow. Consciousness as analysis can open possibilities as well as close them.

Brenner's reevocation of childhood piety elicits comparison with Feierberg's version of the same material in *Whither?* The fascination with the spiritual heroes and villains of the aggadah, the enchanted world of the *mitsvot* in which every sign discloses hidden meanings, the insatiability for secret lore about the messiah, the struggle with the Evil Urge as a soldier in God's army, the great privilege of Jewishness and the feeling of superiority over other boys—all these Feierbergian themes reappear here in condensed form with no effort to conceal their provenance. Feierberg, in a sense, owns this territory, as readers would realize when they came across *In Winter* in the pages of *Hashiloah* only five years after the publication of *Whither?* in the same journal. (The novella was published in 1899, immediately following Feierberg's death at the age of twenty-five.) What, then, is Brenner up to in these chapters? Aside from a possible *hommage* to his precursor, what differences are we urged to see in such a close echoing of materials? The answer is traceable to Brenner's desire, through his narrator, to put his own stamp on the by-now familiar story of the boy's upbringing within the world of tradition. This cognitive code, which carries themes of belief and ideology in the novel, does not exist merely in order to be appropriated by and reduced to a psychological reunderstanding of existence. For a moment in the novel the cognitive code stands alone.

In Brenner's retelling, this story undergoes a surprising revision. Feierberg had already represented a substantial departure from the Haskalah's indictment of the the tradition of imposing irrational and rote learning upon the clean slate of the child's mind. For Feierberg, this critique was beside the point because the metaphysical underpinnings of the tradition had collapsed calamitously, and the reforms of the Haskalah were of little use in comparison. The heder and beit midrash and the inner religious world of the child are presented in *Whither?* as if they existed "always already" under the sign of catastrophe. All these institutions and experiences are moribund and lead inevitably to constriction and entombment. The surprise is that in *In Winter* vitality is restored to these experiences. The exploits of aggadic heroes provide a fertile source for imaginative pleasures. ("Esau, Laban, Bilam—even the villains appeared in a special, magnificent aspect!" [ch 4, p. 16].) The interlocking worlds of symbolic gestures and sacred texts create an inexhaustibly meaningful system of signs ("In my life there was no such thing as unmeaningful practices; everything was spiritually alive . . . and everything reverberated in the upper spheres" [ch 6, p. 23].) The child's messianic fantasies do not lead to a sense of disorienting impotence, nor do they promote a dangerous grandiosity. Pride in being chosen and pity for non-Jews who must live without the commandments are signs of being securely anchored in the universe. ("Whenever I met a gentile I was overcome by pity. What a poor thing this creature is! . . . Not so the Jew; . . . for him the whole world was created and he stands at its center" [ch 4, p. 16].) Moreover, although the style of these pages owes much to the Feierbergian reverie with its vivid sense of inner movement, there is nothing here of the reverie's inevitable collapse into dispirited skepticism, as yet another desperate step is taken along the road to apostasy.[20]

In this reevocation of the inner religious world of childhood, one might hear an anticipation of the famous opening of Georg Lukács's *The Theory of the Novel*, written ten years later in 1914–15:

> Happy are those ages when the starry sky is the map of all possible paths—
> ages whose paths are illuminated by the light of the stars. Everything in such
> ages is new yet familiar, full of adventure yet their own. The world is wide and
> yet it is like a home, for the fire that burns in the soul is of the same essential
> nature as the stars; the world and the self, the light and the fire, are sharply
> distinct, yet they never become permanent strangers to one another, for fire is
> the soul of all light and all fire clothes itself in light.[21]

This happy unity between subject and object, inside and outside, is imagined by Lukács to have belonged to the experience of early Greek epic, and it is the disappearance of this world that later gives rise to the fallen-epic form of the novel. Although for Brenner's narrator this happy time was only ten or twelve years ago, it might just as well have been located in remote antiquity for all the relevance it bears to his present life. This is the difference between Feierberg and Brenner. For Feierberg, the wound is still open and the whole of existence has become contaminated; it is no longer possible to imagine early experiences as ever having been free of the infecting agent that led to a consumptive apostasy. Brenner's narrator speaks from the other side of the divide. He can appreciate, if not celebrate, the lost world precisely by virtue of the finality of the loss. Because that component of the past is finished and self-enclosed, it does not project itself into the present as an aching absence. For the narrator, in any case, the loss of faith was not the catastrophe it was for Feierberg's Nahman; a painful rite of passage, yes, but one all the more bearable for its now common occurrence and literary precedent. The real "dark night of the soul" comes for Feuerman later on, when he enters the flux of student society and is exposed to the manifold temptations to bad faith. But as for the religious world of childhood, the animus has been drained from it and the judgment neutralized.

In Winter makes an important distinction between the world of the fathers and the world of the father.[22] While the world of religious tradition may be viewed neutrally, even nostalgically, the reality of a particular father, *this* father, in his psychological individuality, is not a subject that puts judgment to rest. In chapter 6 Brenner brings these two dimensions into a neat intersection. The chapter pushes to a climax the sympathetic exploration of naïve piety in a description of the Days of Awe as experienced in the narrator's eleventh year. (Compare the use to which this season is put in *Whither?*) Released from heder during these weeks, he is at liberty to devote himself to studies of his own choosing and to luxuriate in the exalted beauty of the special penitential poems [*seliḥot*] recited in the synagogue before dawn. The beauty of the seliḥot awakens in him the desire to write his own sacred verses and to see his name spelled out in them as an alphabetical acrostic. The desire becomes a habit. The boy composes poems for special holidays and writes sketches of life at school and at home and dreams of the great treatises and commentaries on the Talmud and its codes he will one day publish. At this point the father intervenes and grips the boy in a cruel double bind. On the one hand, he shows the poems around town and brags about them as a way of enhancing his own status. On the other hand, he tightly controls Yirmiah's output ("According to him it is enough to write one big poem to show to people— no more is necessary" [ch 6, p. 25]), and he forces the boy to revise his work according to the father's dictates. When Yirmiah protests that he writes for himself and not for others, he is slapped in the face and ridiculed for thinking that writing can have any purpose other than display. In these scenes the motif of writing as self-expression is given an interesting twist. Writing is placed under attack *not* because it conceals the seeds of secularity that will later grow into apostasy. On the contrary, writing is depicted here as a natural outgrowth of the exposure by a sensitive soul to the poetry of religion. When the hand of repression strikes, the source of the blow is not the tradition but the pathology of the father, a psychological exigency conditioned by time and place yet in the end rooted in the shame of inadequacy and resentment.[23]

Contrasted to the father's shame are the pride and potency of Rabbi Hanan-Natan, the town's rabbinic authority and Yirmiah's teacher. Coming immediately after the story of the suppression of the son's writing by the father, chapter 7 is devoted wholly to presenting a portrait of the rabbi. The chapter is notable for the fact that in it the scrutiny of the analytic mode is almost entirely suspended; instead, the chapter is lavish in its use of the full battery of scenic techniques: sketch, anecdote, dialogue, and dramatic monologue. The portrait that emerges is of a man who embodies, powerfully and genuinely, the figure of the rabbi as scholar and teacher. Moreover, in terms of the world he inhabits he is the picture of a productive and generative man. He has created a yeshiva in the town and attracted students on the strength of his authority and charisma as a teacher. He is a writer known beyond local horizons for his erudition and his worthiness as an adversary in the scholarly controversies of the time. The rabbi is most vividly alive when he closets himself in his library and engages in the study of Torah for its own sake. Time stops; the outside world falls way. The rabbi plunges into the sea of talmudic learning and brings his powerful mind to bear in charting a course among contending interpretations. This is nothing less than an act of self-transcendence. He is a man who also inspires love in those close to him. An affecting monologue (p. 50), which is delivered by his wife the rebbitzen and which expresses her admiration of her husband and her pride in his learning, contrasts poignantly with the same expectations, so bitterly disappointed, that Yirmiah's mother has of *her* husband.

Taken as a whole, the figure of the rabbi in this chapter is an unusual presence in the novel. It serves no plot function; it is not ironic. It presents a way of living in the world which is neither double nor impaired. Moreover, all the sectors of his activity are suffused with and empowered by strong libidinal energies. The rabbi, in short, is an incarnation of being. Because the likes of him are attested to nowhere else in *In Winter*, the figure of the rabbi becomes a kind of benchmark in the system of existential values elaborated by the novel. That this embodiment of authority stands with feet firmly planted in the world of tradition should not be surprising—nor for that matter should it be binding. The narrator will later have to take the measure of his own authenticity under the very different conditions that obtain *after* the world of tradition, and the horizon of fulfillment will also, sadly, be different. Yet there is no longing for the lost world, just as there is no condemnation of it. Existence, both before and after, has undergone a reduction to a single existential-psychological standard, as well as a process of relativization. The father, in that world and at that time, fails to meet the standard; the rabbi succeeds. The novel asks the inevitable question: What, in *his* world and in *his* time, will be the narrator's record?

The trial, however, does not come during the first third of *In Winter*. The narrator-hero must first leave the domain of his parents and enter the world after faith in order to be so tested. This transfer of realms does not come about quickly. Some time after becoming bar mitsvah, Yirmiah goes off to a senior yeshiva in another town for some two years (the exact duration is unclear), until he is expelled for clandestine maskilic activities.[24] After returning home for two months, he sets off again for a year's study in a *kloiz* (a study house without the formal structure of a yeshiva), and returns home another time. It is only then that he finally makes his way to the metropolis, the provincial capital, where the crucial middle section, part two, of the novel will unfold. These comings and goings would seem to be the fledgling hesitations that precede the final flight of independence. The fact that this is *not* the case is the great structural surprise of the novel, as well as its greatest puzzle. In the last third of the novel, part three, the narrator goes home again, for no obvious reason, and the great journey outward that we have been prepared for all along becomes a journey that returns upon itself.

The account of the yeshiva years, which includes the attraction to Haskalah and the crisis of faith, is telescoped and elliptical. The entire period stretching between the year of the bar mitsvah to the post-yeshiva departure for the metropolis is covered by only two long chapters (9 and 10, pp. 33–45). The story of these years, which was presented with such high pathos and high drama by Lilienblum and Feierberg, elicits from Brenner little more than a sketchy treatment that fills in the gap between moments more central to the novel. It is as if the groping and desperation of these years, no matter how wrenching in actuality, have become a stale and familiar topos in the writing of them, such that the imagining of the ordeal can safely be left to the literary competence of the reader, who may if he wishes fill in the details from the literature of the time. Brenner, of course, does not refrain from putting something of his own stamp on this material, and it is worth noting a number points that are either special to his account or linked to larger themes in *In Winter*. Art, to begin with, plays a catalytic role in the narrator's fall into apostasy. A single, slight literary sketch which describes life truthfully and simply affects him much more deeply than massive tomes that strive to reconcile Torah with secular learning (p. 35). In publishing the little journal whose discovery brings about his expulsion from the yeshiva, the narrator serves as editor; he experiences this role, which he ennobles with the title *Redactor*, as if it were a sacred service and he a priest (p. 38). When the expulsion finally comes, the scene contrasts the venality of the narrator's fellow students with the dignified pathos of the yeshiva's principal, who is more hurt and be-wildered than righteously angered (pp. 38–39). The "absolute crisis" of religious faith, as we discussed in the opening of this chapter, makes its appearance as an absence in the text, merely a slight tear in its continuity. Finally, in his eventual haste to leave home for the metropolis, the narrator never ceases to feel empathy for his mother's anguish over his defection.

The Erotic Code: Desire and Shame

The narrator's departure for the metropolis brings to a conclusion part one of *In Winter*. Throughout this section we have traced the interplay between the cognitive and psychological codes. The cognitive code represents a revision of earlier accounts of religious development, while at the same time the psychological code rewrites the cognitive code according to a set of existential ciphers. Yet what of the erotic code, the code which figures so prominently in the last third of the novel and which functions so signifi-cantly to differentiate between the narrational and authorial frames of reference? In these early sections are we prepared for the later importance of the erotic code? The answer is that we are given a single narrative unit, chapter 5, which the narrator devotes to an attempt to locate the origins of his present troubles with women in the shame and awkwardness he experienced as a child. The chapter stands by itself and is not interwoven with the cognitive and psychological codes. Moreover, this is virtually the only instance in the novel in which the narrator addresses the erotic theme frontally, self-consciously, and analytically; for later in the novel the theme is acted out rather than thought about and remains entirely immanent in dramatic action. The dialectical and self-vitiating rationalizations that comprise chapter 5 make it a rich source for our understanding of the narrator's conscious and unconscious attitudes toward women and sexuality.[25]

The chapter as a whole is spoken as an involuntary digression. The narrator is in the course of describing his religious development when his account is shunted onto another track. Chapters 5 and 6 both begin with the same sentence, "I was then about ten years old and the youngest [chapter 6 adds: and poorest] of Rabbi Hanan-Natan's students" (pp. 18 and 22). The narrator had *intended* to discuss his studies, as he in fact does in chapter 6, but despite his opening gesture the first time around in chapter 5, he ends up talking about his shame in the presence of women. A subject has, ungovernably, asserted itself; and this is a subject for which there was apparently no room and no place in the narrator's plan for his presentation. This usurpation indicates the presence of a confessional pressure that burdens the narrator in the present time of the writing. Whether the pressure derives from the norms of other and earlier autobiographical works or from the more immediate inner turmoil of unresolved conflicts, the need to make a statement and put himself on the record cannot be resisted.

After pages of arguments and disclosures, the digression—and with it the chapter—comes to an abrupt halt with a self-administered reprimand.

> But enough. What is wanted here is craftsmanship, a quality whose absence the preceding pages bear witness to. I've covered a sheet with words and words— but I've said nothing. Yes, it's true that I have a burning desire to tell all. Yet the more I add color upon color the more the main thing remains hidden deep inside me, shrouded and elusive. . . .
> Yes, enough. It's necessary to return to the subject. Since this won't turn out to be an interesting novel in any case, perhaps the *un*interesting glimmers of memory are best after all. (p. 22)

The self-rebuke turns on a distinction between craft or art [*omanut*] and confession. The former demands discipline and structure, while the apologetic rationalizations of the preceding pages seem to him conspicuously lacking in these qualities. The narrator's literary code, we may assume from his remarks, calls for vigilance against ungovernable confessional urges, against—to apply the terms developed here—self-analysis run riot as opposed to the more disciplined objectification of scenic discourse. (The loss of control is, of course, only self-ascribed; the reader relishes the lapse and sees in it the "artful" hand of the author controlling the release of information about the narrator's character and consciousness.) Yet it is not simply a question of method. Even if he were to strive for the correct coloration and nuance, that "main thing" [*hadavar ha'ikari*], the very subject of sexuality, remains inaccessible.[26] Without it, however, there is not much chance of producing an "interesting novel," interesting at least in the conventional sense of the term. (There is a play here between the noun *'inyani*, "my subject, the subject of the book, which is me," and the adjective *me'anyen*, "interesting.") The narrator long ago reconciled himself to this eventuality; the opening words of *In Winter,* it may be recalled, announce rather proudly that the work which follows is not a novel nor does it relate heroic or amorous exploits. In short, because the narrator's brief life has known no real experience of women, the subject has no rightful place in his story, a story which must base itself on the "glimmers of memory" of things that did happen rather than on the febrile desire for those that did not.

What does manage to get said before the digression is terminated is, as it happens, quite a lot. The narrator makes statements about four topics: his shameful feelings about girls as a child, the conviction of his ugliness as a continuity in his life, his deep intellectual ambivalence toward women as a group, and the even deeper confusion he experiences in relation to women as individuals. In the course of the chapter, each of these topics in turn suffers the same fate. Although the narrator begins his exposition in declarative tones intended to set the record straight, something inevitably goes awry, and the argument is undercut and then collapses. The agent of the mischief in each case is some aspect of erotic conflict which, presumably resolved, remains very much unpacified and irrepressible. In the first section of the chapter, for example, the narrator describes his apartness from the flirtations that took place between the other students of Rabbi Hanan-Natan and three sisters who lived next door. In the face of all such encounters as a child Yirmiah stood painfully abashed. Convinced of his ugliness, he interprets every girlish giggle to be at his expense. And in view of the stern admonitions against impure thoughts, thoughts for which one can lose one's place in the World to Come in but a moment, Yirmiah tries to be grateful that, in making him unattractive, God has taken him out of the game and thereby saved him from sin. The narrator's point, then, is that unlike other children he was removed from this category of experience and knew little of it. This picture is undone, however, by an unstilled voice that betrays the boy's obsession with sexuality and his dread over the mortal consequences of his thoughts. Though he be ugly and apart—and he knows and accepts his fate—he cannot stop wanting and desiring. "I am incapable of keeping the sacred promise I made countless times not to look at girls; I must be counted an incorrigible sinner, for how many times did I shed oceans of tears in contrition and make an absolute vow to steer clear of sin—*the* sin—only to fail the test" (pp. 19–20).

The narrator's conviction of his ugliness is linked to his mother's disfigurement by smallpox. As this cruel blow of fate put her at a disadvantage in life and delivered her into the hands of her husband, so the son believes that his disability makes him repellent to women and bars him from participation in romantic relations. He points to the slovenliness of his dress and the awkwardness of his manners as comprising a thread of continuity between his life in yeshiva and his years as an extern in the metropolis, where he kept to the long *kapota* well after realizing he should be wearing more Western dress. The narrator collaborates in this negative self-presentation; that is to say that he acts and dresses in a way which confirms and amplifies the unsightliness which, if we are to believe him, fate has visited upon him. The diagnosis, I think, is clear. Without minimizing the anguish resulting from this self-perception, it is a fair guess that Feuerman uses his appearance, both endowed and cultivated, as a way of justifying his avoidance of erotic entanglement. The entrenchment of this defense is evident in the elaborate ideological justifications he brings to bear: talmudic dicta disparaging vanity and sensuality, the championing of Hebraic justice over Hellenic beauty, and, especially, the polemics against aesthetics by such Russian writers of the 1860s as Pisarev. But again, the formidable argument constructed by the narrator founders and breaks apart on the very evidence it has adduced. His delight in reading Pisarev's pronouncements turns into self-doubt when he glances at Pisarev's handsome likeness in a portrait. He reasons that Piserev, as a handsome man, has the luxury of denouncing aesthetics, while he, the narrator, is open to the charge of resentment. The narrator becomes mired in the dialectic of bad faith, and the section trails off into the stuttering protests of a man trying to shore up a collapsed position.

The presentation of a self-sabotaging defense becomes even more conspicuous in the next section, in which the narrator surveys the history of his attitudes toward women as a group (pp. 20-21). The narrator's purpose is ostensibly to demonstrate that his ambivalence is not self-invented but derives from cleavages inherent in the two intellectual systems that have shaped his views and attitudes. The Talmud lavishes praise upon the matriarchs and other righteous women, yet at the same time it disqualifies women from performing many sacred tasks and questions their seriousness and reliability. When the narrator leaves Jewish for Russian literature, he finds the same contradiction. Woman in the abstract may be idealized and extolled but individual women are portrayed as calculating, vain, and incapable of critical thought. As if to illustrate the inescapable influence of these doctrines upon him, the narrator switches from the expositional manner in which he has been writing until this point and stages a dramatized debate on the topic of the emancipation of women. The debate is wittily put on. The narrator argues both sides himself; the arguments, mere fragments of ideas in quick succession, make for a parody of intellectual discourse; and the apparatus of the exchange apes talmudic casuistry (*anu lemeidim . . .*). The chief lesson of the debate, however, is to underscore the fact that there is in actuality no debate at all. Just as the seemingly balanced assertions of Jewish and Russian literature are really a cover for a deeply ingrained misogyny, so too the narrator's intellectual prevarications disguise a barely buried fear and resentment of women.

His enmity is openly admitted in the chapter's final section. He confesses his hostility to conventionally beautiful women, "because they ignore me entirely, mock me, and scorn my overtures" (p. 22). Nor does he entertain more positive feeling for the mannish and emancipated New

Woman, "perhaps because I have known more of them, or perhaps because they have lost the kind of feminine charm that interests me" (p. 22). Agitated by the feelings raised by these associations, the narrator gives up the attempt to shape the flow of his words into an analytic argument on his behalf. He breaks down into a confession which is the closest thing we have in the novel to a conscious understanding of his situation. Despite pretenses to a worked-out intellectual position concerning women or to an aloofness in their presence, the narrator finds himself in a constant state of pain. "The bonfires of hell burn in me. I could cry out and moan like an animal felled by a shot" (p. 22). Why this ordeal?

> Like a torch there burns within me the desire *to be in love*, even if only anguish comes from it. Never have I known this feeling that shakes the world! . . . No matter how much I understand, no matter how ridiculous it is, no matter how much I have struggled to say no, no matter how much I have contemplated the dangers brought on by blind desire, I have not been able to free myself from the will to love. (p. 22)

He has knowledge but he cannot act on it. He knows not only that love would be a calamity for him but also that it is impossible to begin with. He is forbidden it. Nonetheless, he goes on wanting, and this desire produces a social existence of misspent emotion and pretense. First, he hates women because of what they arouse in him; then he resents men who succeed with women; and finally he spins a web of intellectualizations around his hatred. He poses as a spirit aloof from entanglements, while all the time his passions are visible for anyone who cares to see. He lives in a constant state of shame, exposed to the world for being what he cannot accept in himself. There cannot be, in short, any greater violation of the existential standard of authenticity that the narrator has laid down in the novel than his own case.

SIX

The Veil of Ideas and the Reduction of Self

Religious crisis behind him, the young hero is free to set out for the big city to pursue an enlightened education and participate in the great issues of the times. His life is now his own to fashion, and what he makes of it in the world beyond the tradition becomes the theme of the autobiographical enterprise. For Lilienblum in the 1870s, this moment was attended less by exhilaration than by despair. Encumbered by an early marriage and sapped by loneliness, Lilienblum fails to master the gymnasium curriculum and is rescued from his ordeal only by a conversion to political Zionism in the wake of the 1881 pogroms. It was in 1881, too, that Brenner was born, and since Lilienblum's time much had changed in the tenor of Jewish student life in the larger cities. By the turn of the century, the road from shtetl to city was much traveled, and a callow youth from the provinces could expect to be received into the ample company of other young men—and now women—who had preceded him in making the journey.[1] The concerns of these "externs" were hardly limited to the getting of an education. This was a milieu electrified by the ideological and political currents of prerevoltionary Russia; socialism, communism, and nationalism, in their various configurations, contended vehemently for the allegiance of Jewish youth. Alongside their claims stood the non-ideological options of emigration to the West and, to the degree that Russian society would permit it, the life of a bourgeois professional.

In Winter is a story about declining these choices—all of them. The novel's protagonist Yirmiah Feuerman refuses to give himself over to any of the new movements and ideas, not to mention the aspiration to worldly comfort and security. He is in the student subculture that surrounds him but not of it. The consciousness he inhabits becomes the lens through which the ideologies of the times are revealed as something other than what they seem to be. The present moment, which seems on the surface to embody the free availability of youthful energies to the hopeful cause of social change, is shown instead to be a great void created by the disappearance of God. In their offer of comprehensive explanatory systems, in their ability to engender belief, and in the sometime sense of fellowship they provide, the new ideologies are parallel in structure and function to the religious traditions they replaced. Yet the verve and innocence with which the narrator's contemporaries deliver themselves to these new movements display little awareness of their function as substitute religions. These young people imagine that they, and the world, have been transformed, whereas in truth they have only exchanged one dispensation for another.[2] It is not as if the narrator rejects the truth-claims of religion, new or old, in themselves, or would not give himself over to an ideology if he could; rather for him, the metaphysical underpinnings of such structures have, simply and irreversibly, collapsed. The option is no longer there. Feuerman observes the devotion of the new true believers and listens to their passionate ideological debates, and what he sees beneath all this is a desperate frenzy to escape the horror of metaphysical absence.

The knowledge that he is no longer capable of belief does not mean that Feuerman cannot be tempted. The middle sections of *In Winter* have the quality of a morality play. Metaphysical absence is indeed horrible: cold, lonely, and bottomless. Each of the youthful socialists or communists who enters the narrator's world has some version of a spiritual refuge to offer, and Feuerman does not remain entirely aloof. "I have known many gods," he admits, "but I contemplated them more than I worshiped them" (ch. 12, p. 56).[3] But his habit of hyperscrutiny *(nakranut),* which seemed like such a liability in the first third of the novel, here stands him in good stead as he dissects the contradictions inherent in the new schemes for salvation. The refusal to abjure his Jewish identity, and its significance for him, provides another yardstick by which the universalist dreams of other young Jews are to be measured. Feuerman is not without his own commitments, but commitment for him never becomes obeisance. His sympathies lie with the Jewish national revival and with the Hebrew language as its vehicle, although apparently *not* with political Zionism or any other redemptive scheme. From his own declarations we learn nothing whatsoever about his opinions. Feuerman's nationalism comes up only as a butt of ridicule among his friends, who can hardly believe that such an intelligent man would hold such regressive views.

It would be a mistake, however, to treat *In Winter* in its middle sections as a drama of ideas. There survives here only the ghost of the kind of Russian novel in which philosophical and theological worldviews engage in a dialectical contest of the most serius sort. Instead of ideas themselves, Brenner is interested in the *fit* between ideas and the self: the spectrum along which sincerity of commitment becomes evasion and hyprocrisy. The total and selfless devotion to historical materialism embodied by a character named Chaimowitch interests the narrator not for the ideological choice it represents, which he finds comically self-hating, but for the innocence it exemplifies. There are at the same time other students who, while busy studying for their professions, pick up and try on opinions as if they were the fashions of the day. The irony underlying these ideological follies is that their notions remain immaculately uncompromised by any action in the real world. Only the unfortunate Chaimowitch makes good on his proletarian commitments by undertaking to become a factory worker. Ideas exist in the novel only as talk, and it is only through this talk that the characters are realized.[4] The seemingly endless discussions among Feuerman's comrades are in fact endless, because they have no beginning or end. These exchanges serve not to confirm or disconfirm any one of a number of ideological tendencies but to illustrate a variety of existential styles, the possible stances the self can adopt in relation to ideas and ideology. Speech is a powerful instanciation in these chapters, and the glib, repetitive, desultory, and coercive way in which characters deliver themselves reveals much about the desperation that lies underneath. Where is the narrator in this babble of voices? At times his laconic interjections have the force of deflating the bombastic certainties of others. When forced to articulate his own convictions, his stuttering half-sentences contrast sharply with the overabundant eloquence that surrounds him. Feuerman's development is marked by a progress toward silence. Withdrawal from the war of discourses—a kind of moral aphasia—can in the end be the only response of a man who has seen the void behind the discourse and has had the courage to abide it.

The city years in *In Winter* are divided into two phases. The first echoes and revises Lilienblum's description of the infantilizing ordeal of going back to school as an adult; in the second phase, with the attempt at education abandoned, Brenner charts his own territory by exploring the option of nonparticipation in the face of the new "religions" of the day. This act of silence, which is presented as a kind of keeping-faith-with-the-void, constitutes the ostensible climax of the novel as a whole. At the level of the existential-psychological code, which represents the limits of the narrator's consciousness of his own situation, Feuerman has successfully withstood a grave test to his authenticity. He has resisted, though at a cost, being caught up in the false surrogates for the religion he has lost. This victory, however, does not remain unchallenged. At the level of the erotic code, which comes to the foreground in the last third of the novel, Feuerman falters seriously in the project of self-knowledge and self-acceptance. His failure has the effect of undermining his earlier achievement and substituting one kind of climax for another. The meaning of this earlier achievement is rendered clearer and more poignant by an interlude inserted between the two stages of Feuerman's experience in the city, the educational phase and the ideological phase. The interlude focuses on the figure of Chaimowitch, who is the only individualized presence amidst the chorus of voices in the metropolis. The innocence and sincerity of his devotion to historical materialism make Chaimowitch into a principle of pure impurity against which Feuerman can better understand himself.

Feuerman's situation upon his arrival in the city is miserable but in no way remarkable. The background will be familiar from previous texts in the autobiographical tradition. As an extern, that is, a student who is not matriculated in the gymnasium, Feuerman must master the curriculum on his own before he can think of attending a school of higher learning. Since he has little Russian and no benefit of preparatory studies in classical languages, geography, and mathematics, the task is an overwhelming one and unthinkable without help from tutors. The only available tutors are the Jewish gymnasium students, the pampered sons of Russified middle-class families; they in turn have nothing but contempt for these awkward and bedraggled ex-yeshiva students, several years their senior, who must beg them for free lessons. As part of Feuerman's humiliation, he is forced to become a tutor as well as a tutee. The means of supporting himself during this period is offering lessons to the unwilling children of assimilating mercantile Jewish families in just those religious subjects he has recently rejected and lost faith in. Even with the money from tutoring, it is a life of destitution and makeshift arrangements. Like autobiographical heroes who preceded him, Feuerman must face these pressures with few resources from his own past. His mastery over the erudite world of talmudic learning, for which he labored so long, counts for nothing in the new regime of secular studies; once a prodigy, he is now behind himself, an aging student of rudimentary subjects. Even crueler perhaps is the indifference of the city to his newly won identity. By publishing an underground maskilic journal in his yeshiva and by leaving his parents' home, Feuerman made a dramatic break with the a world to which he made a difference and where his defection strongly registered. In the city, however, his rejections and affirmations mean little. The Philistine merchant families and the radicalized student ideologues alike find Feuerman quaintly typical and his commitment to the Jewish national revival and the Hebrew language irrelevant.

However conventionalized the milieu in which Brenner places his narrator, Feuerman's mind remains a source of fresh perspectives. His responses have something more to tell us than did Lilienblum's when he first described this by-now familiar setting thirty years earlier. Lilienblum was, to be sure, a keen observer of his emotions: the loneliness of isolation in the city, the hurt over the invisibility of his importance to those around him, and the frustration from his failing attempts to master basic academic studies. Yet although he recorded his pain, Lilienblum understood little of its meaning. For Feuerman, on the other hand, the suffering that attends this stage in his development, in all its awefulness, is not perceived as differing at bottom from the pain of his earlier life.

> I was lower in my own estimation than any man on the face of the earth. I would avert my eyes and suffer distress if anyone looked at me. I knew, to be sure, that I was not without some talent. But . . . from all the attainments I had so painstakingly accumulated since childhood, nothing was left. In my eighteenth year I felt as if I was still a child. (ch. 11, p. 46)

The humiliation, the vulnerability, and the dispossession that overwhelms the narrator as a young man form a complex that is not fundamentally different in kind from his childhood ordeals as the town's prodigy put on display by his father. Nor, in fact, does it differ from the needs that motivate his mother's dependence upon his father's regard, nor the father's dependence upon the opinion of the world. All these are expressions of a modal state of abashment in which the self experiences itself as standing exposed before the world. Starting out alone and emptyhanded in the big city is simply another manifestation of an unchanging human situation founded upon shame and dependence.

The familiarity of pain does not make it any less painful, nor any easier to bear. These sections of *In Winter* are particularly rich in their exploration of the evasions engaged in both by the young Feuerman in the midst of his city years and by the only slightly less young Feuerman who tells the story. For the former, the narrator-as-character, the misery of the present hour can be submerged in reveries of future achievement. "My eyes were fixed on the future, and I felt within me the power and strength to take possession of it" (ch. 11, p. 46).[5] The glittering prizes that are sure to reward his perseverance enable the narrator to transfigure his real privations into a kind of "ecstasy of the agony."

> In this change in my life, in my loneliness, in my near-destitute state, I experienced an exaltation, the nearing of an ideal, an ennobling poetry. When I used to speak to people about that time, my voice would become empassioned, angry, and on occasion despairing, . . . but under no circumstances would I ever complain, despite my lack of shelter, food, and a tutor. (ch. 11, p. 47)

It proves no less difficult, though difficult in a different way, for the retrospective narrator to face the extremity of *his* situation even at a remove in time. The account of this period in his life begins forthrightly enough with an apology and an assertion which together echo the opening lines of the novel. My past, he admits, is wretched, dim, and lowly; it is nevertheless who I am and all I have to offer. Yet instead of proceeding straightway to delineate the terms of his misery, the narrator pauses over the associations raised by the word "wretched" [*umlal*] and is soon lost in a baggy digression on the role of thinking as the natural enemy of the will to live. The pseudo-philosophical ruminations are so transparently ridiculous and derivative that the narrator cuts himself off by exclaiming: "Enough! Where did I begin? Yes, with the fact that I was wretched" (p. 46). He then gets on with the business of making his wretchedness concretely imaginable.

The digression and the recovery from it are instances of a by-now familiar pattern in the composition of *In Winter:* the shift from analysis to scene. Each time the narrator undertakes to describe a new stage in his development, he avoids engaging emotionally difficult material directly. He first generalizes and philosophizes about his condition and only then is he moved to reevoke events and feelings. The recourse to scenic representation, moreover, usually results in a gain in empathy realized by the narrator as a greater measure of self-acceptance. In these sections on Feuerman's failed attempts at getting a secular education, the special strategy employed is comic pathos. The humilating rituals of tutelage become less horrible in retrospect because the goal of all these efforts is made to seem not a little ridiculous. Faced by the prospect of having to acquire a tutor, for example, Feuerman is mortified by the image he will present to a well-groomed and self-satisfied gymnasium student. He involuntarily repeats to himself the word "dust rag" [*smartut*] over and over again, and in an anticipatory imagining of the scene, he undergoes a Kafkaesque metamorphosis: "I am like a worm in their eyes, not a man but a worm, crawling, ridiculous, pathetic, cowed" (p. 50). (The image of the worm will recur at a crucial point later in the novel.) When in fact he finally secures the services of a tutor, the reality turns out to be almost as bad as he imagined. In the tutor's household he is treated, literally, like dirt and required to clean himself off before being admitted to the boy's room. He is kept waiting for their meeting, which is often canceled if the least opportunity for alternative amusement should arise. In the anxiety of waiting Feuerman's mind goes blank and he is treated by his tutor to a lecture on the necessity of hard work and industrious application to one's studies. Yet in the retrospective presentation of this scene, the tyranny of the tutor is qualified, if not wholly undercut. This is a spoiled and patronizing adolescent whose authority over Feuerman derives solely from the fact that his middle-class family is a half-generation along in the process of Russification. For all this, Feuerman's self-abasement at the time was no less excruciating, but at least in his later incarnation as narrator this ordeal can be made to devolve into a comedy of social embarrassment.

The worthiness of the ordeal is again the issue. What is so important about the Russian gymnasium curriculum that so much pain should be endured on its behalf? This is perhaps the most quintessentially Lilienblumian moment in Brenner's novel. Much of *Sins of Youth* is devoted to its author's painstaking efforts, with repeated setbacks, to master the rudimentary curriculum, only to have the importance of his goal swept away by the pogroms of 1881 and the national reawakening. Yet whereas the account of Lilienblum's ordeal takes up a large portion of his autobiography and is told with pathos and self-pity, Brenner dispatches this phase in a few ironic pages. And whereas Lilienblum's dilemma is "solved" by a kind of *deus ex machina* in the form of an historical event that massively impinges upon his life, Brenner's hero remains stuck inside his situation, untransformed and unredeemed. It is not as if Feuerman is not tempted. He briefly entertains a reverie of glorious service to his people: "Society is waiting for me . . .—the Jewish nation, for whom I must live and sacrifice myself, awaits my arrival so that I can save it" (p. 53).

The reverie soon collapses and makes room for less exalted moods. "This period, however, in which I was abrim with ideas, viewpoints, and new information, suddenly fizzled and gave way to its opposite: a period of reflection, doubts, and immense boredom" (pp. 53–54). What the narrator means by reflection (he makes self-conscious use of the European term in transliteration) is not introspective meditation but a morbid state of indecision in which the mind is pulled back and forth between extremes. The scenic technique employed here is the interior monologue.[6] After returning home from giving Hebrew lessons, Feuerman attempts to apply himself to his geometry books, as he yields to one diversion after another. His attention glances off the opaque school texts and drifts to thoughts of Tolstoy's literary judgments, to the difficulty for him of Russian literature, the joys of those who can read literature in their mother tongue, and, of course, the poverty of Hebrew literature. He catches himself and forces his mind back to the theorems and the formulas, which he repeats without comprehension. He becomes outraged at the irrelevancy of his studies and declares his intention to become a kind of Jewish narodnik, wandering the villages and preaching to the simple folk. "I sink into boredom for a week, two weeks, a whole month, I'm incapable of doing anything. I sleep days as well as nights, . . . fifteen hours at a stretch in my clothes and shoes" (p. 55). But there are still times when he will suddenly awake in the middle of the night, full of energy as never before, and fall upon his books with a ravenous hunger that abates only after hours of uninterrupted study.

This manic-depressive cycle, with its moments of study, avoidance, boredom, lethargy, and frenzied recommitment, describes the process of a relationship coming undone. From the beginning, Feuerman's commitment to his studies had never been unreserved. He had been enacting the collective expectation that the break with home and tradition is followed by the getting of enlightenment in the form of Western academic studies. But for Feuerman, the inner connection cannot be made. He is a hero born either too late or too perverse for education, in the conventional sense, to be the answer to his condition.

The narrator's *sentimental* education, however, is hardly arrested. The next move takes him from education to ideology. As Feuerman lets go of his identity as a belated gymnasium student, he enters the maelstrom of social and political ideas churning up Russian Jewish student society. Yet for Brenner, through his narrator, these ideas hold little interest as such. Rather than being laid out and placed in competition, ideological positions are reduced to fragments of discourse which then function in the novel as existential signatures. A good example is Tolstoy, who is the object of Feuerman's first blush of ideological passion. He is attracted by Tolstoy's critique of Western decadence, his simple and heartfelt appeal to human goodness, his conception of society as made up of individual souls, and his glorification of crafts and agricultural labor. Feuerman, to the great amusement of local carpenters and cobblers, even goes around town hoping to be taken on as an apprentice and thereby escape the ignominy of his employment as a Hebrew tutor. Now, the romance of Tolstoyan ideas is not adduced in the novel simply to document a stage in the progress of the hero's social opinions. By means of the supple analytic skills of the narrator, these youthful enthusiams are approached from another angle. They are understood as the products of a jejeune narcissism. "I had few acquaintances at the time, and then only by accident; I had no regular human society because of my intentional isolation, my avoidance of self-disclosure, and my extreme shyness, a quality which derived from an overweaning self-love combined with a smallness of soul" (ch. 12, p. 60). It is this pathological fear of contact, argues the narrator-analyst, which is responsible for Feuerman's attraction to a doctrine which places the individual, his moral world, and its capacity for perfection at the center of a conception of society; similarly in the case of Tolstoy's hopes for a "kingdom of heaven" upon earth. This vision appeals naturally to a soul which, unlike the narrator's, so far knows nothing of the grim struggle for existence in which the effort to dominate the other rarely abates. In these acts of demystification we see the workings of a process familiar from the first sections of *In Winter:* the transformation of the cognitive code into the psychological code. Whereas earlier it was religious beliefs and institutions that comprised the cognitive materials, it is now political and social ideas and ideologies. The context has been transposed but the mechanism remains the same.

The weight of this retrospective wisdom is enormous. The features and physiognomy of the young Feuerman are barely perceptible beneath the closely argued interpretations presented by the older narrator. We discover less about the beliefs held at the time than about their motives, puzzled over and tortuously construed, at a later remove. This is the analytic indulgence that opens many of these sections of the novel, and it is accompanied in this instance by an especially acute attack of self-loathing. The issue again is the unwanted but inalienable habit of *nakranut*, hyperscrutiny: "I am indeed hypercritical and peck around in my own rubbish. I am incapable of letting pass the most transient feeling or the most trivial thought without an analysis that penetrates to the depths. And one thought evokes subsidiary thoughts, one heaped on top of the other" (ch. 12, p. 57). The threat of paralysis and engulfment is averted this time by the narrator's attempt to reach outside his own subjectivity and to present to the reader the reality of another person—his friend Chaimowitch.[7] Even this release is nearly subverted: "Take, for example, my feeling of friendship toward Chaimowitch. What ostensible reasons for faultfinding could there be here? Nevertheless, how many times did I probe in this area and analyze my slightest feelings?" (p. 57). The narrator does manage to get on with the presentation of Chaimowitch, and in doing so Brenner demonstrates, as he did in the description of the mother and father earlier in the novel, a vital difference between his enterprise and Lilienblum's autobiography: the dimension of intersubjectivity. For all of Brenner's admiration for *Sins of Youth*, he was aware that Lilienblum was limited by his capacity "to know only himself and not others. Psychological penetration regarding other people was foreign to him."[8] This is not to say that the centripetal forces of self-absorption are not strong in *In Winter* as well, but the struggle to resist them, and the occasional successes in doing so, are raised to a level of consciousness and thematized.

Chaimowitch is the son of a once well-off Russified Jewish family whose fortunes are in decline. Although educated in Jewish schools, he has retained little knowledge and less consciousness of Judiasm. He was tutored privately with a view to his entering the university, but he twice failed the entrance examinations and disappointed the expectations placed in him. Chaimowitch's political outlook is straightforwardly communist-materialist. For him all issues boil down to the question of whether or not a given course of action will put bread on the table of the masses. Statistics and economic analysis are his basic tools for understanding reality, and all philosophical ideas can be explained by their origin in a particular social class. Nationalisms, and Zionism in particular, are a regressive mystification which brings no practical amelioration to the people. Yet, he allows, the Jews as a group are persecuted, but only because of their anomalous economic position, and they will save themselves only by identifying their true interests with those of the proletariat rather than seeking refuge in the bourgeois utopianism of Zionism.

Now, Feuerman is not easily fooled. He knows that there is much in Chaimowitch's outlook that is simply wrong. The grand reductiveness of the analysis, to begin with, gives offense to Feuerman's sense of complexity: "For Chaimowitch everything is as clear as day. The two terms 'bourgeoisie' and 'proletariat' consume him entirely. All the questions of life are subsumed for him under the question of labor and property, or, more accurately, there *is* no other question in life" (ch. 12, p. 63). He is also aware of the large measure of Jewish self-hatred involved in Chaimowitch's dissociating himself from his origins, and Feuerman further recognizes the psychological motives for his remaking himself as a radical. Yet for all this, Feuerman loves Chaimowitch, who becomes his one true friend in his sojourn in the city. The attractiveness of Chaimowitch derives in part from factors of temperament which are not only unrelated to his austere ideological position but at odds with it, and in part, paradoxically, from the very totality of his identification with that ideology. Chaimowitch is a genuinely affectionate and kind person. He gives Feuerman a place to live when he needs it and encourages him to do something with his life even if it takes a direction not to his liking. He is possessed of a thoroughgoing joy of living which leads him continually to draw others into conversation. He exists in a constant state of nervous agitation: "The smallest fact would set off an effusion of sympathy or an attack of indignation. His excitement was that of a child" (p. 57).

It is this childlike quality that supplies the connection between

Chaimowitch's temperament and his politics. What impresses Feuerman most about Chaimowitch is his innocence. This is "a curious and special innocence that seemed to be guileless—but perhaps not" (ch. 12, p. 57). This quality, the narrator implies, is the innocence of a true believer. The disembodied voices of the many communists, socialists, assimilationists, and Zionists are heard throughout *In Winter,* but none except for Chaimowitch's is allowed to become incarnated in the world of the novel. Perhaps because he was not born into the world of faith as was Feuerman, Chaimowitch can be a true and happy convert to one of the new nineteenth-century secular religions. The doctrines of Chaimowitch's religion are in many ways, though obviously not in others, beside the point; the fact that the system as a whole is founded on bad faith does not take away from the possibility, once inside, of pure faith and pure faithfulness. However kind and affectionate Chaimowitch may be by nature, his *animation,* his being full of life, is fueled from roots that tap into a reservoir of ontological security. The future of *this* illusion is not clear. The judgment the novel makes on the viability of the option represented by Chaimowitch remains equivocal. He drops from sight and only two facts about him are later reported: out of identification with the workers he has gone to work in a factory and later he is forced to flee arrest as a radical. He seems to remain faithful, and it is implied that his end may also be a religious consummation: a martyrdom.[9]

Chaimowitch's serenity has a devastating effect on Feuerman's intellectual world. The latter's attraction to Tolstoyan humanism makes the easiest of targets for Chaimowitch's materialist dialectics. Feuerman's Jewish commitments, however, are of course more deeply rooted in sentiment and personal history, and when these foundations are eventually shaken by Chaimowitch's arguments, the potential for destruction proves much greater. Like many other former yeshiva students who have lost their faith, Feuerman closely identifies with the cultural Zionist analysis of the crisis of Judaism and with a vision of Jewish national revival which places a modern literature in Hebrew at its center. What is surprising is that, given the appropriateness of these convictions on many counts, they should turn out to be so easily swept aside. The implication is that even these values— shared, incidentally, by the small Hebrew-reading public of the time—are in some essential way irrelevant to the self and they act as a kind of filler insulating man from the true bareness of existence. In adopting the ideals of Jewish nationalism Feuerman has merely exchanged one dispensation for another; although the substance has been humanized, the metaphysics of belief persists. The point is made through language, specifically the manipulation of rhetoric, and the contrast of discourses that takes place between Chaimowitch and Feuerman sets the stage for the next several chapters.

The distance separating these beliefs from Feuerman's self is already evident in the way they present themselves to his consciousness as slogans rather than ideas. In discussing Chaimowitch's indifference to Jewish concerns, the narrator lists the issues important to him as a young Jewish intellectual.

> "The sons who were banished from their Father's table"; the great and curious historical tragedy of an ancient people expiring for thousands of years without dying; the war between its ideals and the outside world with its alien perceptions; the excellent sons of this people who rot in the cellar and leave [the people] for other worlds as the memory fades from mind; the scorn and privation bequeathed by the world to this humbled giant; its awakening to new life and the possibility of redemption; its literature and thought, bursting out. . . . (p. 61)

The inflated and awkward rhetoric of this catalogue is clear, as is the fact that it *is* a catalogue, an inventorying of ideas rather than a thinking of them. Even without the benefit of the Hebrew, the pathos and hyperboles of these formulations set them off, violently, from the ironic understatement characteristic of both the narrator and his earlier incarnations. These slogans, taken from controversies in the Hebrew periodical press of the time, have the status in Feuerman's consciousness of quotations, and they never cease to suggest sketches of discourse that have been borrowed from another context and never assimilated. What follows is a further reduction in which these grandiloquent formulations are shrunken down to a rag-tag of phrases that bang about in Feuerman's head: "renaissance of the nation . . . the ideals of Judaism . . . national consciousness . . . evolution according to the national spirit. . . ." The slogans become labels, and it takes very little for Chaimowitch simply to peel them off. In launching his voluble and good-natured tirades against Feuerman's benighted notions, Chaimowitch believes he is merely clearing a space and sweeping aside the ideological debris so that a proper set of values can be set up and installed. The consequences, however, are quite otherwise. In the space swept clean in Feuerman's soul *nothing* can be implanted any longer. "Before long all my 'former values' fell apart. . . . There then arose within me a black despair concerning the life I was stuck in, and then I realized that this despair was nothing other than an embodiment of my life" (p. 63).

In his blithe self-assurance, Chaimowitch characteristically misreads Feuerman's situation, and, at the same time, offers him a way out. When Feuerman inveighs against books and ideologies whose competing messages cancel each other out and in the end come to nothing, Chaimowitch labels this outcry a form of pessimism. For Chaimowitch, pessimism is the self-pitying complaint of a displaced class, the bitter lament of the bourgeoisie as it views its world crumbling and being replaced by more vital forces. The pessimism Feuerman is experiencing, however, has little to do with class. It is moreover not a worldview or a philosophy but an existential state into which Feuerman has fallen because of the collapsed plausibility of worldviews and philosophies as substitutes for the world of faith which has been lost to him. "In my mind there is no idea, no memory, not even the rustle of desiring. In my heart there is vacancy, nothingness, complete lassitude, the realization that my breathing is unnecessary and my stuttering words profitless" (ch. 14, p. 69). Mired in his pessimism, which is presented as less of a stance than a nausea, Feuerman is neutralized; he bestirs himself neither to act nor to think.

The way out offered by Chaimowitch is striking both in its generosity and in its appositeness to the deep themes of the novel. As a rebuke to Feuerman's nausea Chaimowitch remarks, "Pessimism, eh? This is a curious proposition: to write in Hebrew and to be a pessimist!" And a few moments later he exhorts, "Feuerman, O Feuerman! Hebrew writer, awake and hark!" (p. 70). Chaimowitch's admonishment is generous because it suggests a solution to Feuerman's predicament that is attentive to commitments of Feuerman's which he does not share. Chaimowitch himself clearly has no use for the sentimental and elitist appeal to a revived Hebrew language as a vehicle for Jewish nationalism; even Yiddish recommends itself to him only for its temporary utility in persuading the masses. Chaimowitch's remarks serve the additional function of providing us with a piece of knowledge which the narrator vouchsafes to us in no other instance; this is the fact that apparently at this time, long after the maskilic dabbling in the yeshiva, Feuerman is producing Hebrew literature of some sort. From the perspective of an outsider to the world of Hebrew literature—and this is Chaimowitch's perspective—to write in Hebrew means to write in an antique language which represents no existing human community and has no connection to the real world, which is spoken by no one, and which is read only by a few. To do so, then, is evidence not of pessimism but of faith in unseen worlds and visionary futures.

Chaimowitch's prompting, however, is not picked up. Feuerman may or may not continue to write in Hebrew; we do not hear any more about it. But he certainly takes no comfort from Chaimowitch's refutation of hopelessness, as evinced by his deeper slide into despair in the course of the next three chapters. The fact that Feuerman declines to take advantage of the way out offered him by Chaimowitch makes an important statement about the kind of first novel Brenner chose *not* to write. Writing at roughly the same time about a not-so-different society, Joyce had Stephen Daedalus disentangle himself from the bonds of church and family in order to devote himself in exile to recreating the conscience of his race through art. The rebirth into the priesthood of art, which consummates *The Portrait of the Artist as a Young Man*, is never treated as a possibility in *In Winter*. Writing, it is true, is not thematized in the novel; yet given the form in which it is cast, the retrospective autobiographical narrative, the activity of writing is an unavoidable presence.[10] (Though not a first-person narrative, Brenner's second novel, *Beside the Point*, [*Misaviv lanekudah*, 1904], *does* emphasize the protagonist's identity as a Hebrew writer.) The opening line of *In Winter* describes the narrator's preparing for himself a fresh tablet of writing paper on which to record "some impressions and sketches from 'my life.'" As a character within the narrative, Feuerman seems to write Hebrew and associate himself with the new literature. And for the reader familiar with Brenner's biography, it is difficult not to conjure up the sad and brave image of the author as a miserable conscript in the Czarist army stealing time to labor over his first novel only to have to reconstruct it and rewrite it after the loss of the manuscript. Yet for all this, writing never becomes a source of deliverance. For Brenner and his creations, writing is a difficult duty, and perhaps a necessity. One writes under the pressure of the need to understand and express one's situation, but in no sense is the situation transfigured by being written about, nor does the vocation of writer privilege its practitioner or offer him any exemption from the painful dilemmas that have engulfed his generation as a whole. For the *Hebrew* writer to decline this option is doubly significant. At the turn of the century in Hebrew literature, which is after all the writing of the new Jewish nationalism, the rhetoric of rebirth is everywhere: the resurrection of the Jewish people, the revival of the Hebrew language, and so on. The unredeemed souls who inhabit Brenner's fictional world make the contemporary rhetoric of rebirth seem nothing if not ironic.

By renouncing the options of ideological belief and artistic transcendence, Feuerman comes face to face in chapters 15, 16, and 17 with the true experience of absence which resides at the center of *In Winter.* That a specific point has been reached in the progress of the novel is indicated by both compositional and thematic markers. Measured by the pace of the story, that is, the ratio of represented time (the hours or days of lived events described in the text) to narrated time (the amount of space measured in pages that it takes to narrate those events), these sections represent a kind of stillpoint. Three chapters comprising thirteen pages are devoted to the events of a single evening. Although we are not told the exact length of Feuerman's sojourn in the metropolis (one year? two years?), the evening in question is specifically cited as belonging to the last summer of his stay (ch. 15, p. 71). By this time, the narrator admits, he was no longer lacking "for shelter, food, or clothing"; the deprivations and abasements that had so sorely abraded his self-worth in the first period of his story have receded. With these material concerns in the background, the stage is set for an encounter that is more purely metaphysical in nature. The encounter, which unfolds in chapters 15–17, is presented in entirely scenic and dramatic terms, and there are no analytic interventions to indicate how the narrator intends this sequence to be read. Yet what is missing here is supplied earlier on. In the general introduction to part two of *In Winter* (chapter 11), the narrator surveys the whole expanse of his stay in the city and divides it into two stages of experience. Of the first stage he says that in addition to his privations and humiliations he felt an exhilarated sense of anticipation.

My eyes were fixed on the future and I felt within me the strength and power to take possession of it. I positively rejoiced in the release of my spirit from the shackles of religion, in the freedom and liberty I had been given, in the yoke that been lifted from upon me. To conduct myself with utter freedom, not to believe in nonsense—this to me was a kind of positive and joyful creed. *The emptiness that negation had left behind in my heart had not yet revealed itself to me with all its terrors. I had not yet felt the dread that comes from an existence without God, and even the space that had been hollowed out inside me and contracted in pain longed for something new that would come and fill it up.* (p. 47, emphasis added)

The reason why this explanation comes five chapters in advance of the event itself (in chapter 15) should be perfectly clear. This kind of global insight is the exclusive possession of retrospective wisdom; it is available to the narrator only well after the terror of its immediacy has waned. The capacity to take up the subject with articulate composure is precisely what is missing in the moment itself, in which, as we shall see, language decomposes into essential elements of silence and manic outcry. What is striking about this retrospective passage is its explicitness: it gives a name to the terror. When the narrator speaks of "the dread that comes from an existence without God," the words carry none of the ironic deflation that attaches to the generational slogans spouted by Feuerman in his debates with Chaimowitch (chapter 12, p. 61). The phrase is meant to provide a conceptual explanatory key to the real nature of Feuerman's crisis. The spatial metaphor is part of the instruction. Think not, the reader is told, of a resilient force ready to spring free after long constriction; think rather of a pit excavated by the work of apostasy which can be filled in only with cheap, and ultimately dangerous, substitutes for what has been taken away.[11]

If this is the retrospective wisdom which is experienced viscerally later on—and it indeed seems to be—then the moment before us has a strong claim to being regarded as the climax of the novel. The claim is indeed a strong one, but one, I would argue, which is not unqualified. The point of qualification derives from the polyvalent nature of *In Winter*, in which several narrative codes are intertwined. In terms of the psychological-existential code that dominates the middle sections of the novel, the discovery of God's absence from the world, experienced in its full horror for the first time, is indeed a true consummation. This code, to be sure, represents the highest level of the narrator's consciousness, and into its values he toils to translate and absorb the ideological discourse delivered so freely and self-importantly by the other voices in part two. Yet we know from the childhood sections of the novel that the psychological-existential code, despite its importance, is not sovereign. An erotic code operates in an authorial dimension beyond the narrator's consciousness and control, and it is this code which prevents the pivotal insight concerning the absence of God from remaining pivotal. Where we would expect this discovery to shape decisively the course of Feuerman's life-choices and to confirm the finality of his break with traditon and family, the opposite takes place. Feuerman returns home and becomes reinvolved with just those institutions from which he had sought to disentangle himself, and all this takes place under the pressure of unconscious sexual forces. This decentering is a critical moment in the disposition of the novel, and we shall have occasion shortly to take it up more fully in introducing part three of *In Winter,* whose subject is the return home. In the meantime, the concluding sections of part two (chapters 15–17) describe something of what it is like to fall into the void and why it is scarcely possible to abide it. Chapter 15 is an excellent example of Brenner's ability to write in several different styles whose contrasts make a thematic statement. The styles represent different forms of consciousness and speech, and the statement made by their juxtaposition bears on the essentially linguistic nature of the moment of loss. I propose to read this chapter in some detail not only because it constitutes the culmination of the existential-psychological code, but also because it represents the refinement of Brenner's fictional technique.

After the opening temporal markers (the last summer of the sojourn in the city), the chapter is divided into four movements. The first (p. 71) is a strange presence in Brenner's writing: a slice-of-life scene composed in a purely descriptive language attentive to the peculiarities of place and the physical quality of objects. (This metonymic realism, incidentally, is a kind of quotation from the Mahalakh Hadash school of fiction, the chief contemporary competitor to Brenner's psychological realism.) These paragraphs consitute a pure presentness of perception on the part of Feuerman, as he sits in his room looking out. The external world, as it registers itself on his mind, is impressive in its solidity: the firm coordinates of walls, jail, churches, synagogues, and the hum of unselfconscious life going about its business in all its variety. The scene of perception then swings abruptly from outside to inside in the second movement (pp. 71–72). The fullness of life beyond the window, no matter how ordinary, contrasts with the utter vacancy within; it was only by virtue of this vacancy, we now realize, that the picture of the city at work impressed itself on Feuerman's mind like a photographic image on blank film.

The style shifts to a representation of consciousness which borders on derangement, and it is conveyed as a series of truncated associations: "In my brain there arises a mound of rot and upon it worms crawl. . . . They all complain about the desolation; they complain and look for tricks to blot it out . . . carousing, dancing, circuses, theaters, books. . . . Let them be cursed!" (p. 72). This is an image of ennui pushed to pathological extremity. The vacancy of consciousness is in fact experienced not as being truly vacant but as the site of an active putrefaction (*gal shel rikavon*), in which even the maggots are bored and desperately seek diversion. Feuerman next tries out on himself, via a snatch of neoromantic poetry, the desire to be alone and commune with his destitution. (The verses Feuerman picks come from a contemporary poem by Bialik: "Beyom kayits, yom ham" ("On a Warm Summer's Day"), written in 1897 and published in 1900.) But in a true exercise of his penchant for hyperscrutiny *(nakranut)* he discovers that "in the depths of my self, at a point even deeper than the place where his desire for solitude lurks, there breathes the shadow of longing for someone—anyone!—to come in the door" (p. 72). Abiding the vacancy is simply too painful, and Feuerman recoils from it in a double movement of bad faith: first a romanticizing of aloneness and then a longing for rescue by the presence of others. There are masochistic overtones here: Feuerman recognizes something pleasurable in his agony which he is not willing to let go, and he accuses himself of an even more flagrant display of bad faith: "Even my suffering is a sham, a hypocrisy, a kind of bragging, as if my status would be enhanced because of it!" (p. 72).

Feuerman longs for anyone to come through the door, and anyone is who he gets, in the form of a visit from Fiessman and Klienstein. These two are the most vulgar and shallow of Feuerman's acquaintances, as their names imply ("Footman" and "Pebble"). One studies dentistry, the other pharmacy, and together their appearance is marked by the stock interchangeability of a Rosencrantz and Guildenstern. A comic dimension here in the third movement of the chapter (pp. 72–73) is not lacking. Fiessman is described as a man who delights in his illness, complains how he has been treated by life, and considers himself a great skeptic. He is, in other words, Feuerman's double, the ridiculous figure Feuerman would cut if his depth and pathos were taken away from him. The joke is deepened by the fact that it is the search for entertainment and diversion that brings the two of them to Feuerman's doorstep, that scene of bottomless ennui. The conversation they settle for once inside serves as a good example of how skillfully Brenner works with dialogue in the middle sections of *In Winter.* The first part is an exchange among the three of them on the themes of boredom and work, and the dialogue is presented in a way that suggests a one-to-one ratio between the actual speech and the reported speech; that is to say, we are given the full conversation with its repartee, repetitions, and sense of timing. After a lull, the conversation continues in a very different form. Feuerman drops out, and the exchange between Fiessman and Klienstein is presented not in full but in condensed form. Snatches of dialogue separated by ellipses are run together as a series of fragmentary topics with no individual speakers identified.[12]

Feuerman's withdrawal from the conversation is critically situated and critically motivated. Pronouncing aloud the word "boredom" *(shi'imum),* which he has used in a joke, names the very thing he has been trying to escape, and this triggers a sense of self-disgust. "I was much afflicted over having desecrated my silence, and I became loathsome in my own eyes. I withdrew into a corner" (p. 73). This is the moment in which Feuerman realizes that, in his desperation to evade the genuine emptiness inside himself, he has become ensnared in the cheap emptiness of Fiessman and Klienstein's banter and has become no better than they. The epitomized quality of the second part of their conversation takes its form, then, from the point of perception of one who has taken himself out and looks on from the distance. From this perspective, their exchange becomes a cartoon-like caricature of serious conversation. The theme is modern Russian literature, Tolstoy in particular, and the discussion, such as it is, comprises a collection of fragmentary critical commonplaces, largely deprecatory, about Tolstoy's work and its influence. Again, inside and outside are reversed; the report of Fiessman and Klienstein's desultory patter imperceptibly modulates into Feuerman's own unspoken thoughts. Their facile game of playing the critic with Tolstoy leads Feuerman into his own chain of cynical meditations about the futility of writing books about books. And thus he is drawn downward into a vortex of despair about the possibility of utterance.

The fourth and final movement of chapter 15 is delivered in the form of a "mad monologue" (*monolog metoraf,* pp. 74–75). The term is the narrator's, and its use indicates his acute awareness of the role played by language and the forms of speech in Feuerman's crisis. The shape of the monologue is further specified as being broken in two; the first half is interior speech and the second is spoken aloud in the presence of Fiessman and Klienstein but not *to* them.[13] "The second half of my mad monologue I mumbled as if before myself [*kemo lifnei 'atsmi*]." This is not strictly speaking a soliloquy, in which thoughts are spoken aloud; through some quasi-schizophrenic self-division, Feuerman makes himself the auditor-addressee of his own discourse. By labeling this speech as mad, the narrator signals us to invoke a set of reading procedures used to naturalized literary madness, that is, a set of seemingly disconnected utterances which we know to conceal truths central to a work's message.[14] That these utterances are presented in a fragmentary form resembling Fiessman and Klienstein's banalities about literature only underscores the distinction between meaning and non-meaning. Both speeches are composed of snippets of discourse strung together in a series of ellipses. In one case, the fragments are stand-ins for cultural cliches in need of no elaboration, and the ellipses serve simply to indicate the direction of arguments whose devolution is entirely predictable. In the case of Feuerman's speech, however, these disjunctions are signs of crucial mental events taking place at that moment with the rapidity of firing synapses. Feuerman is in thrall to a series of involuntary realizations and negative epiphanies. His truncated utterances are the surface markers in a chain of associations whose deep structure is crucial to the novel's thematic axis.

The passage—here the first, interior half of the monologue—is composed in the style of the "poetry of madness" which figures centrally in the climactic moments of Brenner's later novels, especially *Breakdown and Bereavement (Shekhol vekhishalon).*

Who are these people sitting here with me? Why did they come? Why don't they leave me to myself? But what difference does it make? . . . Ah, at last I am able to think about my own inner affairs. . . . Like a child idiot. . . . Absorbed in small-mindedness. . . . Small-mindedness—then what is large-mindedness? Oh my brain is jumbled. . . . I can't think at all. . . . I have been frozen. . . . Yes, yes, yes, it is hard to live, life is hard, a life like this. . . . My room is full of spider webs. . . . A lizard sucks the brains of flies. . . . It's cold, cold living without God. . . . Cold—but bourgeois warmth, what help is it to me? . . . "The End." . . . Other people. . . . One should live courageously. . . . If this means living for the true and the exalted, isn't all life the same? . . . "Should"—that familiar should. . . . "Afflictions"—which afflictions? . . . "Courageously"— what courage? What am I doing putting on airs to myself? . . . Ohhh, all my thoughts are purposeless. . . . There is no "should." . . . It's all one, one, one. . . . A total wasteland. . . . "Wasteland"—what wasteland? No, no, no. . . . "Nothingness!" I suddenly cry out with a loud laugh. (p. 74)

The monologue begins with a shudder of awareness, as if Feuerman has suddenly awakened to the realization that he is sitting in the company of the likes of Fiessman and Klienstein. He dissociates himself from their presence and turns inward to take stock. He finds himself mired in "small-mindedness" [*katnut*], a term from hasidic thought designating the state of the soul when it is prevented by distraction from cleaving to God. Feuerman's mind is approaching a state of paralysis, experienced first as mental confusion and then as a cessation of thought. Cognition gives way to feeling, Feuerman's statement about the difficulty of living comes across less as a complaint than an admission. The spider's web and the sucked-out brains of flies are affecting metonyms for Feuerman's situation. The frozen state of the mind without thought becomes the chill state of existence without God from which the comforts of home and hearth provide only a cheap escape. The advice offered by other people, who somehow manage to live their lives, is a glib version of the stiff-upper-lip attitude. This platitude about man's duty to face life bravely is dismantled term by term to show its speciousness. The impulse of linguistic analysis does not stop here but rushes on unrestrained to demolish even the concept of nothingness or desolation by which Feuerman has succeeded in giving his condition a name.

Until this point Feuerman's speech has been unspoken, a pure interior monologue. His outburst turns the scene into a comedy of perceptions based on the ethics of speech. While Feuerman has been engaged in this harrowing introspection, his friends have presumably continued to chatter away; so when he suddenly erupts with the cry "Nothing!" [*re'ut ruah*], Fiessman and Klienstein are shaken and grab hold of Feuerman to calm him; they listen astonished as he stammers out his "mad" condemnation of the "moaning and blubbering" of his contemporaries over their pseudo-afflictions. The mad monologue brings to a climax the morality play about language and speech that has been enacted in the middle section of *In Winter*. The self-confident articulation of Chaimowitch, the fraudulent politeness of Borsif, the vulgar sophistry of Fiessman and Klienstein, the ideological cant and contests of chapters 16 and 17—all these instantiate the rhetoric of evasion in its many variations. In this rhetoric, the real underlying contradictions of the present moment and the true terror of an existence without God have been defused and domesticated into manipulable verbal icons and into a kind of cheap currency that can be easily inflated and exchanged. In contrast to the pointless and endless talk, Feuerman's barely articulate stammering represents a more authentic relation between existence and expression. The truth is heard only in the muffled outcry of paroxysm.

Coming after this "climax," chapters 16 and 17, which conclude part two of *In Winter*, have the force of a dispirited denouement. The action, it should be remembered, takes place all in one evening and creates the effect of an epic "last night" in the city. Feuerman first visits Chaimowitch's rooms and then those of a friend Dawidowsky. The two settings represent two different kinds of student societies, and they are meant to be contrasted. At Chaimowitch's, the crowd is political and ideological, and the talk is of economic factors, the historical process, and the coming catastrophe of the bourgeoisie, with Zionism serving as the butt of everyone's sarcasm. At Dawidowsky's, the talk is more philosophical and artistic: the relationship between science and art, the influence of literature on life, the philosophy of Nietzsche, the contemporary theater, and the careers of prominent actors. Each group is distinctive in its atmosphere and conduct. Because they share a set of beliefs in common, the gathering at Chaimowitch's gives the sense of a church meeting: the issues of theory and practice are expounded among the faithful, and then there is a round of communal singing followed by a period of conscientious reading. Those gathered at Dawidowsky's, however, miss out on any chance for communion because they lack a shared creed. The group there is divided into cliques, and efforts at communal singing fail abysmally. (The scorn for Zionism here is the same; they sing a parody of Hatikvah.) Everyone begins drinking and the party quickly descends into drunkenness. The point of the comparison is in fact not to hold up one over the other, but the opposite—to show that the two in the end come to the same thing. If the solidarity were taken away from Chaimowitch's people, their gathering would not look any different from Dawidowsky's. Through Feuerman's eyes, the perception of the meetings shifts in focus from the substance of the talk to what the talk covers over. There is a moment in all of these evenings, observes the narrator, "when the empassioned debaters suddenly fall silent in the middle of the cries of 'Let me point out . . .!' and exhausted and bathed in sweat with scratchy throats, they face each other with an aching emptiness" (p. 78). This a moment pregnant with those same deep unspoken fears of insignificance that the *narrator* is not afraid of voicing: "Why? Why do we gather here? Is it so that each one, in addition to his own boredom, should feel the boredom of others? . . . We have nothing to say to each other. . . . We have no god that unites us and exalts our souls" (p. 78). It is doubtful whether the other participants are aware of just how deeply frightened they are supposed to be. But Feuerman knows, and his knowledge puts a definitive stamp on these leave-taking scenes.

Before concluding our discussion of part two, a word needs to be said about the virtual absence of the erotic code from the middle sections of *In Winter*. Although the main drama in part one centered on the translation of the cognitive code into the psychological code, there were nonetheless descriptions of the boy's early responses to girls and a lengthy excursus by the narrator concerning his deeply conflicted attitude toward the modern liberated woman, in addition to expressions of radical self-doubt about his own attractiveness. And we shall soon see that in part three of *In Winter* the question of sexual desire moves decisively to the foreground. It is only here at the novel's center that the theme is nearly effaced. The several references which do arise either serve to prepare us for a later development in the story or reflect on the displacement of erotic feeling.

So, for example, when soon after arriving in the city (chapter 11) Feuerman receives a letter from his father proposing an arranged marriage, the function of the episode, in addition to its comic inappropriateness, is to set up the storyline of the failed romance around which the events of part three revolve. Borsif, the eroticized male figure who will play a central role in the culmination of that plot, is introduced—and then dropped—in chapter 13 for similar reasons. Although Chaimowitch's female friend Lerner also appears in the working-out of the novel's conclusion, her appearance is more rooted in the middle theme of *In Winter*. She is a woman of middle-class origins who is cut off from her family and lives two years on her own in the city; Chaimowitch has taken responsibility for molding and educating her according to his lights. Their relationship is tender but sexless, a bond based on solidarity and pity, and it stands as an example of the kind of de-eroticized revolutionary marriage which might have been a solution for Feuerman if he had been more successful both in serving other gods and in scourging his "evil impulse."

The last and most significant instance concerns Dawidowsky, a vaguely drawn character who is familiar to Brenner readers from a more central role in the author's second novel, *Beside the Point*.[15] During the long last night in the city, Feuerman escapes the air of political rectitude at Chaimowitch's gathering and goes to sit alone with Dawidowsky in his rooms before the gang of students arrives. The two men sit in the darkness, content in the wordless empathy that emanates from each other's presence. Then, "very slowly, in a kind of concealed, nearly inarticulate murmur, there begins between us an outpouring of confession, barely spoken, about the state of our souls, our impressions" (p. 78). The intimacy of this self-disclosure has no precedent in the novel, and its authenticity is underscored by the fact that in the surrounding din of rhetorical evasions and posturings, this is an encounter that begins in silence and moves no further than halting, half-formed phrases. Chaimowitch may be a good friend and Feuerman may love and admire him, but it is only in this moment with Dawidowsky that one can speak of intimacy. The quality of this intimacy is suggested by the narrator in a comparison used to describe their surprise when they hear the footsteps of the other students coming to visit. Feuerman and Dawidowsky "resemble a little two lovers hiding in the thickets of the forest when they hear people approaching" (p. 79). This is, in short, a kind of homosexual moment, yet one which is neither enacted nor repeated. It functions to locate the distribution and displacement of libidinal energies in Feuerman's world. As we shall see directly, the sort of unacknowledged erotic attraction to women that is Feuerman's undoing in part three of *In Winter* has nothing to do with the tender exchange of inner feelings. The experience of intimacy escapes him altogether, except for this one moment when it becomes possible only with a man.

SEVEN

The Erotic Subversion

It is a truth universally acknowledged that a young autobiographical hero, after going off to the big city, cannot go home again. He must move onward and outward to explore his identity and possess his destiny. To return home is to place at risk the fragile autonomy wrested at a great cost from the seductions of parental love and the oppression of provincial stupidity. Yet this is precisely what Brenner's protagonist Yirmiah Feuerman does in the last third of *In Winter*. Feuerman knows it is a mistake to return to his home town; he knows it is dangerous to his spiritual well-being. But he goes anyway, and by this recursive movement Brenner decisively revises the existing autobiographical model in Hebrew fiction. The great outward voyage never takes place as expected within the boundaries of the novel. When Feuerman finally leaves home at the end of the story—or more precisely when he leaves home *again*—his leaving is more on the order of a bewildered decampment then a journey of discovery.[1]

Brenner accomplishes a great deal by having Feuerman return home. In the city, Feuerman had been *in* the contentious student society that surrounded him but not *of* it. For the very best of reasons he had hung back and watched his peers rush to embrace the new ideologies that presumed to inherit the prerogatives of religion. At home, however, among his family and the young men who grew up alongside him, he can hardly remain aloof. He is forced to become embroiled in the social medium and thereby have the durability of his new identity tested. It is not only Feuerman, moreover, who has changed. In the years he has been away at yeshiva and in the city, his home town has ceased being the timeless shtetl it seemed from the perspective of childhood. The arrival of the Zionist movement has made over the life of the community into a complex web of ideological assertions, assimilation, class distinctions, and various degrees of religious accommodation. This political organism encourages us to compare it not only to the earlier and simpler version of itself in the first part of the novel but also to the student society of the metropolis in the second. This pattern underscores the essentially tripartite structure of *In Winter* and the three-term analogy by which the novel asks to be read. Finally, by means of Feuerman's return, Brenner demonstrates that the business of leaving home is not simple and it is not necessarily accomplished on one try. Feuerman is more entangled than he thinks and for reasons he barely understands. Before leaving, Feuerman has to come to understand and accept the way he will always be bound to this place and this people.

Feuerman's own understanding of his motives for returning remains befuddled. "Now, even after a certain amount of time has passed since that journey," admits the retrospective narrator, "I cannot satisfactorily clarify the principal factors that forced me to take the step, even though I knew full well at every moment that it was *forbidden* me to return home" (ch. 18, p. 85, emphasis in text). It is not that he avoids trying to name the reasons. He recalls that in his last summer in the city his life had reached an impasse, and he waited in vain for some new "crisis" to take hold of him and show him the way. He was waiting, in other words, for a kind of Lilienblumian third stage, a transformation of identity that would descend upon him unbidden and deliver him from himself and his profitless existence. When this deliverance fails to materialize, Feuerman takes up the idea of resuming his education and traveling abroad to pursue his studies. To put together enough money to undertake such a project he would have to work as a teacher for a year's time. In this he has two options. He could become a tutor to a Jewish family in an isolated village in the hinterlands; but he rebels against the thought of being without books or friends and becoming a prisoner to provincial stupidity and torpor. Alternatively, he could return to his home town, where he could get paying pupils because he is known there; this, too, he initially rejects as impossible. As his friend Chaimowitch puts it, there is "no more potent bourgeois poison than the solicitude of a family for its own offspring" (ch. 18, p. 85). Further dissuasion comes in the form of letters he receives at this time from his father and from Ovadiah, the rabbi's son and his school companion. Each is written in an absurdly exaggerated Hebrew style, the one a parody of learned language of medieval rabbis and the other a take-off on the *melitsah*-laden biblicism of the maskilim. Each writer beckons Feuerman home, while the style of the writing, betraying the kind of world he would be drawn into if he did, drives him away.

And yet he goes home. Why? The narrator is willing to allow that it might have had something to do with his interest in a certain young woman, Rahil Moiseyevna, although he claims (falsely, as it turns out) that his attraction to her was conceived only after he had already returned. The relationship, he argues, is not especially useful as explanation for his movements. He has difficulty in bringing himself to believe that such an attraction could even have taken place, not to mention its having been the prime cause for a fateful decision in his life. To recall the affair is more painful than "probing a wound," but since in any case it was all one-sided and nothing even happened, there should be no cause for histrionics. "It was, in truth," he concludes, "just a typical occurrence, one that fades and has nothing *to contribute* to an understanding of myself—a matter of no account ['*urva parah*]" (ch. 19, p. 86, emphasis in text). This last phrase is a patent allusion to Berdichevsky's autobiographical story of the same name,

'*Urva parah* ("A Raven Flies"), published a few years earlier, which recounts the history of the unrequited attraction of a university student named Elimelekh to a young woman also named Rahil (see chapter 4 above; Rahil is the slavicized pronunciation of Rachel and indicates her aspirations to acculturation). Although the relationship has shaken him to the foundations of his being, Berdichevsky's narrator expunges the affair from his mind and persists in regarding it as a matter of no account.[2] The use of the phrase '*urva parah* thus signals an evasion on the grandest scale. What is denied is in fact the main spring of motivation.

This turns out to be Feuerman's situation as well. As narrator, Feuerman has long accepted the fact that romantic love is forbidden to someone like himself, that is, someone of his origins, his appearance, his temperament. That he should become attracted to a beautiful woman like Rahil, a woman entirely inappropriate to him, and beyond him as well, is not only an inconceivable proposition but also a laughable one. If such a thing did happen, Feuerman implies, then it must be accounted a lapse, a misstep, which can shed little light on the main business of his life.

The truth, of course, is quite otherwise. The attraction to Rahil is the principal factor which, against all the counsels of reason and self-interest, brings Feuerman home again. Once back, the attraction becomes an engulfing obsession. Because of it Feuerman is drawn into the company of people he loathes; he sinks into the masochistic pleasure of daily contact with an unobtainable object of desire; and he is led to the humiliation of voyeurism. Worst of all, Feuerman permits himself to indulge in just those fantasies of romantic love—of *being* loved—that he knows are the quintessence of illusion and bad faith. The obsession compromises him on other fronts as well. Out of the need to justify his stay in town, Feuerman must seek paying pupils, and to do so he has to curry favor with the town's notables, who are already more than dimly aware of the true degree of his disaffection from Judaism. Feuerman's secret desire, moreover, makes him easy prey for his father's comic machinations, which take the form of nothing less than a plan to bring off a matrimonial match between Feuerman and Rahil.[3]

This behavior is so at odds with Feuerman's own high standards that for the narrator it simply does not bear examining. Its motives originate in a place located, literally, *beneath* scrutiny. Until this point, the narrative of Feuerman's life had been frequently intruded upon by the voice of the "mature" narrator, which would probe for hidden motives, test for the veracity of statements, discourse on the nature of memory and telling, and sum up stages of development. This we termed the analytic as opposed to the scenic mode in the composition of the novel. The significant change that takes place in the last third of *In Winter* is a shift in the rough balance between these modes. It is in chapter 18, from which we quoted above, that the narrator confesses his perplexity in comprehending the reasons for his return home, and this marks virtually the last interruption by the retrospective analytic voice until the novel's conclusion. In this long interval, which comprises most of part three of *In Winter*, the flow of incidents proceeds unimpeded. The absence of inwardness and introspection makes these sections the most conventionally novelistic in the novel. The marriage plot with its comic misunderstandings adds a quality of a provincial novel of manners. But this novel-likeness, we should recall, is not a sign of achievement. In the preface to *In Winter* the narrator declares his intention to write a fragmentary kind of *anti*-novel; so the presence of such comforting novelistic properties as sequence, complication, and resolution—plot, in a word—should put us on the alert.

The significance of the shift can be best understood by reference to the play of codes. The middle section of the novel, which is set in the metropolis, was composed by the interplay of two codes to the virtual exclusion of the third. The cognitive code presented both the failed attempt at acquiring a gymnasium education and the array of ideological and cultural solutions to the Jewish problem. The dominant existential-psychological code presented these changes as they affected the formation of the self: the experience of shame and exposure in the transition from yeshiva student to extern, and the deep loneliness of Feuerman's struggle to decline the seductions of replacements for God. The erotic code was absent. As in the first section of *In Winter*, the codes in the second part were not simply two perspectives that existed side by side; the relationship was more aggressive. The existential-psychological code was in a constant process of translating the cognitive code and absorbing it into itself. This ascendancy represented the narrator's greatest achievement, according to his own lights: revealing the true level of reality at which life is lived and remaining faithful to its severe but necessary teaching of illusionlessness and renunciation.

Now in the last part of *In Winter* it is the existential-psychological code that is largely absent. This kind of insight is applied to Feuerman's mother and father but not to Feuerman himself. Instead, the action is driven by the cognitive code and the erotic code: on the one hand, the petty controversies among the town's religious and political groupings, and, on the other, the untoward consequences of Feuerman's obsession with Rahil. The gap between these two is evident—and easily collapsible. It is not hard to understand why the story moves along so briskly and scenically in these chapters. Fueled by desire and unencumbered by introspection, plot events can be neatly unraveled. Yet this appealing facility turns out to be a great delusion. The unwilled suspension of the self-critical faculty marks a defeat for the narrator's program. The high standard of existential awareness and conduct, which he has labored so hard to achieve, has been anaesthetized and put to sleep. A rude awakening cannot be far off. To follow the movements of Feuerman's evasion and its consequences, we shall first examine the cognitive code as expressed in the political and ideological changes that have taken place in Feuerman's home town; then the weakened existential-psychological code as applied to the parents; and, finally and most important, the erotic code as enacted in Feuerman's obsession.

The town Feuerman returns to scarcely resembles the town he left. What once seemed like a typical God-fearing shtetl has now changed into a hotbed of Zionist intrigue. How did this come about? Could so much have changed in the course of a few years? (Just how many years is never specified; it seems like four or five.) The velocity of this change would seem, in the end, to owe more to the acceleration in Feuerman's development than to any sudden transformation in the social landscape. Seen from a child's perspective in the first third of *In Winter,* the town is understandably experienced as the milieu of rabbis and melamdim, hadarim, and synagogues. Yet seen from the perspective of a world-weary veteran of the great ideological debates in the capital, as indeed we find Feuerman here at the beginning of the novel's final third, the town presents itself in a different guise. Withdrawn from the scene is Rabbi Hanan-Natan, whose genuine spiritual authority pervaded Feuerman's childhood. The eminence of this scholar-controversialist has been eclipsed by the new political stirrings, and entangled in them as well. The position of the town's chief householder had been formerly held by Katzin; it was to his holiday table that Feuerman's father was flattered to be invited instead of returning home to his wife and child. Katzin is not mentioned again, and it is a sign of the times that the father has found a new class of monied leadership before whom to scrape and bow. The Zionist cause has taken root in the town. The voices raised in opposition have been stilled, and now the national idea is taken for granted (ch. 20, p. 93).

The best indicator of this transition is a figure whose illustrative presence is felt in both the early and the late parts of the novel: Ovadiah, the rabbi's son. The less bright Ovadiah had been Feuerman's shadow. The two boys were tutored together by the rabbi and then expelled together from the yeshiva when they published a secret maskilic journal. But whereas this small rebellion was for Feuerman just a stage along the way to a more radical alienation, for Ovadiah it was the stage at which he got off. Instead of proceeding on to the big city, he returned home, took on pupils to teach, and prepared himself to make a good match. He now remains loyal to religion at the same time as he champions the cause of nation revival; the stamp of Zionism he espouses is cultural rather than political. He praises the purity and superiority of the Hebrew language but (in his letter to Feuerman in chapter 18) composes the most mawkish and ornate *melitsot.* Ovadiah, in short, is a figure of accommodation who has absorbed and domesticated some of the new currents of the time without the painful dislocation entailed in breaking with the surrounding social and religious norms.

Ovadiah's leadership of the cultural faction is overshadowed by the dominance of the political Zionists, led by Elimelekh the moneylender. In the face of Ovadiah's flowery visions of cultural and literary renaissance, Elimelekh embodies the brute fact of power and money. His advocacy of settlement in Palestine is not given at the expense of his adherence to Orthodoxy. He remains a figure of reaction who knows how to use the veil of Zionist rhetoric to protect more essential interests. His hero is the Malbim, the contentious rabbinical figure from earlier in the century who fought the Reformers on their own ground by refuting biblical criticism. Elimelekh is a shrewd manipulator who is aware of the new nexus between the recently monied classes and Zionist politics and who is determined to be a player in this new game. And he is one of the few people in town who has picked up on the true subversiveness of Feuerman's disaffection from the tradition. He understands that one who has lost his faith (an *epikoris*) such as Feuerman is a much greater threat than one who is merely rebelling (a *mufkar*); the latter's rebellion can subside and he can return, but for the former there is no hope (ch. 24, p. 104).

Opposed to the Zionist camp, cultural and political factions alike, are the forces of what Ovadiah derisively calls the assimilationists, led by the Borsif family. The controversy of the moment in the town involves a call for the establishment of a community library. Elimelekh has no use for the idea, but Ovadiah views it as a high cultural priority and argues that it should contain only Jewish books since the town already boasts a Russian library. The younger Borsif brother, however, objects. He advocates Jewish participation in the general stream of Russian society, and he therefore see no warrant for parochial restrictions.

Caught in the toils between these two camps is the prosperous Obedman family. The son Jacob is a contemporary of Feuerman who has remained in the town and become a spokesman for the Zionist cause, and who is influenced alternately by Ovadiah and Elimelekh. The high point in his young life has been a number of letters he has had published in the Hebrew periodical press about local Zionist affairs, and his self-seriousness leads the narrator to bestow on him the sobriquet the Correspondent. Another story altogether is his sister Rahel, or Rahil Moiseyevna as she prefers to be called. She has fallen prey to the Borsifs and their "assimilationist" seductions. Her alliance with the elder Borsif brother Aleksander was already provocatively established in the metropolis. Rahil is of course the object of Feuerman's obsession and the chief motive for his return home. Her "capture" by the Borsif camp forms a bridge between the cognitive code and the erotic narrative that becomes dominant at the end of *In Winter*.

These rather densely observed social and political divisions would on first flush seem to stand in stark opposition to the ideological debates Feuerman encountered in the city. There the Jewish national agenda was a matter of ridicule which was hardly allowed to figure among the overriding concerns of universalist import. Here in the shtetl, by contrast, on Feuerman's home ground, the conflicts and controversies revolve exclusively around the Jewish people and the dilemma of its survival. Yet from the retrospective point of view of the narrator of *In Winter,* this opposition is replaced by a functional equivalence. It is as if Feuerman's experience becomes a literal realization of the talmudic saying mentioned at the beginning of chapter 18 (p. 83): *sadna' di'ara' ḥad hu* ("the earth is all one parcel"); that is to say, human existence does not change from place to place. In both town and city, ideological conviction serves as a mask for the manipulation of power and as a smokescreen to hide the avoidance of meaningful action. The local celebrity won by Jacob Obedman as the Correspondent is not so different from the way in which Chaimowitch arrogates importance to his own political choices.

But the true equivalence lies in the unresolved drama of the "salvation" of Feuerman's soul. The middle section of the novel was presented as a kind of morality play in which the young hero passed before a series of temptations urging him to substitute some new ideological adherence for his lost faith in God. In a different guise, a similar set of seductions is presented to Feuerman on his return home. As the town's prodigy grown up and as a young man fresh from a sojourn in the metropolis, Feuerman is a prize for whatever faction can enlist him. Ovadiah understandably feels he is a natural ally for the culturists' cause. Elimelekh scrutinizes Feuerman for his general usefulness in furthering his own interests. And of course Feuerman's father wants desperately for his son to take a leading role in local affairs so as to recuperate his own wretched sense of social inferiority.

Surprisingly, Feuerman gives in, and not just to one but to all. In the city Feuerman had undergone the darkest ordeals of the soul and managed to resist temptations. Yet here he falters. He allows himself to be enlisted as Ovadiah's confidant. In order to get paying pupils he puts himself into his father's hands, who in turn entangles him in the far-reaching tentacles of Elimelekh's patronage. The taking of pupils and teaching them the traditional course of Torah studies constitutes a move which not only requires Feuerman to represent the system he has broken with but also throws him back—as a kind of recurrence of his father's life—upon the despised dependence of the melamed's life. Nor are the "assimilationists" denied Feuerman's presence. His attraction to Rahil makes him a fixture in the Obedman household when Borsif is discoursing on the folly both of ideological convictions and of Jewish passions.

Feuerman remains sublimely unaware of his capitulation. The critical faculty which was so unremittingly trained on his own shortcomings heretofore has now been lulled to sleep. Yet almost as a compensation, the narrator's attention is abundantly turned once again to the lives of his mother and father. It is only here that we find the operation of the psychological code, the code which is dominant elsewhere in *In Winter.* Representing his parents presents the narrator with an inherently difficult task; his relationship to them at this time is fraught with unavoidable conflict. The son's prospects remain the father's one desperate hope for salvation, and, in a different sense, her son's continued Jewishness remains the mother's sole consolation for a life of sacrifice and affliction. These are expectations that Feuerman must of necessity disappoint. Despite his unchanged traditional garb, the fact of Feuerman's apostasy cannot be long concealed. Although he allows his return home to be interpreted by his parents as a willingness to conform, the true motives for his return are unalterably subversive and eventually lead to expulsion from his parents' home. From the midst of this turmoil (whose effects cannot have worn off) it is no small accomplishment, then, for the narrator to take account of his parents' lives in a way that is both penetrating *and* empathetic. There are differences between the parents, to be sure. The burden of hostility to be overcome toward the father can go only so far as being neutralized, whereas in the portrayal of the mother the narrator has to struggle with a guilt-ridden over-identification with her suffering. In both instances, the narrator's tactic for working toward objectivity is to distil character into speech and present the parents through the art of the monologue. Stripped of their plot function, and therefore of their immediate entanglement in Feuerman's life, the parents are disembodied and reembodied as free articulating voices. Yet their freedom is equivocal, like that of all monologuists. It is their turn to speak, and they are given the floor, as it were, to say their minds unimpededly, yet it is the very pattern of their speech, with its slips and digressions, that gives them away. And underlying all is the fact that this freedom of speech is a gift bestowed by another hand, which gives and then takes away.

In both the early and late parts of *In Winter* the father is portrayed as essentially venal, yet the perception of venality undergoes a change. In part one the father's relentless pursuit of recognition had the effect of cruelly sacrificing the son's interests to his own and systematically denying his wife the acknowledgment she desperately needed. His behavior could be redeemed only to the degree that it could be understood as driven by a set of psychological needs, the same burden of inferiority which is the narrator's unhappy inheritance. In part three the father continues to scrape and bow and wheedle, but the effects of his cravenness on others are not half so destructive, and he seems to be hurting no one but himself. The absence of other victims this time permits the narrator to go further in recuperating the figure of the father and even to bring his portrayal under the aspect of comedy. The comic effect produced by the depiction of the father belongs to the variety based on repetition. Like the cartoon character who, after being trounced, returns for more punishment through a different door, the father never learns. He is just as indefatigable in fabricating new schemes for his deliverance as he is in absorbing their reversals. He is forever picking himself up and starting again.

His plans, of course, are always centered on his son. Raising the boy was like husbanding a prize animal. The prodigy would grow into a rabbi-scholar whose status and marriageability would redeem the father from his lowliness. But when his investment becomes "spoiled" by the "rot" of Haskalah, these hopes are dashed. Yet rather than being crushed or standing unswayed behind the honor of the Torah, the father simply redeploys. If Feuerman has disqualified himself as a rabbi, there are other ways, even more fashionable and advantageous, for him to be presented to the world. The father is quick to sense that in the new Zionist currents astir in the town, Feuerman's outside learning and cosmopolitan experience can be turned into an asset. In the frequent public meetings held to debate national issues, his son might cut quite a figure. Furthermore, as a prospective son-in-law to a newly wealthy businessman he might present the very image of a modern young man, and one far less forbidding than a religious scholar. The father now becomes fixated on the idea of getting his son married, and his imagination is aglow with the generous dowry that might spell the end to his misery. The suitable match he eventually sets his sights on is none other than Rahil Obedman. This piece of plotting is a stroke of genius on Brenner's part. It makes the father, for reasons entirely of his own, the chief abettor in Feuerman's own secret and supremely inappropriate fantasies. The father's tireless machinations in promoting this scheme fuel a conventionally comic marriage plot which unfolds at the same time as, on a deeper level, Feuerman writhes in the toils of degradation and obsession.

Yet again, the father's fantasies are one thing and the son's disposition another. Rather than bestirring himself to impress the younger local intellegentsia and become their natural leader, Feuerman withholds his opinions and awkwardly shrinks from contact. He declines to take up Elimelekh's grand offer to preach in the synagogue on the theme of the Zionist idea. Most infuriating, he scornfully dismisses the idea of marrying with a dowry. One might think that such a series of rebuffs and refusals would be enough to bring home the message that the son cannot be looked to as a source of deliverance. But it is the father's nature to deny the inevitable and try another tack. He suppresses his rage and sets out on a campaign of quiet persuasion. He means to talk to his son like a father offering friendly counsel. Here he advises Feuerman on how to rectify the effects of his ill manners during a visit paid to him by Ovadiah and Jacob:

> Don't worry; you will go to Jacob's house and there you will make it right, Yirmiah. . . . You will still be witness, Yirmiah, to their being humbled before you. And so it shall be if only you will it; they will be humbled like the dust of the earth. . . . Verily, like the dust of the earth. . . . If you can only accustom yourself to them. . . . All is accommodation, I tell you. (ch. 22, p. 99)

This fatherly advice, of course, shows not a whit of comprehension of Feuerman's situation and reveals instead the father's unchanging philosophy of life. One is either among the humbled or among those who cause others to be humbled, and if your sad lot is to be counted among the former, then the best path open to you is to adapt to the expectations of others. At the opening of the novel, the narrator might have stressed the wretched humiliation from which the father speaks. Here, however, the emphasis is on the resilience of his stupidity. His hope for social rehabilitation is perennial. Yet within this Menahem-Mendl-like irrepressibility, there remains a darker side. Within this same fatherly monologue, the example chosen of the successful young man is none other than Feuerman's nemesis, the elder Borsif brother. While Feuerman frittered away his time in the city, the father helpfully points out, this handsome fellow completed the gymnasium curriculum and is well on the path to a distinguished career. That Borsif has discarded his Jewishness along the way seems not to matter. The taunt has been delivered.

The depiction of Judith, Feuerman's mother, plays on a very different set of vulnerabilities. In part one the reasons for her misery were assigned not only to her being orphaned and her disfigurement but also to her husband's continued failure to accord her the least recognition or dignity. In part three, however, the responsibility rests squarely upon the shoulders of none other than the narrator himself. Her investment in her son is, in a sense, greater than her husband's and just as demanding. Whereas the father wants to use Feuerman to enhance his own position, the mother wants him for himself. She needs him to console her badly wounded esteem by vindicating her sacrifice, and she needs him in a practical sense to help the family through hard times. Flushed with pride over Feuerman's return, she speaks at length with her neighbors "of her abiding belief that 'her Yirmiah' would not forget her forever, that he is not like others who fail to recall all the tears and blood shed for them by their mothers" (ch. 19, p. 91). Her need is genuine, far more so than her husband's, yet what she asks for—and what she can obtain only from her son—is precisely what it is most difficult for him to give. His break with the tradition and his further crisis of spirit have decreed upon him homelessness and wandering. Although *he* knows his return home is only a lapse, it teases the mother with the prospect of true reconciliation, and this knowledge in turn makes him vulnerable to her appeals. Feuerman must eventually leave, and the consolation enjoyed by the mother will be withdrawn. There is no way to soften the brutality; his mother must of necessity be the chief victim of his freedom.

Owning up to this responsibility, then, is no small task. Like the early sections of *In Winter* there obtains here a dialectic of distance and empathy, but unlike them, the retrospective gap between the present and the past is much narrower and the degree of adult accountability that much greater. Chapter 23, in which this problem is taken up, turns on the difference between self-pity and empathy. Alone with his mother during the final hours of the Sabbath, that twilight time his mother used to fill in his childhood with wonder tales and legends, Feuerman's general alienation is weakened and he is forced to admit to himself that "In spite of everything, it cannot be denied that there are hidden silk threads that tie me to life" (ch. 23, p. 100). Once touched, Feuerman's emotions are kindled, but the subject of this effusion takes a surprising turn.

> A strange agitation began to beat in my heart. I wanted to weep, to weep for the whole of existence, for the destruction of my own world, for the deprivation of life, to weep without end, without cease. My mother's reminder that the hour had come to recite the evening prayer, struck me as simple, natural, and necessary. Afterwards, emboldened by the look of tenderness and kindness in my eyes, she began to talk with me and tell me various details about her life in order to demonstrate that it would not be a sin if I were aroused to give support to them [the family]. All I could feel was a strong sense of guilt, guilt and shame! (ch. 23, pp. 99–100)

Feuerman's sadness is at first focused on himself. When his aloofness is undermined and he is put back in touch with the throb of human experience, his impulse is to weep over the calamity of his own life, its impoverishment and destruction. The visible imprint of these emotions gives the mother an opening to approach him. She reminds him to pray, which apparently he does, and then she speaks to him. Her speech, the monologue that takes up the concluding pages of the chapter, triggers a transfer of pathos from him to his mother. His response does not stop here but crosses over from pathos to guilt. He is ashamed, so it is implied, over his self-preoccupation and over the difference between the nature of his mother's suffering—a suffering born of poverty and adversity—and his own.

This is a guilt for which there is, and can be, no expiation within the bounds of the story. Feuerman must go, and in going leave the family to its own devices. Some repair, however, can be offered by the retrospective narrator after the fact; if he cannot change the "facts," he can, looking back, shape their perception. This he does by giving his mother the long monologue in chapter 23, which has no plot function other than to dramatize his mother's plight and to underscore the costs of his desertion. Guilt is thereby turned into representation, and this conversion becomes in itself a sign of the narrator's acceptance of responsibility for the payments made by others for his choices. Once given the freedom of her monologue, the mother reveals herself through her speech in ways very distinct from her husband. While his rambling shifts from scheme to scheme and from one fantasy of vindication to another, her speech is an ordered narrative about events that have in fact taken place. Neither confrontational nor ingratiating to Feuerman, her manner of speaking is more persuasive in its indirection. By mentioning along the way, for example, that God had given her the strength to live with her husband's insults, she places in proper perspective her son's largely spiritual miseries and his difficulty in accepting them.

Behind the motherly patter, the self-effacement and the diffidence, there is a horror story that gets told with exemplary precision. The story concerns a crisis precipitated by the mother's illness the previous spring. The family's usual hand-to-mouth survival had been further undermined by the non-payment of tuition for two pupils. Exhausted by the Passover labors and by ministering to a sick daughter, the mother collapsed and took to her bed for several weeks. This was physical and emotional breakdown rather than a specific illness. It was, as the mother succinctly puts it, that "my strength had ebbed away" (ch. 23, p. 100); she had reached a point where there was simply nothing left in her to give. The state of misery and chaos into which the family quickly slipped is a sign of how much depends on her active presence. Perhaps the greatest tribute to her is that she makes neither her suffering nor her importance the final point of the narrative. The second half of the story moves the center of attention from her to her husband. Without the means to summon a doctor or obtain remedies for his wife and rebuffed in attempts to collect on debts owed him, Shalom-Getsl suffers his own breakdown. But instead of collapsing into bed he is seized by a violent frenzy, and it is all his children, and ultimately his wife climbing down from her sickbed can do to keep him from wreaking havoc against those neighbors who had shown him no kindness. Finally, he does collapse, sobbing like a child. "And as for his face," she concludes, "I have seen prettier ones on a corpse" (ch. 23, p. 101). In the end, then, Feuerman's mother gives up her monologue to the larger purposes of reconciliation. Purchasing sympathy for herself is easily enough done; bringing a son closer to a father who is repellant by nature is a task of a different order.

The mother's monologue is a privileged moment in the novel, and it is one which quickly passes as mother and son resume their roles as inevitable antagonists in a drama that climaxes in the expulsion scene. But the pathos of this bond is kept in the reader's awareness in many ways, among them two vignettes about ducks and geese told later in the novel. The seeming extraneousness of these stories provides an illustration of the tightness of Brenner's control of the symbolic texture of the narrative. The first vignette is a conversation Feuerman overhears early one morning while his parents are still in bed (ch. 26, pp. 112–13). His mother, it should be recalled, had started a small business of preparing geese for market as a way—futile, sadly enough—of demonstrating her usefulness to her husband. This morning she awakens with the dreadful premonition that a fine-looking goose she has bought from a peasant might turn out not to be kosher. And so the rabbi decrees: *Nitraf!* The second vignette is told by Feuerman's sister as an illustration of the value of preventing *tsa'ar ba'alei hayyim*, cruelty to animals (ch. 31, p. 122). The story is of a hen which is placed upon a nest of duck eggs. The eggs hatch and the ducklings grow up and go off to paddle in the river. Like a bereaved mother, the hen, only a barnyard fowl, is terror-stricken. "She can neither bring her beloved fledglings back to her nor can she reach them herself."[4]

The emphasis in both these vignettes falls on the fated helplessness of the mother. The first, about the nonkosher goose, implies that her investment in her son and his future is no less desperate than her husband's; like the profits anticipated from the goose, Feuerman's achievements are counted on to purchase a modest amount of dignity. That all her efforts should be in vain and that Feuerman should turn out to be "unfit" and therefore transferred into gentile hands—all this is an outcome that could in no way have been anticipated, because the signs of unfitness were internal and invisible. The term *nitraf* resonates deeply in Hebrew. In addition to ritual unsuitability, it connotes being mutilated by wild animals and, by extension, going mad. The mother's loss, then, is matched by her son's fate. In the story of the hen and the ducklings, unnaturalness is inscribed in the relationship between mother and offspring. The offspring are not only not her own issue but belong to a different species. The separation is inevitable, but its inevitability is hidden from the mother, who has treated them as her own, and it comes over her as a sudden tragedy. In this instance the payment is clearly one-sided: the ducklings swim off to freedom while the surrogate mother shrieks. The use of the story as a didactic illustration of creature cruelty brings up another question: the justice of the world—and its creator—that places such mothers and such offspring together.

Yet for all this resourceful exploration of the parents' situation, this is not the new and critical element in the last third of *In Winter;* it is rather the emergence into the foreground of the erotic theme. This emergence is very sudden, as if to mimic the eruption of forces long suppressed. It is undeniable as well, although these experiences—erotic need, erotic expectation, and erotic fantasy—are all ones Feuerman had either forbade himself as inappropriate or judged himself incapable of sustaining. The existential code of value that Feuerman had worked so hard to adopt is mortally threatened by this new development. The question posed by this section of the novel, then, is how Feuerman will respond to the sudden destabilizing of his world. Will his self-perception and his code of conduct be altered to take account of this new dimension? Will he take action to contain the threat and seek to return to his former life? Or will he be drawn more deeply into the web of erotic feeling?

When the moment arrives for the return of the repressed, the sign is given in a hyperliteral form. In the middle of chapter 24, Feuerman is lured to Jacob Obedman's home by the prospect of seeing Rahil alone, that is, without the presence of Borsif. Once inside, the sight of her provokes a description saturated by the kind of idealization that is so notably lacking from the rest of the narrator's discourse. "She was wearing a dark blue dress, and by the light of the lamp she was the quintessence of life, sparkle, and beauty" (p. 105). Even though he knows that she is waiting for Borsif, "the strings of my heart were stirred with poesy." But it is not only poesy that stirred later in the evening when, after being gently mocked by the bored Rahil, Feuerman suddenly finds it necessary to excuse himself.

> When I apologized for rushing to return home by saying, "I cannot stay any longer," I was not lying. I would have in fact been happy to give up everything I own just to sit there, if only some thing had been in a different position. But this thing was as it was and it aroused in me a powerful desire to hide myself in the darkness outside. (ch. 24, p. 106)

The identity of this "thing" [*davar*] whose awkward position forces Feuerman's hasty departure is not specified, and the reader who is not aware of the operations of the erotic code is likely to see here a general allusion to Feuerman's social embarrassment and confusion. The case can be made, however, that the reference is to nothing other than Feuerman's penis, whose untoward behavior is the true source of his discomfiture.[5]

This is a remarkable scene in several ways. In representing this moment, Brenner makes what is revealed in this discovery scene not a symbolic substitution but, as it were, the thing itself. Rather than a metonymic description of desire, Feuerman is confronted by the literal embodiment of desire. It is a material presence which cannot be controlled by thoughts of appropriateness and inappropriateness. Feuerman's penis gives witness as well. The narrator had long denied not only the acceptability of Feuerman's interest in women but also his very capacity for desire. He believes himself to be damaged and impaired by the deprivations of his upbringing and the calamities of his spirit. Yet behold the first incontrovertible evidence of a desire—and perhaps a potency—that will not be stilled. The irony of Feuerman's desire, as presented in this scene, is that it has the immediate ironic effect of separating him from his source of pleasure. His pleasure comes from the silent contemplation of Rahil, and this he must reluctantly forego when he becomes aware of his erection. We shall see that this passive and one-sided reverie of contemplation, first evident in this passage, becomes the stance that Feuerman seeks to return to and maintain as long as possible. The strange incompatibility between desire and pleasure, which the narrative will explore later on, is expressed at the conclusion of the passage by a curious displacement. The language used to describe Feuerman's compulsion to escape into the night and to escape the possibility of detection ("it aroused in me a powerful desire [*teshukah 'azah*]") is the language that belongs to the experience of desire rather than to its concealment.

The desire for his pleasure turns out to be greater than the shame of his desire. After decamping from the Obedman household, Feuerman seeks, and finds, a way to keep Rahil in his sight without exposing his need. But before he does this he attempts valiantly to dissuade himself from being drawn in any further.

What is this tragedy that I want to create for myself? This is a yeshiva boy! I am alien to any young woman—that is all. One only needs *to know* this. . . . I must overcome all of this so that I don't play the comic hero. These silly notions have come over me from an overindulgence in reading novels! (ch. 24, p. 107, emphasis in text)

The arguments Feuerman mobilizes are a good summary of the conscious existential code that he believes he lives by. Taken for granted, to begin with, is the assumption that for someone of his background the entire sphere of women and sexuality is beyond reach. There is the further assumption of the sufficiency of knowledge and will. That he *knows* about his incapacity should be enough to summon up the courage to resist this temptation to overreaching and bad faith. The fear of looking the fool here is not the same as the primitive dread of sexual exposure that Feuerman had experienced just before. It is connected instead to image and self-perception, and it is associated with the realm of popular fiction. Feuerman fears becoming a ridiculous character in the kind of conventional novel of which *In Winter* is supposed to be the antithesis.

But Feuerman cannot resist, and to the problem of seeing and not being seen he finds the classic solution: voyeurism. Having almost reached home, he turns on his heels and stations himself outside a window of the Obedman house. Through the window Rahil "was visible in her entirety and her full height. She was leaning against the table languidly, yet everything about her shone as if vibrating. Blood coursed through her face like strings of pearls" (ch. 24, p. 107). The object Feuerman contemplates is clearly eroticized. The importance to him of visual access to her body in its fullness is underscored here. The object is transfigured as well. What Rahil is in fact is a tired and bored young woman waiting distractedly for the arrival of her lover. What Feuerman sees is a source of radiant light pulsing with vital intensity. The passage now switches from the object of desire to the observer. "My heartbeats were like hammer blows. All thought disappeared. Trembling but at the same time lifeless, I stood my ground" (p. 107).

What Feuerman is experiencing is sexual arousal and more. He is being shaken to the core of his being in such a way that, for the first time in his life, his rational, consciousness-producing faculty has been obliterated. He has become transfixed. Yet the totality of the experience is not enough after a moment to protect him from self-accusation: "Only in my conscience I was like one who was ascending the gallows. A free man like me! Tied and trussed, . . . unable to move. . . . Truly there can be no issue from all this. . . . no second act to this ridiculous drama" (p. 107). With the lucidity of a man who observes himself about to step into the abyss, Feuerman fatalistically acknowledges the reality that is rushing toward him. As if separated from himself, he glimpses the sad and ridiculous spectacle of free will in the process of delivering itself up to compulsion. The process is soon complete. "I have been subjugated, obliterated [*nitbatalti*]. . . . She can do with me whatever she wishes. . . . Truly? Yes, yes, yes. . . . She can, she can!" (p. 107). But there is one more jolt before Feuerman's ordeal comes to an end. He had until now been standing before the window enveloped in a voyeuristic reverie. Suddenly he hears steps—the voyeur is being viewed! Although it turns out to be an ordinary passer-by, Feuerman automatically assumes that it is *"He,"* Borsif, the real possessor of Rahil. Caught in the act, if only in his imagination, Feuerman is engulfed by shame and reduced to a "vessel full of shame, jealousy, stupidity, cowardice, and vulgarity" (p. 107).

What happens to Feuerman in this chapter is transformative. These events can be seen as the climax of part three of *In Winter* and its dominant code, if not of the novel as a whole. The subsequent chapter (25) opens with the portentous biblical formula, "After these things . . ." [*aharei hadevarim ha'eleh*], as if to indicate that a dividing line has been crossed beyond which the very terms of Feuerman's life will be different. From this point on (again the number of days or weeks is not clear) Feuerman's experience will be ruled by the logic of erotic obsession. Life in the throes of obsession is a phenomenon we have come across previously in the Hebrew autobiographical tradition. The young heroes of this literature, suddenly uprooted from the world of tradition, find the empty spaces in their souls particularly vulnerable to invasion by sexual fantasy and dependence. Feuerman's fate in Brenner's *In Winter* unmistakably evokes Elimelekh's ordeal in Berdichevsky's *A Raven Flies*. For both characters, life within obsession creates a similar structure of experience: an unworthy object is transfigured and idealized; the self, shorn of its previous identity, is re-duced to a state of being possessed and controlled by the other; there is an ever-present dread of the shame of exposure; the obsessive relation to the object is unilateral, passive, and fantasy-laden; the greatest fear is that this low threshold of sexuality be violated by a more active relationship to the object with the result that the reverie will be shattered and the pleasure taken away. Finally, there is the more-than-coincidental fact of a shared name; both Elimelekh and Feuerman are in thrall to the enchantments of a Rahel/Rahil. There are of course differences as well. These are dictated by the broader scope of *In Winter*, which integrates the erotic theme into a complex social and intellectual whole, and by the kind of consciousness Feuerman inhabits. What is shattered when Elimelekh is plunged into obsession is a naive and arrogant rationalism. The nuanced self-awareness and self-analysis attained by Feuerman mean that the nature of *his* "fall" is very different.[6]

The fate of these special qualities of mind under the conditions of obsession is the subject investigated in *In Winter*. The changes are most markedly evident in the nature of Feuerman's response to the events taking place around him. The remaining weeks of his stay in the town are es-pecially full of incident. On the political scene, the controversy over the establishment of a Jewish library heats up. Jacob Obedman celebrates the publication of yet another "correspondence" in the Hebrew press. Borsif airs his assimilationist views and taunts Obedman about the ridiculousness of the Zionist idea. The rabbi's authority is checked and Ovadiah's advantageous marriage is put in jeopardy. Feuerman's father begins actively to promote a match between Feuerman and Rahil, while his mother demurs and has premonitions of disaster. In earlier sections of the novel it would not have been enough for the narrator to render a vivid and ironic account of these developments. The response elicited *in the narrator* by the plot events would have been an inseparable part of the narrative. We would have been told about the complex internal workings of Feuerman's reaction at the time of the events, and we would have been given the self-reflective digressions of the narrator as he ruminates on present feelings provoked by past occurrences and on the difficulty of summoning up the past altogether. Yet here there is nothing of this. The Zionist follies go on and the comic marriage plot works toward a climax as if this were some provincial novel on the order of Trollope's *Barchester Towers*. All is reduced to incident, information, intrigue, and complication—and nothing more.

What is missing, in sum, is the autobiographical element. This is the relentlessly self-analytical temper that distinguishes *In Winter* from other narratives, and it is a function of the psychological-existential code that rules most of the novel. It is this prerogative that Feuerman gives up when he submits to his attraction to Rahil. This renunciation is made with stunning complacency.

> After these things there passed over me days of plain existence [*hayyim stam*], an existence that tended to resemble the life of plants. Every evening I would visit the Obedman house, and sometimes at midday as well. Yet all of my dilemmas, disturbances and thoughts seemed to have departed from me. The enterprise of analysis and scrutiny I forgot. Even my sorrow was softened and made fleeting, a kind of ecstasy of agony. Inside me reigned something like the tranquility of besieged cities before they fall into the hands of their captors. (ch. 25, pp. 107–8)

The life of plants is an apt figure for the vegetal phase Feuerman now enters.[7] Rather than living off his mind, he has been reduced to the most basic kind of biological pulse. Like plants, his nourishment is given, not taken; he passively soaks in Rahil's radiance, and that is enough for him. This new condition has an anaesthetizing—perhaps more precisely, a narcotizing—effect on this man of existential sorrows. The ache of loss and the nausea of uncertainty have been sweetened and made companionable. Pacified as well is the habit of hypercriticism [*nakranut*], which had heretofore clung to Feuerman wherever he went and wherever he looked.

The simile concerning the tranquility of besieged cities is a figure that is realized in the subsequent chapters. Conflicts rage around Feuerman yet he remains impassive. Some issues are petty, some significant. For example, Jacob Obedman, flush from his triumphant appearance as the Correspondent, brings Feuerman to the home of his younger cousin, and there Feuerman is witness to the tensions between father and son over religious issues. But instead of commenting, Feuerman remains disengaged: "With a serene soul I listened to the voices clamoring in the adjoining room" (ch. 25, p. 110). Jacob and Ovadiah go on to discuss in hushed tones the imperative need to accomplish the plan for a Jewish library in the town, while both father and son, their hosts, disparage the plan each in his own way. And Feuerman? "I sit in my seat and take it all in with a composed soul" (p. 110). Yet Feuerman is neutralized even when it comes to matters of much greater emotional valence. "For that limited time even my jealousy and hatred for Borsif were blunted" (p. 110). What is infuriating about Borsif, in addition to his possession of Rahil, is his habit of discounting the seriousness of important issues and turning everything into ironic badinage. Provoked by Obedman's insistence that he finally speak his mind about Zionism and the Jewish question, Borsif answers that the question is no question because the Jews are not a nation but creatures who "crawl like worms, speak jargon, and arouse disgust with their appearance and customs" (ch. 25, p. 111). Obedman, beside himself with rage and yelling "Assimilationist!," appeals to Feuerman. But Feuerman equivocates by attempting to separate Borsif's erroneous conception from the aesthetic impact of his rhetoric. He equivocates again when asked by Rahil if he himself is a Zionist, and his equivocation is mocked by her as being effeminate. Greater insults, both personal and national, can scarcely be imagined. Yet Feuerman manages to maintain his composure, as if to say, "Nothing can affect me. . . . *It is nothing at all.* Nothing" (ch. 25, p. 112, emphasis in text). The conversation continues, and by the end of the chapter Feuerman's serenity has been regained so that he can state that despite the turmoil around him, "All around me there was peace."

Feuerman's withdrawal illustrates the basic message of this section: the interchangeability of eros and interiority. This does not mean that Feuerman's highly nuanced consciousness is merely a compensation for the absence of sexual feelings. But there is no mistaking the fact that his critical awareness of self is put in abeyance the moment he gains access to Rahil's presence. Truly astonishing is that this suppression should be purchased for so little. Feuerman's relationship to her is decidedly erotic; the ungovernable sign of his desire has given him away. Yet no matter how great its impact, the actual level of erotic experience Feuerman contents himself with is extremely low. "Like one deaf and dumb, I would sit at a distance from *her* leafing through a newspaper or a journal, listening to her voice and stealing glances at her. *He* sat close to her, conversing with acquaintances or whispering in her ear affectionate taunts" (ch. 25, p. 111, emphasis in text). Feuerman's experience on his daily visits *inside* the Obedman house represent a kind of continuation of the voyeuristic moment initiated *outside* the Obedman house. He is now not actually invisible to her but practically he is so, because she and the others are barely aware of his presence. To be in Rahil's presence and hold her in his gaze are quite enough. This might not be so little if Feuerman were alone with her, but Rahil cannot be seen without Borsif, who is the unnamed antecedent for the emphasized "he." This man is not simply a competitor but, as will become increasingly evident, nothing less than Feuerman's nemesis and the stereotypical embodiment of the kind of blond beast that stands over and above the meek of the earth. The price Feuerman must pay for maintaining contact with Rahil is being a captive witness to the loveplay between the two of them and to their exchanges of witty endearments. Feuerman has become a domestic lapdog, a pet for their amusement. But so deep is his need that not even this humiliation can be permitted to place the source of his pleasure, such as it is, in jeopardy.

While Feuerman sits transfixed, his father is busily maneuvering to bring about a match between his son and Rahil and to sell the idea to his wife and to Feuerman himself. The father's scheming, on the one hand, and the son's obsession, on the other, represent the erotic code in its aspects of genre and anti-genre. In a conventional novel the marriage plot (whether the match is imposed by society or wished for by the hero) would carry the romantic theme. In the "anti-novel" Brenner is writing, however, marriage is beside the point, not only because it imposes an institutional norm but also because it signifies love that is both mutual and consciously acknowledged. For the hero of *In Winter*, alas, erotic experience can be neither of these things. It must remain one-sided and unacknowledged. For this reason, the intertwining of the conventionally comic marriage plot with the desperate story of Feuerman's inner ordeal generates a wonderful series of ironies. The chief among these is the fact that the match the father is promoting—even pandering—is precisely what Feuerman most deeply desires yet cannot have. When in chapter 26 the father relentlessly questions his son as to why he resists the match, Feuerman can provide no real reasons for rejecting what in fact he really wants. What fuels the father's eagerness for the match, besides the family's wealth, is a perception that, for their many sins, Rahil and Feuerman belong together. Both, he reasons, are apples that have become infected by the same rot of disaffection from traditional Jewish life. If Feuerman has left the yeshiva and dabbled in foreign ideas, and in so doing invalidated his "marketability" as a scholar-rabbi, then let him regain some of his worth by being matched with someone of his ilk. From Feuerman's perspective, however, the idea of Rahil's similarity to himself is absurd. While he struggles to forge an identity in the aftermath of a profound attachment to Jewish belief, she loosens an already loose bond out of assimilatory reveries of escape from the tedium of provincial Jewish life. She is a bored Chekhovian heroine who seems by accident to have alighted in the unfamiliar territory of Hebrew fiction. Feuerman's mother senses the difference and even the danger ("There is something hidden about her," ch. 26, p. 114), although she cannot articulate it. But the father, with the glint of the prize in view, sees nothing but opportunity.

It is at this point in the novel that Feuerman dreams. There are anxious dreams before he spits in Borsif's face and true nightmares afterwards. The dreams are literary dreams in the sense that they serve to bring to light some of the latent and unnamed forces at work in the narrative and to express them in compressed images that resonate with wide networks of motifs. Yet the chief import of these dreams is the juncture at which they occur and the very fact they occur at all. As constructed by Brenner, the mental world of the narrator in *In Winter* is a supremely conscious one. The goal of the narrative is to represent and expose the delusions of youth according to a leavened retrospective wisdom, and this project is accomplished by the dual instruments of analysis and scenic reevocation. Reveries of future happiness are dissected and the stratagems of false consciousness unmasked. But nowhere in his work but here does the narrator have recourse to the kind of primary psychological processes revealed by dreams.

The dreams occur just at the moment when the powers of consciousness are at their lowest ebb. From the beginning of his active infatuation with Rahil the faculty of analysis had been silenced, but now Feuerman reaches a point where the need to suppress even the general exercise of consciousness becomes overwhelming. The sudden awareness that he is being presented to others as a candidate for marriage to Rahil keeps Feuerman at home away from the Obedman household and therefore in a state of being cut off from his connection to her. The production of desire, of course, does not stop. Lying around the house in his self-imposed exile, he sinks into reveries of deliverance. "She and I are on a journey to Switzerland . . . traveling together. . . . Like dew, she revives my lapsed powers, and I enrich her life with my spirit!" (ch. 28, p. 116). (The reverie is an almost exact transcription of Elimelekh's fantasies at the outset of *A Raven Flies*.) "Whole hours would go by," he admits, "in fanciful imaginings without my even being aware of it." Kept at the reverie stage, these daydreams are a way for Feuerman to give himself pleasure while cut off from visual contact with Rahil. But when he falls asleep, the pleasure, with its benign assumption of control, is exchanged for something else altogether. At the core of the dream that follows lies the image of a journey. Yet in contrast to the gratifying mood of the reverie, this journey is arrested. In one sequence of the dream he is traveling in a wagon with family and friends; the wagon stops and all but Feuerman get out. His father shouts at him to step down and make himself a presentable candidate for marriage; he refuses, answering proudly that he is going off to Germany with her (Rahil). Meanwhile, he is left stricken on the ground as the journey recommences without him. In the next sequence he is put off a train or prevented from boarding one for want of a ticket by a conductor who is part the rabbi and part Borsif. He sinks into the ground, unable to move, as he is told that it is his nose that prevents him from moving on. Taken together, the dream material, at whose center is the interrupted journey, reverberates forcefully with the novel's overall pattern of moving onward and returning home; it nicely anticipates as well the novel's closing picture of Feuerman's being put off a train in the middle of nowhere. The very availability of this material to interpretation, which will not be undertaken here, is just the point. The reader is alive to the obvious line of meaning, whereas Feuerman is not. For him, his dreams are messages without meanings. He has sunk into the sleep of reason in which to stop dreaming is not necessarily to awaken.[8]

Feuerman does bestir himself to spit in Borsif's face. Unable to stay away from the Obedman home, he enters to find the entire family taking tea. While conversing politely, Feuerman is overcome by the desire to spit in Borsif's face, only to be riddled by doubts about his nerve and his ability to transcend his crippling self-dissection [*nakranut*]. The subject of Chaimowitch arises; Borsif derides Chaimowitch's identification with the working classes and mocks his idealism. Then Feuerman spits at Borsif and goes out into the night. The incident is important not only for plot reasons but because it constitutes the only initiative undertaken by Feuerman after returning home. All other actions are ones he either declines doing or is drawn into despite himself. Even his leaving the town is more of an expulsion than a decision. The question of the proper interpretation to give this exceptional action is a matter that is thematized within the text. Feuerman's father is certain that the purpose of the act is to scuttle his, the father's, schemes and to cut off his chances forever, while the mother, not a little relieved, hastens to offer support rather than to look for reasons. Feuerman himself offers two contradictory explanations, one before the fact and one after. While screwing up his courage, Feuerman savors the pleasure to himself and the consternation to others that will be caused by Borsif's humiliation. The act has heroic overtones of defiance of false authority applauded by all concerned ("How great a mercy on all of us!," ch. 30, p. 119). All that is lacking is the courage to do the deed. After the fact, however, Feuerman is suffused with shame. Walking through the night-shrouded town he now sees what he did as a "despicable, lowly, loathsome act done by a man-fly to a man-worm" (ch. 30, p. 120). Rather than an assertion of will, his behavior betrayed a loss of control motivated by an indulgence in self-pity.[9]

These two interpretations, which play on the theme of the hero/anti-hero introduced in the prologue to *In Winter,* are urged on us by the narrator. But his insistence need not compel us, and we should recall that in his narrative proximate causes are often passed off as ultimate causes. As the one whose face is spit at, Borsif is the manifest object of Feuerman's resentment. He is the incarnation of all the values Feuerman has set himself against as well as all the natural endowments that he has been denied. Borsif is cold, soulless, and aloof from his people, as well as being well off, successful, and the possessor of a manly bearing attractive to women. His presence in the novel is reduced to three powerfully condensed synechdoches: his manly forelock, his derisive laugh, and the gold button on his tunic. (It is the loathsomeness of the last two of these that gives Feuerman his final spur to action.) Yet in the end it is not these qualities that demonizes Borsif but his connection to Rahil. (The possibility of his being a "daemon" is raised in the conversation between Rahil and Feuerman in chapter 24, p. 106). He is above all else Rahil's lover and therefore the possessor of the object Feuerman most deeply desires. To be sure, sexual jealousy is a powerful emotion, but the hatred deriving from it, though turned toward the successful competitor, finds its ultimate source in the beloved object itself and in its power over the self. Feuerman's uprising against Borsif is an attempt, and not a wholly unsuccessful one, to break the grip of his obsession. By humiliating himself in his attempt to humiliate Borsif, Feuerman not only explodes his father's marriage schemes but causes himself to be permanently banished from Rahil's presence and therefore from the nourishing pleasure of her visual accessibility. Viewed in this way, Feuerman's dramatic insult is exclusively neither defiance nor resentment but something at once more desperate and more effectual: an act of survival. He is roused to sacrifice his pleasure in an effort to rescue his self.

Just how great a risk he runs is revealed in a second dream sequence that takes place some days after the incident. Numbed and apathetic, Feuerman has in the meantime remained at home, enduring his father's rage over the collapse of his plans and his mother's growing anticipation of loss. At night he dreams:

> I am placed inside a filthy sack, sand weighs down my head and heavy rocks my hands and feet. I break out of the sack—but my father strikes me from above. Now I am a fly sporting [metsaḥek] on the cheek of that young woman. . . . She takes me and breaks off my wings. . . . The pain resembles what I used to feel as a child when I saw hell in my dreams. . . . Seventy degrees of ice . . . step after step . . . I climb up and then down . . . everyone mourns me. (ch. 31, p. 123)

The image of the interrupted journey from the earlier dream, with its possibility of renewed movement, has been revoked and inverted into an image of enclosure and imprisonment. The filthy sack in which the dreamer is forcibly restrained represents a potentially lethal impasse; the attempt to be born or reborn is on the verge of being aborted. (Perhaps this is the metamorphosis of the worm into the fly.) The constriction is broken through by dint of an active struggle, only to be greeted by blows from the father. The fly into which the dreamer is suddenly transformed is an image both of insignificance and of freedom. This is a nice representation of one side of Feuerman's relationship to Rahil. He is a creature of no importance to her, a mere annoyance, yet at the same time and for this very reason he can go where he likes and get as close to her as he wishes. *Mitsaḥek,* "sporting," in Hebrew carries an unmistakable sexual connotation.

What happens next, however, represents the darker side of his involvement. Proximity and pleasure ineluctably lead to dismemberment. Although in the dream this violence is depicted as something done to him by her, the hurt is actually inflicted on himself as a result of having given himself over to his obsession and the vulnerabilities it opened in him. The clipping of wings is a standard figure for castration. Already Feuerman has been sexually wounded by exposing sexual feelings that had been concealed and denied, only to find himself shamefully impotent. Yet the damage done is more than sexual. The torn wings represent not only the genitals but that which has replaced the genitals in the organization of Feuerman's mental life. His intelligence, his mind, his language, as well as his capacity for suffering, his honesty, his empathy—all these compensations for the more vital life of the instincts, which have in turn been libidinalized by him, are the forces that have shaped Feuerman's spirit, deformed and abnormal as it may or may not be. It is these qualities of consciousness that are taken from Feuerman when he abandons himself to obsession. They are all he has and they are who he is, and his act of rescue is to recover them.

The self-rescue leads to Feuerman's exit from town. The expulsion scene (chapter 32) ties together with great ironic economy the planes of perception operative throughout part three: Feuerman in his public and social role as perceived by his family, and Feuerman caught in the web of unconscious desires as experienced by himself alone. Throughout his stay at home, the great issue for his father has been marriage; for Feuerman the related but very different issue has been of erotic obsession. The underlying comic irony in these sections is generated by the father's obliviousness to his son's inability to relate to women, and the tragic irony is generated by the son's complicity, brought on by his obsession, in his father's plans. These two lines collide when the father intercepts and opens a letter from the city sent to Feuerman by Rivka Lerner, Chaimowitch's friend. She writes asking for money for Chaimowitch, who has been forced to leave town (presumably because of political agitation), and, destitute herself, begs Feuerman to find her employment in his home town. Unlike Chaimowitch's Russian letters to Feuerman, this one is written in Yiddish and therefore an open book to the father, who seizes upon the female identity of the writer as given away by the closing salutation: "your friend" [*yedidatkha*]. "What is she to you? A lover?" the father demands derisively, goading Feuerman, who replies falsely to the taunt with his own provocation, "Yes, a lover!" (ch. 32, p. 125). To the father it is now clear as day that the match with Rahil failed because Feuerman was in love with another woman whose existence he had concealed from him. To the mother, it similarly becomes clear that her son's loyalty to Jewish religious practice had all along been compromised by his relations with this "free" woman. In the customary gesture of parents whose offspring has been "lost" to the Jewish people, they both begin moaning and bewailing their son as if he were dead. The irony is devastating. Feuerman stands accused of the one sin he—and for that matter all his predecessors in the Hebrew autobiographical tradition—is sadly incapable of committing. The woman with whom he is supposed to have consorted is in fact the most wretched and pathetic of creatures, and has been the asexual companion of another man. She is the kind of woman for whom Feuerman can feel no attraction but only pity. But these stirrings of empathy he does feel for her and for others; he loves them in *this* way. So when he admits to being a lover it is not only provocation but also a perverse but real truth.

The endings of all of Brenner's novels are at once rich and problematic. For the doomed and struggling young men and women Brenner writes of there can be no simple gesture of closure. Deliverance through love or the formation of a new community through marriage were possibilities patently inappropriate. Dismissed as melodramatic were the principal unhappy endings available at the time: madness, suicide, and death by disease. Brenner resists as well the temptation to offer a wisdom ending of the sort that looks back and ruefully acknowledges, "Now I realize. . . ." Brenner's characters know more at the end than they did in the beginning, but their knowledge is rarely redemptive or even consoling. The most that can be said about these figures—and after what they have gone through it is not a little—is that they manage to go on, and this without having completed some neatly defined "stage" in life's journey and without knowing exactly what will come next. The most Brenner can do is to attempt to represent this sense of survival and the moment of pause in the onrush of life in which it occurs. A study of the changes in how Brenner devises these endings throughout his career—and the techniques by which the ending are bound to the body of the novels—would tell us much about the development of Brenner's art.[10] In the case of *In Winter*, Brenner's first novel, two intertwined lines of closure are offered: one tightly continuous with the work's poetics (chapters 34 and 36) and one provocatively at odds with it (chapters 33 and 35). The first of these gives us briefly two incidents that followed Feuerman's departure from his home town: his meeting with Rivka Lerner and his being put off the train. The meeting with Lerner takes place in the big city, to which he has now returned. Penniless and bereft of Chaimowitch's guidance and support, Lerner has suffered a breakdown leaving her barely able to take care of herself. There is no help to be sought from her parents, who view her as degenerate and wayward. Why the novel should end with such a minor character and one so distantly connected to Feuerman is a question answered by the way she is presented here: she is Feuerman's double. She is now what Feuerman would have become if he were born a woman and if he lacked his special endowments of mind. He and she are of the same species; she is simply one of the weaker fish in the sea who is not equipped for survival. Feuerman's response to her is equivocal; he is first repelled and then overcome by pity. But even this emotion is eclipsed by a more insistent image: the memory of Rahil. While in Lerner's presence, Feuerman's mind drifts off into a comparison between Rahil's life and Lerner's. While one suffers and will go on suffering, the other, always loved and indulged, will go off to Switzerland, have Borsif's children, and live the life of the bored rich. Yet the true purpose of the reverie, with which the chapter ends, is not its manifest subject, the pitying of Lerner, but rather the way in which that subject is quickly displaced by obsessive thoughts of Rahil. The fact that he has saved himself by escaping from her presence does not shield him from the persistence of desire and its ungovernable reassertions. As an ending, then, chapter 34 underscores the decisiveness of the erotic moment in Feuerman's life, a moment whose consequences Feuerman will have no choice but to struggle with from now on.

Similarly, the brilliant final chapter of *In Winter* (36) manages within the compass of half a page to recapitulate, and in a sense take leave from, some of the major movements that shape the novel. This is an ending which as pure scene, free of comment and free of description, stands in a starkly metonymical relation to all that has gone before. On a rainy night, Feuerman is discovered concealed and ticketless on a train traveling away from the big city. Spewing antisemitic remarks, the authorities order him put off the train at a tiny station in the middle of nowhere. He gets off, crosses the tracks, and finds a woodpile behind which to lie down as the rain and snow fall on the ground. That *In Winter* should end with an image of an arrested journey should not be surprising. Implicit in the novel are movements in two directions. As a novel of childhood and youth and therefore a kind of *Bildungsroman*, the work creates the expectation of a linear growth (albeit with setbacks) in the direction of greater awareness and maturity. Yet patterns of departing from home and returning to home deflect the linear movement inward and bend it into the prospect of circular repetition. Brenner's next novel will be called *Misaviv lanekudah*, "Movement in Place." In *In Winter*, that circularity is anticipated but not yet realized, and therefore the picture of Feuerman's being put off the train is particularly effective in registering the indeterminacy of the hero's future. He has managed, after all, to break away from home and from Rahil and is en route to a new destination (designated, perhaps appropriately, only by the Hebrew letter *alef*). His journey is interrupted but at least it has been undertaken. The ending implies that the process of journeying and being stopped from journeying will go on and on. For the moment there is cessation, a sense of pause, and, as Feuerman lies down in the rain by the woodpile, a posture of acceptance.

Significantly, it is an outside force that interdicts his initiative. The specter of antisemitism raised on the last page of *In Winter* compels us to reflect on how small a role is played in the novel by the gentile world and its hostility toward the Jews. Feuerman's ordeals—his deprivations, his loss of faith, his existential trials, his struggles with sexuality—unfold as a drama which at times is distinctly and internally Jewish and at times belongs to the human condition in general. The sense of impending catastrophe in *In Winter* hovers over the soul of the Jew rather than over the collectivity of Israel in its historical and political reality. Because this is the rule, the exception in the novel's closing moment becomes an ironic gesture, one which opens up a possible but unrealized perspective. It is as if Brenner is saying that although he has written a work all about Jewish self-exploration and self-doubt, one cannot lose sight of the larger and forbidding framework in which these dramas are played out. There are limits to self-judgment. The irony is further compounded. After being put off the train at least in part for being a Jew, Feuerman ends up not back with his people but at a station whose closest village has no Jews at all. He is, for the moment, literally, nowhere.

If this were all there was to the conclusion of *In Winter*, the novel would end with two beautifully minimalist images, one conveying the deconstructive persistence of desire (chapter 34) and the other stressing the ambiguity of movement (chapter 36). Both are tightly integrated into the diction and discourse of the novel. But this is not quite all. Of the four-chapter ending of *In Winter*, the long fourth-to-last chapter and the brief penultimate chapter are written with an expressive abandon largely at odds with what has come before. The peculiarity of these sections presents considerable interpretive difficulties, which have led Brenner critics to exaggerate the importance of the statements made in the chapters and to see in them, especially in the wintry mood of chapter 33, a summary of the novel's wisdom. I would like to suggest that the opposite tack be taken. The anomaly of these chapters, conveyed in their expressively heightened diction, offers examples of the kind of writing in which Brenner chose *not* to compose *In Winter*. The chapters describe two extreme and opposing dispositions of the narrative consciousness, the one sardonic and moribund and the other abandoned and exultant. Rather than disclosing the ultimate meaning of Feuerman's ordeal, they offer insights into what the novel cannot be about and remain a novel.[11]

Chapter 33 is composed of a series of meditations about the stony apathy that takes hold of the human spirit after efforts and aspirations have come to nought. The chapter is set off from others by being explicitly identified as an eruption of the narrative present into the job of relating the past. Nearing the end of his story, the narrator breaks into the story to describe his present state of mind before quieting himself and resuming the last three chapters of his narrative. From the very beginning, then, this section is presented as an outburst of uncontrollable feelings and as a violation of the self-discipline necessary to discharge the burden of narration. These charged emotions flow from a conviction of futility about writing and from the life experiences it is supposed to describe.[12] The narrator alludes to the little notebook referred to in the very first line of the novel in which he meant to jot down "a few impressions and sketches." The notebook still has many empty pages, but he is convinced that any description of his future life will be merely a repetition of what is already recorded. The reason he writes, however, is because he cannot do otherwise. "I write only because it is impossible for me not to cry out the old woe, because I shall never cease bewailing the old pain. . . . let me shout! Let me shout out a great and bitter complaint!" (ch. 33, p. 126). From this shriek, the narrator passes on to meditations about winter as a metaphor for the soul, about death and the seduction of suicide, and about the blind struggle for survival. The chapter concludes by edging off into the kind of sardonic laughter that raises the prospect of madness. "This is a laughter that resembles the sound made by a mad dog" (p. 127).

It is tempting to take these existential broodings, conveniently gathered together at the novel's close, as a window into the soul of the hero-novelist (the two merge at this point). Attention to the style and tone in which these statements are uttered, however, should bring us to the opposite conclusion: Before us is a *parody* of sententiousness rather than sententiousness itself. The short, choppy, often one-line paragraphs produce the effect of stammering and speaking by association. Sentences either end abruptly with exclamation marks or trail off unfinished. This is writing as existential howl. Ejaculations abound; "oh's" and "woe's" stud the page. The emotionally charged language speaks only of extreme states of being— and non-being. In sum, the canons of craft and discipline set up by Brenner throughout the novel would urge us to judge chapter 33 not as an excrescence of insight but simply as bad writing. Its badness derives from the giving way to feeling. It is not as if the wretchedness of spirit is not real—it is. But the achievement of the narrator throughout *In Winter* has consisted in the successful containment of this pain. By the willed exertion of intelligence and empathy, the narrator has been able to turn his misery into art. Throughout the story there are moments when this pressure, which issues from the present instance of the writing, threatens to drown the narrative in existential outcry; but the narrator pulls back and regains control. The melancholic broodings about breakdown and suicide in chapter 33 stand, then, as a reminder of what was overcome and not given into in order to produce the story we have just read. We are reminded as well not to adopt any facile view of narration as therapy and consolation. Feuerman is not to be counted among those narrators who, having confessed their past and given it shape, are now free of its hold. If anything, the location of this outcry at the end of the novel indicates how immense has been the task of self-control and how difficult to keep the floodgates shut now that the task has been accomplished.

The twin to this outcry is chapter 35. It is written in the same exclamatory mode, except its mood is the exact opposite: joyous, celebratory, embracing of life. This time the exclamation arises not from the time of the writing (the narrator living as a tutor in an isolated village) but from the penultimate moment in the narrated action of the story, that is, as Feuerman is about to depart from the big city a second time after his brief return. The outpouring comes in the form of a letter to Dawidowsky that is never posted. "Today the sun will shine," the letter begins, "Not the winter sun with the weak and pale face of a young woman, but a summer sun so great, bold, and brilliant that a man's eyes cannot behold it" (ch. 35, p. 129). Feuerman goes on to proclaim that he loves life, that his heart is overflowing, and that he knows that what will come next will be different from what has come before. He declares life to be too abundant and complex to be grasped by the "dissecting knives" of analysis. As the child of suffering he knows that further suffering awaits him in the future, but he is not afraid and gladly faces his wanderings and his loneliness.

This is certainly happier news than Feuerman's melancholic ruminations, but like them, it is, as far as the novel is concerned, news from nowhere. Again, this is not to say that these transcendent feelings are not genuinely held, or that they cannot be understood, as Kurzweil does, as the exaltation of a man who has survived his torments,[13] or as Zemach does, as a reassertion of the vital instincts once possessed in childhood.[14] Yet there is no more warrant for reading this passage as a message of redemption than there is for taking chapter 33 as an oracle of collapse. The ode to the new sun shining embodies the dithyrambic and breathless style in which *In Winter* was not, and could not, be written.[15]

"What are these dissecting knives to me?" asks Feuerman in his paean to light (ch. 35, p. 129). A great deal, the novel answers. The exercise of critical intelligence is the hallmark of the narrator's method. He uses his powers of consciousness to conceive the past and understand it, and in so doing allows himself to be moved to empathy by the visions of himself and others that he has summoned up and analyzed. This sort of confrontation with the past, which requires the constant application of mind and craft, describes the difficult commitment to narration sustained by Brenner's narrator. This is a commitment that will of necessity at times fall into the slough of despond and entertain fantasies of escape into madness and death and at times ascend to visions of radiance and plenitude. The twin epiphanies, one negative and one positive, that are braided into the conclusion of the novel represent such necessary and deserved moments of evasion and remission. Yet it is not they who have the last word. The true and final ending to *In Winter* belongs to the huddled figure behind the woodpile in the rain who before long will pick himself up and begin telling his story.

CONCLUSION

The Vagaries of the
Autobiographical Impulse

This study has examined a brief but significant moment in which the crisis of Judaism in the modern age was given a very specific literary expression. This expression, the autobiographical mode of writing after the example of Rousseau and Maimon, was adopted to tell the story of a generation of young men who grew up within the piety of East European Jewish society only to lose their faith and be condemned to find their way in a world without God. The intertwining of these two, the autobiographical mode and the apostasy narrative, is an example of how a particular literary form can be suited to the exigencies of historical experience. The pain and upheaval caused by the collapse of traditional belief was a crisis for a whole generation, yet the ordeal was experienced by individuals whose consciousness had been sensitized by the experience itself. Autobiography as a form answered to needs that arose on both these levels. As confession, autobiography allowed the individual to give shape to the anguished feelings that arose from his own situation. At the same time, the very presumption of writing about oneself assumed that the individual's ordeal was representative of a collective crisis and therefore significant on those larger grounds.

When the nature of the historical crisis shifts (in ways we shall look at in a moment), the knot binding the autobiographical mode and the apostasy narrative comes undone, and each strand undergoes a separate course of development. The career embarked upon by autobiography evinces a clear withdrawal from a commitment to individualized introspection and inwardness. One line of development is writers' autobiographies, a category which includes Abramowitsch's *Bayamin hahem* (1897–1911, *Of Bygone Days*, 1973), in Yiddish Shalom Aleichem's *Motl Peyse dem ḥazans* (1916–17, *The Great Fair*, 1955), and in the same mode much later Dov Sadan's *Mimeḥoz hayaldut* (1938, "From the Province of Childhood") and *Mima'agal hane'urim* (1981, "From the Province of Youth"). The spirit of all of these works is ethnographic rather than existential. They seek to evoke a way of life and a social world that have been overtaken by historical change. The image these authors present of themselves is meant to be paradigmatic of that world; the self is not conceived of as a complex and individual organism in tension with its environment. The segments of life represented tend to

203

come from the early stages of personhood, so that the question of how the child became a writer, with all that implies, is kept well at a distance.

Another line of development in autobiography shifts the focus from the author to the events he witnessed. World War One, the Russian Revolution, and the Russian Civil War were all events that had the most profound, and usually destructive, impact on Jewish society. Jews led revolutionary movements, fought on both sides in the wars, and became victims of widespread pogroms and dislocations. In the many first-person accounts of these upheavals written in Hebrew, the true "heroes" are the events themselves. The author's life is an armature around which history is recounted; he remains a witness rather than a subject. The outstanding example of this kind of autobiography is Avigdor Hameiri's *Hashiga'on hagadol* (1929, *The Great Madness*, 1952, 1984), which tells the story of what he witnessed as a soldier in World War One. In a related kind of autobiography, which tends toward the memoir, the author is indeed important and can lay claim to playing a role in history rather than simply witnessing it. In Hebrew literature this primarily means the great Zionist leaders. Examples include Shmaraya Levin's *Mizikhronot hayyai* (1935–42, *The Arena*, 1952), Arthur Ruppin's *Pirkei hayyai* (1943–46, "Memoirs"), Zalman Shazar's *Kokhvei voker* (1950, *Morning Stars*, 1967), and David Ben-Gurion's *Zikhronot* (1971, "Memoirs"). Some of these are rather dry efforts to document the course of a career, settle old scores, and revise the historical record, while others offer insights, at times genuinely self-reflective, into the mind and motives of historical actors; some are crudely written, while others display a gift for the shaping rhetoric of historical narrative. Yet in all of these autobiographies-memoirs the object of self-portraiture is restricted to the public self. These are not works in which to look for reflection on domestic relations, romantic experience, crises of self-doubt or of belief in the cause—which is to say all the themes of the private self that have arisen from the autobiographical texts discussed in this study.

It is in the later development of the apostasy narrative once it is disentangled from autobiography that the private dimension can be found. The apostasy narrative as such—the story of the break with traditional Jewish faith—disappears; what persists is the sensibility upon which it was based. The apostasy narrative disappears, I would suggest, for two reasons. The first relates to the influence of literary generations. From the nineteenth century to the present there have been continual waves of young Jewish men and women who have undergone a shattering crisis of faith. Yet within the development of Hebrew literature as a system, that crisis is identified with Brenner's generation, the generation that came of age after the demise of the Haskalah and before the consolidation of the Jewish national movement. Religious belief as a problem "belongs" to that generation in the self-conception of Hebrew literature; the issue recedes thereafter. A second, related reason stems from the suffocating force of Brenner's *In Winter* as a work of art. We have examined in depth the way in which *In Winter* breaks down the autobiographical tradition into its component themes, rewrites them, and recombines them into a new whole. The mastery with which Brenner revises the tradition is an instance in literary history of a work whose authority seems to exhaust the possibilities of a genre and discourage further attempts at development.

The sensibility that persists, after the topic of apostasy loses its relevance, expresses itself in the focus on inner experience. The stage of life represented in writing is no longer the immediate aftermath of the loss of faith with its throbbing disorientation. The heroes are instead men and women in their twenties and thirties who are already longtime denizens of the void. Their faithlessness is the accustomed condition of their lives, and the break with religion, if it was anything more than a rite of passage to begin with, is barely recalled. The existential and psychological exploration of these dispossessed souls takes place in the later fiction of Brenner himself and in the fiction of several of his contemporaries: U. N. Gnessin, G. Schoffman, and Jacob Steinberg. Only in Brenner, especially in his last novel *Shekhol vekhishalon* (1920, *Breakdown and Bereavement*, 1971), does this inner scrutiny remain both Jewish and religious. Brenner's characters are deeply embroiled in the contemporary struggles of Jewish life, and they continue to be tormented by religious and metaphysical needs long after they have ceased believing in the God of Israel. In contrast, the fiction of Gnessin, Schoffman, and Steinberg may be set in provincial bourgeois Jewish society, but the dilemmas faced by their heroes have little to do with Jewish issues. They experience vague sexual longings and the urge toward some creative self-realization, yet all their desires seem destined to remain unfulfilled because of a failure of will and a romantic absorption in illusion. Even if the world of these characters is touched by an entropic movement toward death, the literary representation of their lives can be very vital. In Gnessin especially the vivid and subtle observation of mental sensations and interior consciousness creates an aesthetic texture that is alive on its own terms. Taken as a whole, however, the writing of this group describes a world *created by* apostasy but no longer quickened by its particular thematics.

When it comes to the use of the autobiographical mode in serious writing, we discover a surprisingly prolonged absence. With the exceptions of Agnon and Lisitzky, there are few if any significant examples of autobiographical writing in Hebrew literature from before World War One until Pinhas Sadeh's *Ḥayyim kemashal* (1954, *Life as a Parable,* 1966). Even this work turns out to be exceptional; the general absence continues through the 1970s.[1] This generalization is of course qualified by a definition of terms. As used here, autobiography excludes memoiristic writing as well as fiction that is fed from autobiographical sources but not expressed in that mode. Even with these qualifications, the phenomenon is a striking one. It tests the widespread assumption that autobiography writing is a universal "impulse" in the self-conscious modern world created by the breakdown of traditional society. Seen from this perspective, the works of Guenzburg, Lilienblum, Feierberg, Berdichevsky, and Brenner that have been discussed in this volume constitute a moment that came and went in the life of Hebrew literature rather than the beginning of a basic shift in orientation.

Why this should be so is a problem with so many variables it can not be approached here. Some direction is indicated by the historical status of autobiography described in the introduction. In contrast to the Christian European tradition, we saw that there is almost no autobiography to speak of in classical and medieval Judaism; the self-writing undertaken in the early modern period (Modena and Emden) was never circulated beyond manuscript form, and it was not until the end of the eighteenth century that Maimon, under the influence of Rousseau, provided a public model of true autobiographical writing. The relative alienness of autobiography to Jewish culture, we conjectured, results from the secondary status of the individual in Judaism. Although the individual is responsible for his actions, the meaning of his life is absorbed in collective structures and collective myths. With the partial exception of mystical testimonies in the kabbalistic tradition, Judaism, unlike Christianity, does not know the deeply personal experience of conversion nor the nuanced inner drama of individual salvation.

To be sure, the Jewish national movement in modern times, whose imaginative expression is Hebrew literature, is not continuous with classical Judaism. Yet in its distinct emphasis on the role of the nation in the realization of the individual, a pronounced continuity can be observed. The establishment of a Jewish state in Palestine was to be a solution for the Jewish people as a whole and a normalization of the anomic inner gropings of the Jewish intellectual. There is nothing coincidental about the fact that Lilienblum brings the story of his anguished searchings to a close just at the moment that the truth of political Zionism is revealed to him. Once the Yishuv is firmly established, the force of collective ideology never ceases to be paramount. Even when writers speak in the first person, their "I" is often simply a more poignant way of saying "we."

The Hebrew autobiographical tradition stands, then, as something of an aberration. The normative mode of Jewish literature, before the modern period and after it, is unremittingly collective, whereas in autobiography, as we have surveyed it, the inner turmoil of the individual is unrelieved by being part of a larger national process. Yet far from detracting from the significance of the phenomenon, this fact should make us appreciate its paradigm-breaking power even more.

We observed that there are few examples of true autobiography in Hebrew literature after Brenner. There are several significant exceptions to this rule, and each of them tells us something different about the conditions for autobiographical expression in an essentially non-autobiographical national literature.

Ephraim E. Lisitzky's *Elleh toldot adam* (1949, *In the Grip of Cross-Currents*, 1959),[2] to begin with, is written from the periphery of the periphery of Hebrew literature. As a poet, Lisitzky played an important role in Hebrew literature in America, but he wrote not from New York or another Jewish metropolis but from New Orleans. His autobiography follows his life from his years as a yeshiva student in Slutsk, Lithuania, to his encounter as a young man with America. The America he discovered was not only the immigrant neighborhoods of Boston with poor Jews and their Zionist and socialist clubs but a much broader canvas: rural Jewish communities in upstate New York and isolated Jews living in the frontier settlements of northern Ontario. This is, literally, uncharted territory for the Hebrew writer, and it would seem that this conviction of uniqueness is one of the springs of the narrative. One of the constraints on autobiography in Hebrew is the sense that the members of a generation have all undergone the same experiences and passed through the same scenes. If at the age of fifteen Lisitzky had ended up in Jaffa rather than Boston, he too may have felt that his story would be merely a retelling.

In the Grip of Cross-Currents is far from being a travelogue. The work is marked by a balance between recording the sights and sounds of his new life and observing the deep changes in his private self. In themes and images reminiscent of Bialik, Lisitzky recounts the early emotional deprivation that marked his life. His mother died when he was seven, and his father left for America a few months later, leaving the boy in the care of a hastily married step-mother. It was eight years before the father sent for his family, and during this time the boy found a second home in the world of the heder and the yeshiva, in which he excelled. But the world of Torah and a future as a scholar seemed irrelevant in Boston, where Jews were absorbed in the struggle to make a living. Lisitzky's story, then, is about a double deprivation: the loss of primary love and security as a child and then the sudden obsolescence of the calling he had seized upon as a substitute. His wanderings off the beaten path in America, from far north to deep south, are not simply the expression of a *wanderlust* but an effort to find a home and a vocation. The special pathos of this quest, for a Hebrew writer, is that it takes place in America, the country that compassionately opened its doors to the huddled masses and then promptly eradicated their languages and culture.

Lisitzky does eventually succeed in his calling as a Hebrew poet and a Jewish educator and in finding a place to settle in New Orleans. Yet *In the Grip of Cross-Currents* does not conclude with a sense of arrival, however incomplete. The book ends at an indefinite moment in Lisitzky's early adulthood, whose sadness returns us to the author's early deprivations. *In the Grip of Cross-Currents* lacks the kind of double autobiographical perspective characteristic of Brenner's *In Winter*, in which we come to know something of the narrator in his present identity as he meditates upon, and reacts to, his earlier selves. Despite the palpable pain that quickens his story, Lisitzky is not drawn to the exploration of subjectivity as were Brenner and his generation. The self remains oriented toward the outside—a mirror that reflects the spectacle of the world. The vignette, the portrait sketch, and the nature description are among the techniques at which Lisitzky excels, and they are well suited to capturing the sights and wonders that meet the Hebrew writer at large in the New World.

Although written in Israel and a part of the literary scene there, Pinhas Sadeh's autobiography *Ḥayyim kemashal* (1954, *Life as a Parable*, 1966) is in every sense as exceptional. Both Lisitzky and Sadeh are poets who write prose autobiographies based upon the authority of their experience as artists rather than upon the claims of worldly accomplishment. Yet while Lisitzky writes from old age about a formative period in his youth, Sadeh— much in the manner we are familiar with from Lilienblum and Brenner— writes his autobiography at the age of twenty-seven and concentrates on the most recent ten years of his life. Sadeh was brought to Israel from Europe by his parents at the age of five and raised under conditions of cultural deprivation at home and in institutions for troubled youths. He fought in the War of Liberation and worked at many low-paying jobs in Israel and Europe while he wrote poetry. Yet in contrast to Lisitzy, the scenes and sights through which he passes hold no interest for him. Sadeh's eyes are turned inward to the drama of the soul. He presents his life as the record of "the birth of the spirit out of the agonies and yearnings of the flesh" (p. 60).[3] He struggles to free himself from "sin," which he defines as "cleaving to material existence, by means of delights, the cult of the body, the pursuit of gain and luxury" (p. 102). His path toward this freedom is tortuous; he is often mired in his own needs and prone to relationships with women based on "animal delight and disgust." Sadeh is unsparing with himself, and his commitment to "truth," in the grand tradition of autobiography, endows the work with an urgent authenticity.

What makes *Life as a Parable* important is the historical moment in which it was written and the literary-cultural norms with which it takes issue. Sadeh was nineteen years old when the 1948 war broke out, and he fought in it together with other young writers (Yizhar, Shamir, Meged, Gouri), members of what became known as the Palmah Generation. For these writers the war was a defining event that brought to a climax an intense identification between the individual and the nation. Yet for Sadeh the opposite was true. He writes only about the first hour of the first night of the war, and of the remaining two years he states: "Much of what happened to me has no personal meaning, and what has no personal meaning may be considered worthless" (p. 129). For a national literature deeply rooted in a collective historical myth, this is an astonishing assertion, and it is one that is made with clear philosophical and theological awareness. The bond between individual experience and collective destiny is expressed by the insistence in classical Judaism that the individual will be redeemed only in the messianic age when the people as a whole will be redeemed. Sadeh cannot forgive Judaism (unlike Christianity) this failure to acknowledge the possibility of individual salvation. For him this is the only goal that matters. To take up his quest he therefore looks for guidance from masters beyond the bounds of normative Judaism: Nathan of Gaza, Jacob Frank, Nietzsche, and above all—Jesus.

There is no mistaking the link between Sadeh's quest for individual salvation and his turn toward autobiography. The other members of his literary generation are absorbed in describing the challenges faced by the new state and the ways in which the individual is enmeshed by collectivist ideology. Only Sadeh stands apart and relegates these struggles to a low rung of importance relative to his, and every man's, search for salvation. Only this kind of cosmic narcissism—the belief in the individuated self as the ultimate locus of meaning—can authorize the writing of genuinely confessional autobiography in such an age as this, when the burden of the collective is so acutely and generally felt. For Sadeh there is another life, the life of the spirit, and to pursue it requires severing oneself from history and national experience. The spirit can be reached through meditation, reading, poetry, the scrutiny of behavior, and above all, through dreams and their analysis. In recording these efforts, Sadeh creates a new kind of mixed text which combines philosophy, poetry, and dreams, as well as narrative. He goes about his task of converting life into a parable and thereby breaking the hold of history.

And in the end there is Agnon, the exception who is not an exception. Any study of Hebrew autobiography would be incomplete without reference to his work; yet mining and refining the autobiographical deposits scattered throughout Agnon's considerable *oeuvre* is its own enterprise requiring its own instruments. I have tried my hand at a piece of the task on another occasion.[4] Some of the specifically autobiographical components of Agnon's work include the artist tales from his years in Jaffa preceding World War One (including "Giv'at haḥol" ["A Hill of Sand"]); the first-person novel *Oreaḥ natah lalun* (1938–39, *A Guest for the Night*, 1968), which describes a year-long return to his native town in Galicia; the persona of the narrator in surreal stories that make up *Sefer hama'asim* (1932–53, "The Book of Deeds"); a self-parodic fragment "Hemdat" (1947); and *'Ad Hena* (1952, "Until Now"), a novella based on the author's experiences in Germany during World War One.

The autobiographical persona changes with the narrator's situation. He is a cherished son about to leave home for the Holy Land, he is an artist among the bohemians of the early Yishuv, he is a young Hebrew writer sojourning in Germany, he is a husband and father separated by circumstance from his wife and children. In all of these guises there is a deflationary irony and even parody. The autobiographical narrator is usually a passive figure to whom things happen, sometimes nightmarish things. When he has plans of his own they are often foolishly aggrandizing.

Sometimes he serves simply as an armature around which tales and anecdotes are spun. He is portrayed as a bourgeois Jewish artist, a kind of religious *moyen hommme sensuel,* whose self-absorption constantly leads to the dereliction of sacred responsibilities. Yet all this self-mockery strengthens rather than undercuts the sovereign sense of self that pervades Agnon's work. He is secure in depicting his weaknesses precisely because he views his life as the embodiment of the ordeal of religious man in the twentieth century.

Agnon's strength of self, his fundamental energizing narcissism, escaped the fate of the earlier writers in the autobiographical tradition we have discussed in this study. Unlike Feierberg, his soul was not consumed in the conflagration of apostasy, and unlike Brenner he did not leave the crisis of faith behind him. Agnon *ingested* the crisis and lived with it in his bones and his mind. Rather than cutting himself off from the tradition, he incorporated the conflict and dramatized it within the dynamics of his own ego. In so doing, he taught us something lasting about the paradoxical connection between the assertions of the self and the integrity of the tradition.

Notes

1. The Turn toward Autobiography in Hebrew Literature

   1. See my *Ḥurban: Responses to Catastrophe in Hebrew Literature* (New York: Columbia University Press, 1984), ch. 2, "Midrash and the Destruction."

   2. The phrase is included (enclosed in quotation marks) in a catalogue of slogans mentioned by Yirmiah Feuerman, the hero and narrator of Brenner's autobiographical first novel *Baḥoref* (1903, In Winter), *Yosef Ḥayyim Brenner: Ketavim* (Tel Aviv, 1978), vol. 2, p. 176.

   3. Georg Misch, *Geschichte der Autobiographie* (Bern and Frankfurt, 1949–1969).

   4. On the centrality of Augustine, see William G. Spengemann, *The Forms of Autobiography* (New Haven: Yale University Press, 1980). This volume also contains an excellent review of the critical literature on autobiography.

   5. See the introductory definitions in Karl Joachim Weintraub, *The Value of the Individual: Self and Circumstance in Autobiography* (Chicago: University of Chicago Press, 1978).

   6. The literature is introduced and excerpted in a useful anthology compiled by Leo W. Schwarz, *Memoirs of My People: Jewish Self-Portraits from the Eleventh to the Twentieth Centuries* (New York: Schocken Books, 1943 and 1963). On Yagel, see David Ruderman's translation of Abraham ben Hananyah Yagel's *Gei' ḥizayyon (Valley of Vision)*, (University of Pennsylvania Press, forthcoming). To this list could be added an extremely brief autobiographical fragment recently discovered: Yisrael Yuval, "An Ashkenazic Autobiography from the Fourteenth Century" [Hebrew], *Tarbiz*, vol. 45, no. 4 (1987), pp. 542–66.

   7. Daniel Carpi, ed., *Ḥayyei Yehudah* (Tel Aviv, 1985).

   8. See the introductory essay by Natalie Zemon Davis to the translation by Mark Cohen of Modena's *The Life of Judah* (Princeton: Princeton University Press, 1988), pp. 50–69. I am grateful to Professor Davis for sharing with me a draft of her essay.

   9. Davis, p. 69.

   10. Abraham Kahana, ed., *Megillat sefer* (Warsaw, 1896).

   11. *Solomon Maimons Lebensgeschichte, von ihm selbst geschreiben* (Berlin, 1793); English translation by J. Clark Murray, *The Autobiography of Solomon Maimon* (Boston, 1888).

   12. The *Lebensgeschichte* was translated into Russian in 1871–72, into Hebrew in 1899, and into Yiddish in 1927. For other translations, see *Kirjat Sepher* XLI (1966): 257–59.

   13. Weintraub, p. 300.

   14. See Fischel Lachower's introduction to Y. L. Baruch (trans.), *Sefer hayyei Shelomo Maimon* (Tel Aviv, 1943 and 1953), p. 25.

   15. Samuel Werses, "Directions in Autobiography in the Haskalah Period" [Hebrew], *Gilyonot* 17 (1945): 175–83.

   16. Mordecai Aaron Guenzburg, *Aviezer* (Tel Aviv, 1967; photoreproduction of first Vilna edition, 1864), pp. 1–2.

   17. Moses Leib Lilienblum, *Ketavim otobiogerafiyim*, ed. Shlomo Breiman (Jerusalem, 1970).

   18. *Aviezer*, p. 2.

   19. Jean-Jacques Rousseau, *The Confessions*, trans. J. M. Cohen (Baltimore: Penguin Books, 1975), p. 17.

   20. Philippe Lejeune, *Le Pacte autobiographique* (Paris, 1975).

   21. On the autobiographical long poem in Tchernichovsky, see Yehudit Bar-El,

" 'Al tel ha'aravah—The Poetics of Tchernichovsky's Long Autobiographical Poëme" [Hebrew], *Meḥkerei yerushalayim besifrut 'ivrit* 9 (1987): 125–47.

22. See Dan Miron, *Hapereidah min ha'ani he'ani: mahalakh behitpatḥut shirato hamukdemet shel Ḥayyim Nahman Bialik* [*Taking Leave of the Impoverished Self: Ch. N. Bialik's Early Poetry, 1891–1901*] (Tel Aviv, 1986).

23. *"Bo'ah, lailah": hasifrut ha'ivrit bein higayon le'igayon* [*"Come, Night": Hebrew Literature between the Rational and the Irrational at the Turn of the Twentieth Century*] (Tel Aviv, 1987).

24. For useful summaries of this literature, see the methodological chapters in Spengemann (note 4 above); Avrom Fleishman, *Figures of Autobiography: The Language of Self-Writing in Victorian and Modern England* (Los Angeles and Berkeley: University of California Press, 1983); and Paul John Eakin, *Fictions in Autobiography: Studies in the Art of Self-Invention* (Princeton: Princeton University Press, 1985).

25. Roy Pascal, *Design and Truth in Autobiography* (Cambridge, MA: Harvard University Press, 1960) and James Olney, *Metaphors of Self: The Meaning of Autobiography* (Princeton: Princeton University Press, 1972).

26. See Jeffrey Mehlman, *A Structural Study of Autobiography* (Ithaca: Cornell University Press, 1974), and Paul De Man, "Autobiography as Defacement," *MLN* 94 (1979): 920–23.

27. See Eakin's judgment on this issue, pp. 275–78.

28. See Weintraub, Introduction.

29. See Dan Miron, *Bodedim bemo'adam: lediyuknah shel harepublikah hasifrutit ha'ivrit biteḥilat hame'ah ha'esrim* [*When Loners Come Together: A Portrait of Hebrew Literature at the Turn of the Twentieth Century*] (Tel Aviv, 1987), pp. 86–111.

30. See Alan Mintz, *George Eliot and the Novel of Vocation* (Cambridge, MA: Harvard University Press, 1978), ch. 2, "The Shape of a Life in Biography and Autobiography," pp. 21–51.

31. Lejeune, p. 14.

32. See Yael Feldman's useful clarifications in "Gender In/Difference in Contemporary Hebrew Fictional Autobiographies," *Biography* 11:3 (1988): 193.

2. The Haskalah Background: In the Toils of Authenticity

1. On the didactic elements of *Aviezer*, especially the use of such neoclassical rhetorical devices as the parable and the example, see the instructive studies by Moshe Pelli, "The Essence of the Hebrew Biography: A Study of *Aviezer* by Mordecai Aaron Guenzburg" [Hebrew], *Hadoar* 62:10 (Jan. 14, 1983): 156–57, and "Life as Parable; Issues in the Didactic Autobiography: A Study of M. A. Guenzburg's *Aviezer*" [Hebrew], *Iyyunim beḥinukh* 41 (Aug. 1985): 167–76.

References are to Mordecai Aaron Guenzburg, *Aviezer* [Hebrew] (Tel Aviv, 1967; photoreproduction of first Vilna edition, 1864). Translations are by the present author.

2. Digressions such as those on Christians and heretics (p. 44), class differences (p. 50), and marriage (p. 52) would seem to be modeled on Maimon's practice in the *Lebensgeschichte*.

3. Moses Leib Lilienblum, *Ketavim otobiogerafiyim*, ed. Shlomo Breiman (Jerusalem, 1970), 2: 109. All references are to this edition according to volume and page (e.g., 2: 109) and are translated by the present writer.

4. In *Sincerity and Authenticity* (Cambridge, Mass.: Harvard University Press, 1971), Lionel Trilling describes the French conception of sincerity as "telling the truth about oneself to oneself and to others; by truth is meant a recognition of such of one's own traits or actions as are morally or socially discreditable and, in conventional course, concealed" (p. 58). See also Henri Peyre, *Literature and Sincerity*

(New Haven, 1963). I use "authenticity" here in the Sartrian sense of acceptance of responsibility for one's liberty through avoidance of bad faith.

5. For an attempt to situate Lilienblum's work within current thinking about autobiography as a literary genre, see Ben-Ami Feingold, "Autobiography as Literature: A Study of M. L. Lilienblum's *Sins of Youth*" [Hebrew], *Meḥkerei yerushalayim besifrut ivrit* 4 (1984): 86–111. Especially valuable is Feingold's use of Lilienblum's letters and diaries to show how "crafted" the work is.

6. See V. V. Zenkovsky, *A History of Russian Philosophy,* tr. George I. Kline (New York: Columbia University Press, 1953), p. 322. Lilienblum mentions Chernychevski's influence on 2: 72.

7. Thomas G. Masaryk, *The Spirit of Russia,* tr. Eden and Cedar Paul, 2nd ed. (New York: Macmillan, 1955), p. 398.

8. Zenkovsky, p. 338.

9. Lilienblum compares his lot to that of Pisarev on 2: 96 (see Breiman's quotation of the manuscript diary in n. 96). Also see Lilienblum's retrospective remarks on Pisarev on 3: 195. In reference to Turgenev, see n. 91, 2: 72.

10. D. I. Pisarev, "Bazarov," in *Sochineniya* 2 (Moscow, 1955): 7–50; tr. Lydia Hooke in the Norton edition of *Fathers and Sons,* ed. Ralph E. Matlaw (New York: Norton Books, 1966), p. 202.

11. Ibid.

12. Ibid., p. 211.

13. What could be more pathetic than Lilienblum's writing a long poem on the occasion of the tenth anniversary of his marriage called "A Prisoner's Lament" ('*Enkat 'asir,* 2: 196–203)?

14. *Kol kitvei Ḥ. Y. Brenner* (Tel Aviv, 1961), 3: 109.

15. On the space of individuality in late nineteenth-century Hebrew literature, see chapter three.

16. See the citation Breiman brings from the manuscript of *The Way Back* (2: 153, n. 34) in which Lilienblum plays with the reader's curiosity concerning the final outcome of the relationship.

17. This seems to be the case for all intents and purposes, though once again Lilienblum plays with the possibility of persistence when he begins the first two letters of *The Way Back,* addressing his correspondent in the feminine as "Yedidati," without giving anything away in the letters themselves (2: 154, 156).

3. Mordecai Ze'ev Feierberg and the Reveries of Redemption

1. Although "apostasy" may seem a strong term to use in this context, I think it is an appropriate equivalent for the Hebrew *kefirah*. As it is used here, apostasy refers not to conversion out of Judaism into another religion but rather loss of faith in the traditional theological structures of Judaism and in the divine authority of Jewish law.

2. A good synthesis of our biographical knowledge of Feierberg is contained in Hillel Halkin's introduction to his translation of Feierberg's fiction, *Whither? and Other Stories* (Philadelphia, 1972). Concerning the important last year of the author's life, see Samuel Werses, "Nahman's Last Speech and Its Sources" [Hebrew], *Moznayim* 48:5/6 (1979): 280–91.

3. On Feierberg's romanticism see Gershon Shaked, *Hasipporet ha'ivrit 1880–1970* [Hebrew Narrative Fiction, 1880–1970], vol. 1 (Tel Aviv, 1977), pp. 206–13.

4. Shaked, p. 209.

5. See Feierberg's letter to Ahad Ha-am (January 5, 1898), reprinted in *Kitvei M. Z. Feierberg,* ed. Eliezer Steinman (Tel Aviv, 1941), pp. 182–83.

6. See "An Open Letter to Mr. Berdichevsky" [Hebrew] in *Kitvei,* pp. 156–61.

7. Samuel Werses, in his chapter on Feierberg in *Sippur veshorsho* [Story and Source] (Ramat Gan, 1971), pp. 88–103, provides a valuable morphology of the various aggadic and legendary ingredients of *Whither?*.

8. Compare Shaked's assertion that there is little development in Feierberg's work, p. 207.

9. First published in *Hatsefirah*, 1897; *Kitvei*, pp. 147–55.

10. The first edition of Feierberg's work was published in Cracow in 1904 ("Hasefer Editions"). Page references here throughout are given according to the 1941 Steinman edition (see note 5)—these are placed second and in italics—and to the English translation by Hillel Halkin (*Whither? and Other Stories*)—placed first. All passages are quoted from the Halkin translation. For the beauty and skillfullness of this translation, the critic as well as the reader owes a great debt of gratitude.

11. Sanhedrin 34a.

12. First appeared in *Luaḥ aḥi'asaf*, 1897–98; Halkin, pp. 51–64; *Kitvei*, 133–42.

13. See Halkin's note on Hofni's names, p. 19.

14. Feierberg had made clear his distaste for such social clubs in a journalistic account of his town published in *Hamelits* (in *Kitvei*, pp. 171–78).

15. First appeared in *Luaḥ aḥi'asaf*, 1897–98; Halkin, pp. 65–71; *Kitvei*, pp. 143–46.

16. First appeared in *Hashiloaḥ* 2 (1897): 433–36; Halkin, pp. 73–80; *Kitvei*, pp. 126–130.

17. First appeared in *Hashiloaḥ* 4 (1898): 501–10; Halkin, pp. 81–104; *Kitvei*, pp. 39–56.

18. The phrase is Halkin's, p. 23.

19. Werses, *Sippur veshorsho*, pp. 94ff.

20. First appeared in *Hashiloaḥ* 4 (1898): 336–41; Halkin, pp. 106–18; *Kitvei*, pp. 56–64.

21. First published in *Hashiloaḥ* 5 (1899): 141–48, 217–32, 311–20, 406–18; Halkin, pp. 121–215; *Kitvei*, pp. 65–127.

22. Joseph Klausner, *Yotsrim uvonim* [Creators and Builders] (Jerusalem, 1929), 3:165ff., and Baruch Kurzweil, *Sifrutenu haḥadashah: hemshekh o mahpekhah* [Modern Hebrew Literature: Continuity or Revolution?] (Jerusalem, 1971), pp. 149ff.

23. Yosef Hayyim Brenner, *Kol kitvei Brenner* (Tel Aviv, 1960), 2:241.

24. *Moznayim*, 1st ser. 1, no. 4 (1929): 2.

25. *Yetser viyetsirah* [Instinct and Creation] (Jerusalem, 1951), p. 241.

26. Feierberg gives us his own catalogue in the form of Nahman's reminiscence about his life: "It had been poor, this life, but it had been rich in fantasies, dreams, visions, ambitions, and hopes instead" (p. 127, 69).

27. The term "reverie" was given currency in critical discourse by Gaston Bachelard, throughout his career and most synthetically in his late work *La poetique de la reverie* (Paris, 1961). (On this see Mary Ann Caws, *Surrealism and the Literary Imagination* [The Hague, 1966].) Bachelard used the term phenomenologically to describe the pleasures of the artistic imagination as it contemplates natural objects. My use of "reverie" to describe a unified series of imaginative moments not within the mind of the artist but within the finished work of art contains only a few similarities to Bachelard's usage. For the non-literary study of the reverie, see Jerome Singer, *Daydreaming* (New York, 1970).

28. Kurzweil, *Sifrutenu haḥadashah*, p. 150.

29. On the description of external reality in Feierberg, see Joseph Ewen, " 'Indistinct Objects and Feelings' in the Landscape Descriptions of M. Z. Feierberg" [Hebrew] *Meḥkerei yerushalayim besifrut 'ivrit* 6 (1981): 105–115.

30. Contrast the situation in Feierberg's story "In the Evening," in which temptation is embodied in a melody that originates from *outside* the circle.

31. See Y. Y. Wohl and A. Cheskis, "Mordecai Ze'ev Feierberg" [Hebrew], *Hashiloaḥ* 5 (1899): 382.

32. On the switch from the mother as the dominant force in the stories, see Moshe Pelli, "Central Motifs in the Stories of Mordecai Ze'ev Feierberg" [Hebrew], *Hadoar* 60:23 (1981): 370–72, 61:18 (1981): 282–83, and 61:19 (1981): 293–95.

33. For the use of this phrase in contemporary Hebrew literary criticism, see above, chapter 1.

34. It is not unlikely that as the prototype for this passage Feierberg had in mind the section of the Mishneh Torah in which Maimonides describes the enlightenment of the prophet and his subsequent separation from ordinary men.

> When one, . . . sanctifying himself, withdrawing himself from the ways of ordinary men who walk in the obscurities of the times, . . . keeping his mind on higher things . . . so as to comprehend the pure and holy form, . . . on such a man the Holy Spirit will promptly descend. . . . He will be changed into another man *(veyehafekh le'adam aher)* and will realize that he is not the same as he had been, and has been exalted over other wise men, even as it is said of Saul "And thou shalt prophesy with them, and shalt be turned into another man" (1 Samuel 10:6). (Hilhot yesodei hatorah, 7:1, trans. Hyamson)

In the bitter irony of the enlightenment Nahman expects and the enlightenment he gets, his situation resembles nothing so much as the primal parents in the Garden story whose eyes are opened only to see their own nakedness.

35. For an analysis of chapter 3 of Lamentations on its own terms, see my *Hurban: Responses to Catastrophe in Hebrew Literature,* chapter 1.

36. For the influences on Feierberg's idea of the Orient and its restorative power, see Werses, "Nahman's Last Speech and Its Sources" [Hebrew], *Moznayim* 48 (1979): 280–291.

37. Gershon Shaked, "Between Vision and Essay" [Hebrew], *'Al hamishmar,* April 4, 1966.

4. Berdichevsky and Erotic Shame

1. A starting point has been provided by the following discussions: Jacob Katz, "Marriage and Sexual Life among Jews at the End of the Middle Ages" [Hebrew], *Zion* 10 (1944): 21–54, and "Family, Kinship, and Marriage among Ashkenazim in the Sixteenth through Eighteenth Centuries," *Journal of Jewish Sociology* 1 (1959): 22–44. See also the paper by Julius Carlebach and the response to it by Marion Kaplan: "Family Structure and the Position of Women," pp. 189–203 in *Revolution and Evolution: 1848 in German-Jewish History,* ed. Mosse, Paucher, and Rurup (Tubingen, 1982).

2. On the awareness of novelistic conventions, see Anita Norich, "Portraits of the Artists in Three Novels by Shalom Aleichem," *Prooftexts* 4:3 (1984): 237–251.

3. For the publishing history of these stories, see Dan Almagor and Samuel Fishman, *Nahalt M.Y.B.: mafteah bibliografi litsirot Mikhah Yosef Berdichevsky (Bin-Gurion) ulehiburim 'al odotav* [A Bibliographical Index to the Work of Mica Yosef Berdichevsky and Critical Writings about It] (Tel Aviv, 1981). While some others of Berdichevsky's early stories such as *Two Camps* have been written about, there has been surprisingly little critical attention paid to *A Raven Flies.* See Y. H. Brenner, "From a Writer's Musings" [Hebrew], *Ketavim* 3:243 (first published in *Revivim* 2, Elul 1907); Y. Klausner, "Belles-Lettres in 1900—A Survey and a Critique" [Hebrew] in Nahum Sokolov (ed.), *Sefer hashanah lemehkar . . .* (Warsaw, 1901), pp. 247–50; Y. Keshet, *M. Y. Berdichevsky (Bin-Gurion): hayyav umif'alo* [M. Y. Berdichevsky (Bin-Gurion): His Life and Work] (Jerusalem, 1958), pp. 165–98.

4. Dan Miron, "The Turning Point in Modern Hebrew Fiction in *Mahanayyim*" [Hebrew] in Zippora Kagan (ed.), *Hagut vesipporet bitsirato shel Berdichevsky* [Thought and Fiction in the Works of Berdichevsky], (Haifa, 1981), pp. 27–52.

5. Page references are to the first edition published by Tushiya (Warsaw, 1900). Translations are my own. There are changes between the first edition and the version of the story in the collected works, beginning with the Shtybel edition of 1921–25. The changes are chiefly found in the first seven chapters, and they mostly involve condensing lengthy descriptions of Elimelekh's mental state. For a standard printing of the text in the Devir edition, see *Kol Kitvei Mikhah Yosef Ben-Gurion (Berdichevsky)*, (Tel Aviv, 1965), pp. 36-51.

6. See Shelomith Rimmon-Kenan, *Narrative Fiction: Contemporary Poetics* (Methuen: London, 1983), chapter 6.

7. See Terrence Doody, *Confession and Community in the Novel* (Louisiana State University Press: Baton Rouge, 1980), pp. 4–5.

8. The meditation is found at the end of every tractate in the standard edition of the Babylonian Talmud: "We thank you, Lord our God and God of our fathers, for making our portion with those who sit in the study house and not with those who sit idle. We rise early and they rise early: we rise early to study Torah and they rise early to pursue worthless affairs. We toil and they toil: we toil and receive our reward and they toil and receive no reward. We hasten and they hasten: we hasten to life eternal and they hasten to the netherworld."

9. Heinz Kohut, *The Analysis of Self* (International Universities Press: New York, 1971), p. 26.

10. P. 106.

11. Miron gives a similarly crucial role to the death of the mother in *Maḥanayyim;* see p. 50.

12. Carl D. Schreider, *Shame, Exposure, and Privacy* (Boston: Beacon, 1977), pp. 18–20.

13. *The Gay Science*, Book 2, Sect. 107, p. 164.

14. *Being and Nothingness*, trans. Hazel Barnes (New York: Citadel Press, 1969), pp. 221–22. See also Helen Lynd, *On Shame and the Search for Identity* (New York: Harcourt, Brace, 1958), and Helen Lewis, *Shame and Guilt in Neurosis* (New York: International Universities Press, 1971).

15. Gerhart Piers and Milton B. Singer, *Shame and Guilt: A Psychoanalytic and Cultural Study* (New York: Norton, 1971), pp. 15–18.

16. Pp. 24–25.

17. Pp. 28–29.

18. Doody, *Confession and Community in the Novel*, pp. 4–5.

19. On the issue of the narratee in the Hebrew literature of the period, see William Cutter, "The Readers in the Text: The Audience of Joseph Hayyim Brenner," *Hebrew Annual Review* 7 (1983): 57–68.

20. "Age and Youth" [Hebrew] in R. Breinin (ed.), *Mimizraḥ umim'arav; me'asef ledivrei ḥokhmah ulesifrut* (Berlin), vol. 4 (1899), p. 112. In the same volume appears another article by Berdichevsky, "The Soul of Hasidism" [Hebrew], pp. 59–64. The contrasts and similarities between these two essays present in miniature the author's spiritual world at this time.

21. See Miron, pp. 51–52, who correctly points out that with the publication of the essay "On Will" Berdichevsky began to moderate his stand on the relationship between the individual and his people. "On Will" was published the same year (1900) as the lead article in the collection *'Al em haderekh—reshimot* [At the Crossroads] (Warsaw, 1900), pp. 7–14.

5. The Revision of Childhood

1. All citations are taken from the Shtybel edition, *Kol kitvei Y. H. Brenner*, vol. 1 (Warsaw, 1924).

2. See Gershon Shaked, *Lelo' motsa'* [Dead End] (Tel Aviv, 1973), p. 81.

3. For the circumstances surrounding the writing and publication of *In Winter,* see Yitzhak Bakon, *Brenner hatsa'ir* [The Young Brenner] (Tel Aviv, 1975), 1:92–120.

4. M. L. Lilienblum, *Ketavin otobiografiyyim* [Autobiographical Writings], ed. Shelomo Breimen (Jerusalem, 1970), pp. 95–96.

5. On the question of the degree of fragmentariness or coherence in *In Winter,* see Shaked, p. 86, and the contemporary reaction of M. Y. Berdichevsky in *Yosef Ḥayyim Brenner: mivḥar ma'amarim al yetsirato hasifrutit* [Yosef Haim Brenner: A Selection of Critical Essays], ed. Yitzhak Bakon (Tel Aviv, 1972), p. 44.

6. Lilienblum, p. 95.

7. The Hebrew reading audience for such works as Brenner's was, in fact, extremely limited and had undergone an attrition at the end of the century. See Dan Miron, *Bodedim bemo'adam: lediyuknah shel harepublikah hasifrutut ha'ivrit biteḥilat hame'ah ha'esrim* [When Loners Come Together: A Portrait of Hebrew Literature at the Turn of the Twentieth Century], Tel Aviv, 1987, pp. 86–111.

8. Shaked, p. 79. Despite Brenner's rejection of the term, referring to *In Winter* as a novel is justified—and unavoidable—by virtue of the subsequent development of the modernist novel.

9. On the shaping of events in Lilienblum, see above, chapter 2, and Ben-Ami Feingold, "Autobiography as Literature: A Study of Lilienblum's *Sins of Youth*" [Hebrew] in *Meḥkerei yerushalayim besifrut 'ivrit* 4:86–111.

10. For a very useful clarification of when it is proper to speak of fiction as being autobiographical, see Menahem Brinker, "On the Question of Autobiographicality in Brenner's Fiction" [Hebrew] in *Maḥberot Brenner,* ed. M. Dorman and U. Shavit (Tel Aviv, 1984), 3/4: 145–72. Brinker's strictures are a good corrective by which to read Bakon's biographical study *(Brenner hatsa'ir),* which devotes over a hundred pages to *In Winter.* Bakon's historical research into Brenner's early movements in volume 1 is of considerable value, while the interpretive commentary based on these facts in volume 2, which reads more like lecture notes than a finished work, betrays a tendency to confuse the distinctions between events and their representations.

11. It is these opening pages that Berdichevsky found the most appealing in the novel. See Bakon, *Mivḥar ma'amarim,* pp. 43–44.

12. It is important to point out that the negative portrayal of the father in *In Winter* is at odds with the figure of the father in two short stories Brenner wrote at about the same time ("Shama" and "Pa'amayim," published in *Lu'aḥ ahi'asaf,* September, 1903), which are also supposed to be autobiographical. In these sketches the mother is absorbed and distant, whereas the father is compassionately and affectionately related to the child. The divergence in these contemporary texts is an admonition against searching for autobiographical veracity in Brenner's fiction. The purpose of these first-person forms, Brinker reminds us, is to create the *illusion* of autobiographical truth.

13. The narrator of *In Winter* would surely be disinclined to accept Baruch Kurzweil's assertion that "the essence of suffering in Brenner's fiction is specifically Jewish," *Bein ḥazon levein ha'absurdi* [Between Vision and the Absurd] (Tel Aviv, 1973), p. 276.

14. Some aspects of scenic discourse are taken up by Yosef Ewen in *Omanut hasippur shel Y. Ḥ. Brenner* [Y. H. Brenner's Craft of Fiction] (Jerusalem, 1977), ch. 4. As with much of this New Critical study, the observations about formal techniques fail to become connected to the profound thematics of Brenner's work. Compare the different mode of perceiving and telling conveyed by the terms *zikaron* and *yedi'ah* in Ada Zemach, *Tenu'ah binekudah: Brenner vesippurav* [Motion in Place: Brenner and his Fiction] (Tel Aviv, 1984), p. 104.

15. Compare Bakon's treatment of the Yom Tov scene in *Brenner hatsa'ir,* 2:278–82.

16. Again, compare Zemach, p. 104.

17. Talmud Bavli, Shabbat 84a.

18. For the best sustained discussion of the narrator's self-judgment, see Shaked, pp. 87–90.

19. Zemach's argument (pp. 110–16), that this childhood joy is rooted in the strength drawn from the commandments, is convincing.

20. See chapter three above.

21. *Theory of the Novel*, trans. Anna Bostock (Cambridge, MA: M.I.T. Press, 1971), p. 29.

22. See the helpful presentation of the issue in H.Y. Katznelson's 1904 Russian article translated in Bakon, *Mivḥar ma'amarim*, pp. 49, 51–52. This point is expanded upon in Samuel Schneider, '*Olam hamasoret hayehudit bekhitvei Yosef Ḥayyim Brenner* [The Traditional Jewish World in the Writings of Joseph Hayyim Brenner], Ph.D. dissertation, Yeshiva University, 1976, pp. 192–244. Schneider contrasts the absolute negations of religion in Brenner's ideological and publicist writings with his sympathetic portrayal of a number of religious figures in *In Winter*. He correctly takes issue with Bakon's insistence that the rejection of the father and the Father-in-heaven are one in the same. Schneider emphasizes Brenner's distance from the militant maskilic portrayal of religious life and sensitively analyzes the figure of the rabbi as an "authentic personality" (p. 208).

23. In her insightful and nuanced study of Brenner, Ada Zemach argues that the act of writing is the central source of meaning in *In Winter*. Her thesis is presented on pp. 99–101. Life as a source of vitality has been shut off from the hero, and the only outlet left to him is writing. Zemach therefore relies heavily on the description of Yirmiah's early experiments with poetry-writing as a key to the narrator's later identity. While there may be some merit to this line of interpretation in the later novels, I think the point is exaggerated as regards *In Winter*. What is remarkable about the childhood experiences with writing is that they do *not* open up some path toward a new identity or toward some means of self-transcendence. This is also the case when the hero is older, as will be seen in part two of the novel. *In Winter* does not turn into *A Portrait of the Artist as a Young Man*. Writing fails to become a redemptive moment. Of course writing is important to Brenner's narrators; that is a commonplace. But writing remains communication—disclosure to oneself or to others—not self-transcendence through language. Writing and speech are the vehicles for expressing existential modes of being. In this connection, compare Jeffrey Fleck's emphasis on narration as action in *Character in Context: Studies in the Fiction of Abramovitsh, Brenner, and Agnon* (Chico, CA: Scholars Press, 1984). Shaked puts the issue in proper balance by stressing the fact that the entire novel exists within the subjective consciousness of the narrator in contrast to Haskalah narratives in which reality is described "objectively" (p. 86).

24. Bakon notes that Brenner himself left home three years earlier and did not live with his parents between the ages of 10 and 13. *Brenner hatsa'ir*, 2:300.

25. See Dov Sadan's substantial contribution to this subject, chapter 7 below, note 3.

26. See Kurzweil's interesting excursus on the word *davar* as sexual experience, p. 294. Kurzweil's is the most penetrating discussion of the connection between loss of faith and eros, and we shall return to it in chapter 7.

6. The Veil of Ideas and the Reduction of Self

1. On the desire for the journey, see Gila Ramras-Rauch, *Y. Ḥ. Brenner vehasifrut hamodernit* [Y. H. Brenner and Modern Literature] (Tel Aviv, 1979), pp. 49–50. Also, Dan Miron, "Hebrew Literature at the Beginning of the Twentieth Century" [Hebrew], *Me'asef ledivrei sifrut, bikkort, vehagut* (1971) 2:459. Brenner's own early story "Shama" plays on this theme.

2. For a more theoretical discussion of this phenomenon, see chapter 4, above.

3. All citations are taken from the Shtybel edition, *Kol kitvei Y. H. Brenner,* vol. 1 (Warsaw, 1924).

4. See Shaked's perceptive remarks on the reduction to talk in *Lelo' motsa'* [Dead End] (Tel Aviv, 1973), pp. 83–85, 96–97.

5. Ada Zemach would see in these aspirations an expression of the untrammeled spirit Feuerman has preserved from childhood. Yet this is not the way we are urged to see these fantasies by the narrator. See *Tenu'ah binekudah* [Motion in Place] (Tel Aviv, 1984), pp. 114–16.

6. On the different kinds of subjective discourse used by Brenner, see Yosef Ewen, *Omanut hasippur shel Y. H. Brenner* [Y. H. Brenner's Craft of Fiction] (Jerusalem, 1977), pp. 134–62.

7. See Shaked, p. 74, on the structural danger in the novel posed by excessive reflection and discursiveness. See also chapter 5, above.

8. *Kol kitvei Y. H. Brenner* (Tel Aviv, 1961), 3:109.

9. Compare Yitzhak Bakon's suggestion that Chaimowitch is Feuerman's alter ego, his split self, in *Brenner hatsa'ir* [The Young Brenner] (Tel Aviv, 1975), 2:333–37.

10. Compare Zemach, pp. 99–101.

11. On the spatial metaphor, see chapter 4, above.

12. On Brenner's use of scenes to exemplify reality rather than represent it extensively, see Shaked, pp. 81–82.

13. See Ewen, pp. 137–141.

14. Truth delivered in madness is a central device in Brenner's fiction; see Shaked, p. 96.

15. I do not see a basis for Bakon's claim that Feuerman shifts his allegiance from Chaimowitch to Dawidowsky. See *Brenner hasta'ir,* p. 350.

7. The Erotic Subversion

1. Gershon Shaked sees the novel as a parody of the *Bildungsroman* in which the hero's travels signify no gain in knowledge. See *Lelo' motsa'* [Dead End] (Tel Aviv, 1973), pp. 81–82. Gila Ramras-Rauch emphasizes the archetype of the quest underlying the novel's premise. See *Y. H. Brenner vehasifrut hamodernit* [Y. H. Brenner and Modern Literature] (Tel Aviv, 1979), pp. 45–50.

2. On the ambiguities of this title, see chapter 4, above. Dan Miron sees *In Winter* as a parody of *A Raven Flies.* See *Bodedim bemo'adam; lediyuknah shel harepublikah hasifrutit ha'ivrit bitehilat hame'ah ha'esrim* [When Loners Come Together: A Portrait of Hebrew Literature at the Turn of the Twentieth Century] (Tel Aviv, 1987), pp. 232–48. This material came to my attention too late to be dealt with in the body of the text.

3. In a series of pathbreaking studies in the 1930s, Dov Sadan (Stock) applied psychoanalytic theory to Brenner's fiction. Sadan brought examples, especially from chapter 5 of *In Winter,* of description of unconsciously motivated behavior. Sadan sees the first-person form as an expression of the need to confess these hidden motives in public. The frequent daydreams, reveries, and ruminations in Brenner's work provide portals to the unconscious. All articles were published under the title "Episodes in the Psychology of Y. H. Brenner" [Hebrew], in *Ahdut ha'avodah* 3, nos. 1–2 (1931): 103–16; *Davar* (Suppl.), 29 Kislev, 7 Shevat, 1932; *Moznayyim* (1933), nos. 55–59; *Ha'olam* (1933), nos. 30–32. For the purposes of this chapter, Sadan's most important article is "A Woman's Shadow" [Hebrew] in *Davar* (Suppl.), 9 Iyyar 1936. In his depth analysis of Feuerman's psyche, Sadan sees the root of the problem in the mother's taking her son as a replacement for the husband's acknowledgment and affections. All women remind Feuerman of his mother, and men like Borsif, who are sexual competitors, present themselves as

versions of the father. Brenner's characters express a longing to return to a union with the mother that will be unimpeded by the father; they wish, in other words, to return to the womb, and it is the womb that is symbolized by such enclosures as tunnels, sacks, and houses. Feuerman's overwrought rationalizations for returning home, Sadan argues, reflect an inability to understand either his inner needs or his inner inhibitions.

4. See Sadan for the metamorphosis of this tale in Bialik and Mendele, *Davar* (Suppl.), 9 Iyyar 1936. Also compare Yitzhak Bakon, *Brenner hatsa'ir* [The Young Brenner] (Tel Aviv, 1975), 2:305.

5. On Kurzweil's understanding of the word *davar*, "thing," in its sexual connotation, see above, chapter 6.

6. Baruch Kurzweil is the only critic to give full weight to the connection between Feuerman's loss of faith and his erotic dilemma. Kurzweil seems uninterested, however, in the particular nature and structure of this impasse. See *Bein ḥazon levein ha'absurdi* [Between Vision and the Absurd] (Jerusalem, 1973), pp. 289ff.

7. See Kurzweil, pp. 278–80, on vegetal-animal existence in Brenner.

8. Compare Kurzweil, pp. 292–93.

9. See Bakon for a useful discussion of the interrelations among Chaimowitch, Rahil, and Borsif, p. 338.

10. Such a study is being undertaken by Ariel Hirschfeld, of the Department of Hebrew Literature at the Hebrew University, to whom I am grateful for conversations on this topic.

11. Zemach sees chapter 33 as expressing the final loss of Feuerman's childhood hope for becoming an other as well as the acceptance of the failure of his return home (p. 138). Ramras-Rauch, following Kurzweil, takes the chapter as the epitome of Feuerman's fall into an absurd existence, the condition that must inevitably result from the loss of faith in God (p. 52).

12. See Jeffrey Fleck, *Character and Context: Studies in the Writings of Abramovitsh, Brenner, and Agnon* (Chico, CA: Scholars Press, 1984).

13. Kurzweil, p. 79.

14. Kurzweil, p. 142.

15. Fleck sees Feuerman's wintry meditations as a catharsis which vents the "nausea of narration" and in turn makes possible some empathy for others as well as the chapter's elated feelings (pp. 71–72).

Conclusion: The Vagaries of the Autobiographical Impulse

1. See Yael Feldman's interesting speculations about the absence of autobiography in "Gender In/Difference in Contemporary Hebrew Fictional Autobiographies," *Biography* 11:3 (1988): 189–289.

2. Ephraim E. Lisitzky, *Elleh toldot adam* [These Are the Generations of Adam], (Jerusalem, 1949), translated by Moshe Kohn and Jacob Sloan as *In the Grip of Cross-Currents* (New York: Bloch Publishing Co., 1959).

3. Pinhas Sadeh, *Ḥayyim kemashal* (Jerusalem, 1954), translated by Richard Flantz, *Life as a Parable* (London: Anthony Blond, 1966). Page references are to the translation.

4. "Agnon in Jaffa: The Myth of the Artist as a Young Man," *Prooftexts* 1:1 (1981): 62–83.

Index

Abramowitsch, Sh. J. (Mendele), 5, 18, 203
Aggadah, 61, 80
Agnon, Sh. Y., 209–10
Ahad Ha-am, 61
Almagor, Dan, 215
Analytic discourse, 137–38
Apostasy: definition, 4; as narrative theme, 18; in Guenzburg, 26–28; and impotence, 25–26; in Feierberg, 79–80, 82–83, 85–86, 88; in Brenner, 123–24, 148–49, 166–67
Augustine of Hippo, 7
Autobiography: in classical Judaism, 6–7; in Renaissance, 7–10; impact of Rousseau, 6, 11–12; in Haskalah, 14–16; in Revival period, 18–19
—modern tradition: as alternative to novel, 5–6, 16–17, 90, 130–31; generic distinctions, 14–16; Maimon, 15; Lilienblum, 31; Berdichevsky, 116–20; Brenner, 6, 17–18, 128–31 *passim*; *Baḥoref* as consummation of genre, 204–5
—and literary theory: structuralism, 19; deconstruction, 20; confession, 20–21, 116; inwardness, 20; shape of life, 21; rhetoric of authenticity, 21–22; retrospective premise, 22–23, 118–20; audience, 117, 128–30

Bachelard, Gaston, 214
Bakon, Yitzhak, 217–20 *passim*
Bar-El, Yehudit, 211–12
Ben-Zion, Sh., 135
Berdichevsky, M. Y.: biography, 91; ideological program, 91, 119–20; *Mahanayyim*, 11–13; and autobiographical tradition, 16–17; and Feierberg, 61; and Brenner, 190
—'*Urva paraḥ (A Raven Flies)*: summary of themes, 93; specimen chapter commentary, 93–102; inside/outside dichotomy, 96, 98; reveries, 86–88, 89, 101; conceptions of love and marriage, 97, 100; isolation, 98, 102; erotic obsession, 103–7; brother-sister fantasy, 104; sadism and misogyny, 107; eros and religious experience, 107–9; narcissism, 110–13; grandiosity, 112–13; shame, 112–16; confession and addressee, 116–17; retrospective wisdom, 117–18; explanation of title, 118–20
Berkowitch, Y. D., 19
Bialik, H. N., 19
Braudes, R. A., 5
Brenner, Y. H.: *Misaviv lanekudah*, 165; *Shekhol vekhishalon*, 170, 205; "Shama" and "Pa'amayim," 217; and autobiography, 6, 17
—*Baḥoref (In Winter)*, composition of: apos-

tasy scenes, 123–24, 148–49; and autobiographical tradition, 124–26; explanation of thematic codes, 126–28; anti-novelistic conventions, 128–30; novel *vs.* autobiography, 130–31; analytic discourse, 137–38; scenic discourse, 138–39; Yom Tov scene as example, 139–43; images of narration, 142–43; representation of childhood, 143; mad monologues, 170–72; comic plot, 193; problems of closure, 198–202
—*Baḥoref (In Winter)* and belief: apostasy, representation of, 123–24; religious world of the child, 144–47; compared to Feierberg, 146; father compared to rabbi, 147–48; secular studies, 158–60; ideology and authenticity, 160–65; Chaimowitch as paragon, 161–66; art as vocation declined, 165–66; life without God, 166–67
—*Baḥoref (In Winter)*, psychological component in: analysis of parents, 131–33, 181–84; relation to mother, 139–41, 184–87; *nakranut*, 138, 155, 195; leaving home, motif of, 175, 196–97; overcultivation of mental functions, 134–36
—*Baḥoref (In Winter)*, erotic theme in: attitudes toward women, 149–53; obsession, 151–53, 187–90; Dawidowsky and homosexual feeling, 173–74; allusions to Berdichevsky, 176–77; erotic attraction as repressed motive, 177–78; eros and interiority, 191–93; dreams and nightmares, 194, 196; Borsif as competitor, 195–96
Brinker, Menahem, 217

Carlebach, Julius, 215
Carpi, Daniel, 211
Confession, 26, 116
Crews, Mary Ann, 214
Cutter, William, 216

Davis, Natalie Zemon, 8, 9, 211
De Man, Paul, 20
Doody, Terrence, 116–17

Eakin, Paul John, 212
Education, 26–27, 37, 42, 48–50, 53, 134–36, 158–60
Emden, Jacob, 7–10 *passim*
Erotic obsession, 107–9, 177–78, 191–93
Ewen, Yosef, 214, 217, 219

Family and marriage, 27–28, 43–44, 89, 100, 182–84
Feierberg, M. Z.: biography, 57; and autobiographical tradition, 6, 58–60; individual

221